Refugee Law and Durability of Protection

This book examines the link between refugee protection, duration of risk and residency rights. It focuses on two main issues of importance to current state practice: the use of temporary forms of refugee status and residency and the legal criteria for cessation of refugee status under Article 1C(5) of the 1951 Refugee Convention.

In analysing this issue, this book canvasses debates which are pertinent to many other contentious areas of refugee law, including the relationship between the refugee definition and complementary protection, application of the Refugee Convention in situations of armed conflict, and the role of non-state bodies as actors of protection. It also illustrates some of the central problems with the way in which the 1951 Refugee Convention is implemented domestically in key asylum host states. The arguments put forward in this book have particular significance for the return of asylum seekers and refugees to situations of ongoing conflict and post-conflict situations and is therefore highly pertinent to the future development of international refugee law.

Dr Maria O'Sullivan is a Senior Lecturer in the Faculty of Law and Deputy Director of the Castan Centre for Human Rights Law at Monash University, Australia.

Law and Migration

Series Editor
Satvinder S. Juss, King's College London, UK

Migration and its subsets of refugee and asylum policy are rising up the policy agenda at national and international level. Current controversies underline the need for rational and informed debate of this widely misrepresented and little understood area.

Law and Migration contributes to this debate by establishing a monograph series to encourage discussion and help to inform policy in this area. The series provides a forum for leading new research principally from the Law and Legal Studies area but also from related social sciences. The series is broad in scope, covering a wide range of subjects and perspectives.

Other titles in this series:

Law and Asylum
Space, Subject, Resistance
Simon Behrman

Ethical, Legal and Social Aspects of Healthcare for Migrants
Perspectives from the UK and Germany
Edited by Katja Kuehlmeyer, Corinna Klingler and Richard Huxtable

Environmental Change, Forced Displacement and International Law
From Legal Protection Gaps to Protection Solutions
Isabel M. Borges

Conflict Displacement and Legal Protection
Understanding Asylum, Human Rights and Refugee Law
Charlotte Lülf

Refugee Law and Durability of Protection
Temporary Residence and Cessation of Status
Maria O'Sullivan

For more information about this series, please visit: www.routledge.com/Law-and-Migration/book-series/LAWANDMIG

Refugee Law and Durability of Protection

Temporary Residence and Cessation of Status

Maria O'Sullivan

Routledge
Taylor & Francis Group
LONDON AND NEW YORK

First published 2019
by Routledge
2 Park Square, Milton Park, Abingdon, Oxon OX14 4RN

and by Routledge
605 Third Avenue, New York, NY 10017

First issued in paperback 2020

Routledge is an imprint of the Taylor & Francis Group, an informa business

British Library Cataloguing-in-Publication Data
A catalogue record for this book is available from the British Library

Library of Congress Cataloging-in-Publication Data
Names: O'Sullivan, Maria (Law teacher)
Title: Refugee law and durability of protection / Maria O'Sullivan.
Description: Abingdon, Oxon ; New York, NY : Routledge, 2020. | Series: Law and migration | Includes bibliographical references and index. | Based on her thesis (doctoral – Monash University, 2012) issued under title: Cessation of refugee status under article 1 C(5) of the 1951 Refugee Convention : protection from persecution or effective protection?
Identifiers: LCCN 2019001359 | ISBN 9781138303461 (hardback) | ISBN 9780203731079 (ebook)
Subjects: LCSH: Refugees—Legal status, laws, etc. | Responsibility to protect (International law) | Convention Relating to the Status of Refugees (1951 July 28)
Classification: LCC KZ6530 .O78 2020 | DDC 341.4/86—dc23
LC record available at https://lccn.loc.gov/2019001359

ISBN 13: 978-0-367-72918-9 (pbk)
ISBN 13: 978-1-138-30346-1 (hbk)
ISBN 13: 978-0-203-73107-9 (ebk)

Typeset in Galliard
by Apex CoVantage, LLC

Contents

Acknowledgements

This book is based largely on my doctoral thesis, undertaken for the PhD degree at Monash University, under the supervision of Professor Susan Kneebone. I sincerely thank Susan for her encouragement and support of both my PhD and my academic career in general. I particularly note Susan's generosity in opening up her research networks to me and including me in various workshops and conferences overseas, which has greatly assisted me in bringing a much-needed international comparative focus to my work. I also thank the examiners of my PhD thesis, Professor Elspeth Guild and Professor Helene Lambert, who gave me excellent feedback on my doctoral thesis.

I acknowledge that my PhD candidature, upon which this book is based, was generously supported by an Australian Government Scholarship. I also wish to acknowledge the generous support of the Law Faculty of Monash University in assisting me to complete the research for this book. Particular thanks go to the Research Committee for providing me with funds to enable me to present my draft papers at international conferences and seminars to test out my ideas. I would like to make special mention of the participants at the annual conferences of the Refugee Law Initiative at the University of London, who gave me valuable feedback on my analysis. In addition to this, I acknowledge the excellent research assistance work carried out by Gimhani Eriyagolla, who conducted research on temporary residence in Europe, and Aisha Ismail who assisted greatly with editing and feedback on Chapter 7.

Writing a book of this nature requires the support of colleagues, friends and family. I would therefore like to acknowledge and thank my colleagues at the Faculty of Law, Monash University, who assisted me by providing a sounding board for ideas and for their wise advice, particularly Dr Patrick Emerton, Dr Heli Askola and the staff and members of the Castan Centre for Human Rights Law at Monash University. I also thank my Monash teaching co-ordinators HP Lee and Karinne Ludlow who configured my teaching so as to allow me to concentrate on my book. This was extremely important to me and greatly appreciated.

Finally, I would of course like to acknowledge the support of my family. Thank you to my husband, Jeff Crosbie, who provided me with support during my PhD candidature and who looked after our two young children whilst I attended overseas conferences. Finally, I would like to acknowledge the role of my mother,

Catherine O'Sullivan, who inspired me to become a lawyer and who ensured that I was given a high quality education to enable me to fulfil that dream.

Maria O'Sullivan
Melbourne, October 2018

The law is stated as at 31 July 2018, although later developments have been incorporated where possible.

Cases and short names

Case name	*Short name*
Applicant A v. Minister for Immigration and Ethnic Affairs (1997) 190 CLR 225	*Applicant A*
Beldjoudi v. France, 55/1990/246/317; 12083/86, European Court of Human Rights, 26 February 1992	*Beldjoudi v. France*
Bundesverwaltungsgericht (Federal Administrative Court, Germany) BVerwG 10 C 33.07, 7 February 2008	*BVerwG C 33.07*
Fadil Dyli (Protection – UNMIK – Arif – IFA – Art1D) Kosovo CG* [2000] UKIAT 00001, 00/TH/02186, 30 August 2000	*Dyli*
Hoxha v. Secretary of State for the Home Department [2002] EWCA Civ 1403 (England and Wales Court of Appeal)	*Hoxha*, Court of Appeal
In re B (FC) (Appellant) (2002). Regina v. Special Adjudicator, Ex parte Hoxha (FC), [2005] UKHL 19 (House of Lords)	*Hoxha*, House of Lords
Gardi v. Secretary of State for the Home Department [2002] EWCA Civ 750	*Gardi*
Horvath v. Secretary of State for the Home Department [2001] 1 AC 489	*Horvath*
Januzi v. Secretary of State for the Home Department [2006] 2 AC 426	*Januzi*
Matter of Chen, United States Board of Immigration Appeals, 25 April 1989, 20 I. & N. Dec. 16	*Chen*
Minister for Immigration and Multicultural and Indigenous Affairs v. QAAH of 2004 [2006] HCA 53	*QAAH*
MS (Art 1C(5)-Mogadishu) Somalia [2018] UKUT 196 (IAC)	*MS (Mogadishu) Somalia*
Nystrom v. Australia, UN Human Rights Committee, Communication No 1557/2007, UN Doc CCPR/C/102/D/1557/2007 (18 July 2011)	*Nystrom*
R v. Secretary of State for the Home Department; Ex parte Robinson [1998] QB 929	*Robinson*

R v. Secretary of State for the Home Department, Ex parte Adan [1999] 3 WLR 1274 (Court of Appeal)	*Adan* 1999
R v. Secretary of State for the Home Department, Ex parte Adan; R v. Secretary of State for the Home Department Ex parte Aitseguer [2001] 2 AC 477	*Adan* 2001
Salahadin Abdulla and Others v. Bundesrepublik Deutschland, C-175/08; C-176/08; C-178/08 & C-179/08, Court of Justice of the European Union, 2 March 2010	*Abdulla*
Secretary of State for the Home Department v. MA (Somalia) [2018] EWCA Civ 994	*MA (Somalia)*
SF (Sufficiency of Protection-KAA-Michigan Guidelines) Iraq CG [2002] UKIAT 07376	*SF Iraq*
Slivenko v. Latvia (2004) 39 EHRR 24	*Slivenko v. Latvia*
Stewart v. Canada, CCPR/C/58/D/538/1993, UN Human Rights Committee (HRC), 1 November 1996	*Stewart v. Canada*

Abbreviations

AAT	Administrative Appeals Tribunal (Australia)
AsylVfG	*Asylverfahrensgesetz* (Asylum Procedure Law, Germany)
BVerwG	*Entscheidungen des Bundesverwaltungsgerichts* (decisions of the German Federal Administrative Court)
CEAS	Common European Asylum System
CFR	Code of Federal Regulations (USA)
CJEU	Court of Justice of the European Union
CRR	*Commission des recours des réfugiés* (France)
DHA	Department of Home Affairs (Australia)
DIAC	Department of Immigration and Citizenship (Australia)
EC	European Community
ECHR	European Convention for the Protection of Human Rights and Freedoms 1950
ECRE	European Council on Refugees and Exiles
ECtHR	European Court of Human Rights
EU	European Union
EWCA	England and Wales Court of Appeal
ExCom	Executive Committee UNHCR
HC	House of Commons
IARLJ	International Association of Refugee Law Judges
ICCPR	International Covenant on Civil and Political Rights
ICJ	International Court of Justice
IFA	Internal Flight Alternative
INS	Immigration and Naturalization Service (USA)
IRB	Immigration and Refugee Board (Canada)
IRO	International Refugee Organisation
NGO	Non-governmental organisation
OJ	Official Journal (EU)
OAU	Organisation of African Unity
RRT	Refugee Review Tribunal (Australia)
SHEV	Safe Haven Enterprise Visa
TEC	Treaty Establishing the European Community
TFEU	Treaty on the Functioning of the European Union

TPS	Temporary Protected Status (USA)
TPV	Temporary protection visa (Australia)
UDHR	Universal Declaration of Human Rights 1948
UN	United Nations
UNGA	United Nations General Assembly
UNHCR	Office of the United Nations High Commissioner for Refugees
UNHCR	Ex Com Executive Committee of the Programme of the United Nations High Commissioner for Refugees
UNTS	*United Nations Treaty Series*
USC	Unites States Code
VCLT	Vienna Convention on the Law of Treaties

1 Introduction

Key concepts and interpretative framework

This book deals with one of the most pressing and difficult issues of modern times – the way in which the international community should respond to refugee flows and the content of the law which should govern that response. In particular, this book examines the criteria used to grant and revoke refugee status, the nature and length of the protection which should be accorded to recognised refugees and the procedures used in such determinations.

It focuses on a relatively recent and controversial development in state practice of international refugee law: the use of time-limited permits[1] for recognised refuges and the cessation of refugee status due to a change in circumstances in conditions in the refugee's country of nationality under Article 1C(5) of the 1951 Refugee Convention.[2] It queries whether protection and residence of refugees can be temporary. If so, how is this measured against the duration of risk? Importantly, this book examines what happens when an asylum host state seeks to revoke temporary refugee status or residence. What standards govern this decision and should any integrative links which the refugee has acquired or developed in the host state be considered as part of the cessation and deportation decisions?

This book is timely because some states, particularly those in Europe, have expressed an increased interest in utilising cessation as a mechanism to compel refugees to return to their country of origin. This is most starkly reflected in current proposals before the European Parliament to amend the EU Qualification Directive[3] to oblige or encourage EU Member States to use 'status reviews' to

1 I utilise the term 'time-limited visas' in this book to refer to the use of temporary protection for those persons *individually* determined to be refugees under the Convention. This is in contrast to the meaning of temporary protection in its 'traditional' sense, which is used to protect a mass influx of asylum seekers where individual refugee status determination is not undertaken. This is discussed further later in this chapter.

2 Convention relating to the Status of Refugees, Geneva, 28 July 1951, in force 22 April 1954, 1989 UNTS 137, supplemented by the Protocol relating to the Status of Refugees, New York, 31 January 1967, in force 4 October 1967, 19 UST 6223, 6257 (hereinafter Refugee Convention).

3 Directive 2011/95/EU of The European Parliament and of The Council of 13 December 2011 on standards for the qualification of third-country nationals or stateless persons as beneficiaries of international protection, for a uniform status for refugees or for persons eligible

examine whether there have been significant changes in the situation of the relevant country of origin.[4] It is hoped that this book will provide a detailed, robust analysis of cessation which will guide states in utilising such reviews.

Although this book is focused on time-limited protection and cessation, the analysis presented here has broader relevance to global refugee law issues: the way in which international refugee law norms should be interpreted in a modern-day context, the influence of European definitions of refugee law on international law and the balance to be struck between refugee protection and contemporary state imperatives which are increasingly hostile to acceptance of significant numbers of refugees.

Current state practice of temporary residence and cessation

Many states now favour the use of various forms of temporary protection for individualised refugees via time-limited visas and permits. Such practice is important, as it allows states to then *review cases* upon expiry of that permit in accordance with Article 1C(5) of the Convention and to *revoke* refugee status and residence if circumstances in the country of origin have changed.

There are two main examples of state practice in this context which will be used in this book. First, state practice in Australia, which has operated a temporary protection visa (TPV) scheme in various forms since 1999. Under the current legal framework in Australia, a recognised refugee can only be granted a three-year 'temporary protection visa' and is precluded from obtaining a permanent protection visa. The existence of TPVs has enabled Australian authorities to apply Article 1C(5) to holders of those visas.[5] This will therefore be analysed in some depth as a case study throughout the book.

Time-limited residence permits for refugees are also now used in some Member States of the EU. The Qualification Directive[6] is important here as it allows EU Member States to issue three-year residence permits to refugees, rather than permanent residence permits.[7] As a result, a number of European states, including

for subsidiary protection, and for the content of the protection granted (recast), [2011] OJ L 337/9 (hereinafter 2011 Qualification Directive).

4 *Proposal for a regulation of the European Parliament and of the Council on standards for the qualification of third-country nationals or stateless persons as beneficiaries of international protection, for a uniform status for refugees or for persons eligible for subsidiary protection and for the content of the protection granted and amending Council Directive 2003/109/EC of 25 November 2003 concerning the status of third country nationals who are long-term residents*, COM(2016) 466 13.7.2016 2016/0223(COD).

5 This is discussed in Chapter 3 of this book.

6 2011 Qualification Directive, above n 3.

7 Ibid, Article 24. Article 24(1) obliges Member States to issue such a residence permit to refugees '[a]s soon as possible after their status has been granted'.

the United Kingdom (UK),[8] Germany,[9] Netherlands,[10] Finland[11] and Norway,[12] have introduced temporary residence permits for recognised refugees.[13] The EU Qualification Directive also requires Member States to implement cessation provisions similar to those in Article 1C(5) into domestic law[14] and to revoke or refuse to renew refugee status if cessation has occurred.[15]

Interestingly, although many states have cessation provisions in place in domestic legislation, cessation practice is a relatively recent phenomenon. Of all EU countries, only Germany has applied Article 1C(5) to holders of temporary residence permits in significant numbers.[16] Other EU countries have cessation provisions in place in domestic law but have only commenced utilisation of those provisions relatively recently and in comparatively small numbers. This may be due to the resource implications of applying cessation to refugees (which requires decision makers) and the existing backlog of first-instance refugee status decisions in many countries.

In order to understand current state practice on cessation, one must also differentiate between (a) refugee status and (b) the residence or protection permit which *coincides* with that status. Here there is a significant difference across key jurisdictions. In Australia, cessation results in the revocation of both refugee

8 All recognised refugees are granted a 5-year limited leave to remain status: see UK Immigration Rules 339Q(i), <www.ind.homeoffice.gov.uk/lawandpolicy/immigrationrules/>.

9 Recognised refugees are granted a 3-year renewable residence permit: see German Federal Office for Migration and Refugees, 'Legal Consequences of the Decision', 18 January 2011, <www.bamf.de/EN/Migration/AsylFluechtlinge/Asylverfahren/Rechtsfolgen/rechtsfolgen-node.html>.

10 Recognised refugees are granted a 3-year renewable residence permit: Aliens Act 2000 (Complete Revision of the Aliens Act) (Netherlands), 1998–1999; 26 732, 1 April 2001, Sections 26–29, <www.unhcr.org/refworld/docid/3b5fd9491.html>.

11 Alien's Act (Finland), s. 53(b), <www.finlex.fi/fi/laki/kaannokset/2004/en20040301.pdf>.

12 Recognised refugees are granted a 3-year renewable residence permit: Norwegian Directorate of Immigration, pamphlet, 'What Happens If Your Application Is Granted', <www.udi.no/Norwegian-Directorate-of-Immigration/Central-topics/Protection/Procedure-in-asylum-cases/What-happens-if-your-application-is-granted/>.

13 Other jurisdictions continue to give refugees a permanent status or very long residency period. For instance, in France, persons recognised as refugees are granted a 10-year renewable residence permit by the Prefecture: EDAL database, 1 January 2012, <www.asylumlawdatabase.eu/en/content/edal-country-overview-france>.

14 EU Qualification Directive, above n 3, Article 11(1)(e) and (f). The differences between Article 11(1)(e) of the Qualification Directive and Article 1C(5) of the Convention are discussed in Chapter 3 of this book.

15 EU Qualification Directive, above n 3, Article 14. This obliges Member States to 'revoke, end or refuse to renew' the refugee status of a person 'if he or she has ceased to be a refugee in accordance with Article 11'.

16 For instance, the refugee status of over 38,000 refugees was revoked by German authorities due to Article 1C(5) cessation in the period 2005 to 2010: The precise figure for the number of refugees subject to the cessation provisions is 38,556: see H. Dörig, 'Current Problems in Asylum and Protection Law: The German Judicial Perspective', International Association of Refugee Law Judges (IARLJ) World Conference, Bled, 2011, 5.

protection *and* lawful permission to stay. Thus, cessation renders applicants open to deportation. In contrast, under the German system, residence is not revoked automatically following the application of cessation. Further, if residence is revoked, such persons may be protected from immediate return due to applicability of a bar on deportation[17] or they may be eligible for other types of protection, such as complementary protection, humanitarian protection or tolerated (*Duldung*) status, which is a temporary stay on deportation and does not constitute a residence permit).[18] Thus, in Germany it appears that cessation is being used as a means of stripping away the rights of those refugees affected, rather than for the purpose of return to their country of origin.[19] Such 'ceased refugees' may also have an uncertain status in Germany (for instance, if they are given 'tolerated stay' via the grant of *Duldung* status).[20] For instance, as of 2006 (when Germany was utilising cessation widely), there were 186,000 persons in Germany holding *Duldung* status. More than 100,000 of these had been staying in Germany for longer than 6 years.[21] UNHCR also reported that, as at the end 2007, 13% of the 8,380 persons who had their refugee status revoked due to Article 1C(5) were staying in Germany on the basis of toleration permits.[22] As UNHCR has

17 Section 60(7) Residence Act (Germany) provides that 'A foreigner should not be deported to another state in which a substantial concrete danger to his or her life and limb or liberty applies. A foreigner shall not be deported to another state in which he or she will be exposed, as a member of the civilian population, to a substantial individual danger to life or limb as a result of an international or internal armed conflict. Dangers pursuant to sentence 1 or sentence 2 to which the population or the segment of the population to which the foreigner belongs are generally exposed shall receive due consideration in decisions pursuant to Section 60a (1), sentence 1'.

18 Presentation of H. Dörig, 'Judges, Federal Administrative Court of Germany', ELENA Advanced Course on Generalised Violence, Bologna, 4–6 May 2012, notes on file with author.

19 It may well be that they are not being returned due to concerns over ill-treatment in the country of origin which would breach Article 3 of the European Convention on Human Rights. However, if this is so, such refugees should be assessed as such and, if so, granted a form of complementary or subsidiary protection, as provided for in Article 15(c) of the 2011 EU Qualification Directive, above n 3. It should be noted that, while such refugees may not presently be subject to deportation, once their refugee status is revoked, they lose the right to the protection of the *non-refoulement* principle under Article 33 of the Refugee Convention.

20 *Duldung* status is a form of tolerated stay utilised primarily in Germany under which migrants are permitted to stay in the country of residence but have restricted rights. For instance, in Germany holders of *Duldung* have restricted access to employment and receive state benefits at a rate 20% below conventional social welfare payments. They cannot work for a year after the initial grant of *Duldung* status, and work permits stipulate the number of hours that they may work. Children can go to school, but cannot access vocational training. Further, they do not have rights to family reunion: see F. Mansouri, et al., 'Temporary Protection and the Refugee Convention in Australia, Denmark, and Germany' (2009) 26(1) *Refuge*, 135, 140.

21 European Union, *Report by the Commissioner for Human Rights, Mr Thomas Hammarberg, on His Visit to Germany 9–11 and 15–20 October 2006*, CommDH (2007), 11 July 2007, 35 [128] (hereinafter *Hammarberg Report*).

22 *Duldung* permits can be granted to persons who cannot be returned to their country of origin for legal, technical or humanitarian reasons. It does not give a right of residence but

noted, it therefore places the individual in a very weak legal position.[23] This is important for the operation of cessation, as such persons may be residing in a host state but be open to deportation at any time if state authorities decide that their country of origin is now 'safe'. Further, the former EU Commissioner of Human Rights, Thomas Hammarberg has criticised Germany's use of *Duldung*, noting that whilst they may be justified as a short-term measure, 'when they are applied for several years, not to mention over a decade, such an insecure status can become an affront to human dignity'.[24]

The legal questions

The state practice of time-limited visas and permits raises fundamental questions relating to refugee protection: in what circumstances should refugee status be ceased? Should it simply be where the refugee no longer meets the definition of a refugee under the Refugee Convention, or does it require more? Is the test simply absence of persecution or a broader notion of 'effective protection' encompassing criteria such as human rights protections, operation of judicial and administrative structures, and the absence of armed conflict? In other words, what is the relationship between persecution and protection under international refugee law?

The difference between granting and revoking refugee status

One of the fundamental starting points of my analysis is that the granting of refugee status is an important act under both international and domestic law. This may be an obvious point to some readers, but it is worth highlighting because it is a legal act which has ramifications for the way in which states grant protection, and for the test to be used in *revoking* that status.

The definition of a refugee set out in Article 1A(2) of the Refugee Convention states that the term 'refugee' shall apply to any person who:

> owing to well-founded fear of being persecuted for reasons of race, religion, nationality, membership of a particular social group or political opinion, is outside the country of his nationality and is unable or, owing to such fear, is unwilling to avail himself of the protection of that country.[25]

---

rather simply suspends deportation on a temporary basis for a period of 6 months at a time. Persons holding a *Duldung* permit have restricted access to health care, education, work and restricted right of movement: see ibid 35 [128].

23 UNHCR, 'UNHCR Statement on the "Ceased Circumstances" Clause of the EC Qualification Directive' (2008), 11 (footnote 59), <www.unhcr.org/refworld/docid/48a2f0782.html> (hereinafter UNHCR Cessation Statement 2008).

24 *Hammarberg Report*, above n 21, 35 [129].

25 Refugee Convention, above n 2, Article 1A(2). It also covers those 'who, not having a nationality and being outside the country of his former habitual residence as a result of such events, is unable or, owing to such fear, is unwilling to return to it.'

Thus, the refugee definition applies only to those persons who are outside their country of origin and are able to demonstrate that they are unable or unwilling to return to that country due to a well-founded fear of persecution for a Convention reason.

There are two issues which arise from this in terms of the duration and nature of protection granted to refugees under Article 1A(2). First, once refugee status is granted, it is able to be revoked or 'ceased' by a state if the criteria set out in Article 1C of the Refugee Convention are satisfied. One of the criteria upon which a state can cease the refugee status of a person is if there is a sufficient change in circumstances in the refugee's country of nationality ('the ceased circumstances clause'), which is set out in Article 1C(5) of the Refugee Convention. It provides that the Convention may cease to apply to a refugee if:

> he can no longer, because the circumstances in connection with which he has been recognized as a refugee have ceased to exist, continue to refuse to avail himself of the protection of the country of his nationality; Provided that this paragraph shall not apply to a refugee falling under Section 1A(1) of this Article who is able to invoke compelling reasons arising out of previous persecution for refusing to avail himself of the protection of the country of nationality.[26]

Second, the Refugee Convention does not explicitly state that refugee protection granted by a state must be permanent in nature. Historically, the use of temporary protection has generally been recognised as an acceptable response to the particular exigencies of certain situations, such as those of mass influx. However, it is less clear that it should be used outside that special case, where individual refugee status determination is possible. On this point, some commentators have pointed to Article 1C as evidence that protection under the Convention is designed to be temporary only.[27] I argue in this book that whilst temporary residence permits may be granted to refugees, the legal situation becomes more complex as those refugees continue to reside in the asylum host state for a number of years. As such, the practical integration of refugees in an asylum host state may have to be considered as part of any cessation decision (discussed in Chapter 7).

26 Ibid, Article 1C(5).

27 See e.g. M. Kjaerum, 'Temporary Protection in Europe in the 1990s' (1994) 6 *International Journal of Refugee Law* 444, 445–6: 'The 1951 Geneva Convention reflects the temporary nature of refugee status in the cessation clauses of article 1C, especially paragraph 5'. See also J. Fitzpatrick and R. Bonoan, 'Cessation of Refugee Protection', Chapter 8 in E. Feller, V. Türk, and F. Nicholson (eds.), *Refugee Protection in International Law: UNHCR's Global Consultations on International Protection* (Cambridge University Press, 2003), 491, 492; M.A. Castillo and J.C. Hathaway, 'Temporary Protection', in J.C. Hathaway (ed.), *Reconceiving International Refugee Law* (Martinus Nijhoff, 1997), 2.

Persecution and protection, whilst linked in the refugee definition,[28] are two very different concepts under cessation, and indeed under international refugee law more broadly. Acts recognised by state decision makers as constituting persecution vary, but typically include threats to life or physical harm and certain human rights violations.[29] The concept of 'protection' in cessation decisions is a much wider and different concept in that it involves positive attributes, such as, *inter alia*, the provision of physical security and safety; the existence of a functioning government and basic administrative structures, including a functioning legal and judicial system; and an adequate infrastructure to enable residents to exercise their rights.[30] As such, it may not be possible for cessation to be satisfied where the refugee is being returned to a state where there is an ongoing armed conflict or where protection is being provided by a non-state actor.[31]

There are also important procedural questions which arise as to how cessation should be applied. For instance, what should be the burden and standard of proof, what weight should be given to past persecution and what role should UNHCR play in decisions about cessation? In relation to past persecution, there is also a question as to whether 'compelling reasons' for non-return should provide an exception to cessation, as is set out in the proviso to Article 1C(5)[32] and the domestic law of some states.[33]

The notion that a refugee can have his or her refugee status revoked due to a change in circumstances in a country of origin therefore raises difficult and controversial questions. This is particularly so due to the highly politicised context in which refugee law operates.

Controversially, many of those who have had their refugee status revoked due to cessation have been citizens of Iraq, Afghanistan and Somalia – countries which have been the site of serious security problems, political unrest and human rights

28 For instance, the existence of state protection is a key element of the definition of refugee status under Article 1A(2) of the Refugee Convention.

29 See discussion of the varying forms of persecution in G. Goodwin-Gill and J. McAdam, *The Refugee in International Law* (Oxford University Press, 3rd ed., 2007), 92.

30 See UNHCR, *UNHCR Statement on the 'Ceased Circumstances' Clause of the EC Qualification Directive*, 14 August 2008, <www.unhcr.org/48a2f2a42.pdf> (hereinafter UNHCR Cessation Statement 2008). This is discussed in detail in Chapter 2 of this book. As Hathaway and Foster note, 'while the change of circumstances is a condition precedent to contemplating cessation under Art. 1(C)(5)-(6), it is the consequential restoration of *protection* . . . that must be established in order to justify the cessation of refugee status': J.C. Hathaway and M. Foster, *The Law of Refugee Status* (Cambridge University Press, 2nd ed., 2014), 476.

31 These issues are discussed in detail in Chapters 4 and 5 of this book.

32 Refugee Convention, above n 2, Article 1C(5): 'Provided that this paragraph shall not apply to a refugee falling under Section 1A(1) of this Article who is able to invoke compelling reasons arising out of previous persecution for refusing to avail himself of the protection of the country of nationality'. The 'compelling reasons' proviso is discussed in detail in Chapter 6 of this book.

33 For instance, Section 73 of the German *Asylum Procedure Act* and Section 108(4) of the Canadian *Immigration and Refugee Protection Act.*

abuses.[34] Despite concerted efforts to achieve peace and democratisation in these countries, they continue to suffer from protracted civil conflict, political instability and systemic economic problems.[35] Indeed, UNHCR has explicitly stated that the current situation in Afghanistan does not warrant cessation of refugee status on the basis of Article 1C(5) of the Refugee Convention.[36]

The past use of cessation by asylum host states in relation to such countries provides an important illustration of some of the complexities, both legal and political, that arise in deciding the criteria upon which refugee status should be ceased. Cessation of refugee status involves questions not only about refugee law but also geo-political questions about assessing the likely developments in the country situation in the future. For instance, what will be the likely effect of the withdrawal of multinational troops and other international actors upon the durability of change in the country? Are there security and socio-economic factors which may affect the country's future stability?

Because of the importance of the grant of refugee status and the circumstances in which it is made, cessation of refugee status is therefore a serious matter. It may result in return of that person to a country where it has been found that a well-founded fear of persecution previously existed. This involves an evaluation of country information to establish whether or not there has been a sufficient change of circumstances in the country of origin and whether the former refugee can avail themselves of the protection of their country of origin. As noted earlier, such a process is complex and difficult in conflict situations such as those in Iraq

34 See e.g. 'UK Operational Guidance Note: Afghanistan, 2012' [3.7.2]. In relation to Iraq, a 2012 UNHCR report points to, among other things, the 'volatile security situation' in the country: see 'UNHCR Country Operations Profile: Iraq 2012', <www.unhcr.org/pages/49e486426.html>. On Somalia, Amnesty International reports that armed conflict continued in central and southern Somalia between Somali Federal Government (SFG) forces, African Union Mission in Somalia (AMISOM) peacekeepers, and the armed group al-Shabaab: Amnesty International, *Amnesty International Report 2016/17: Somalia*, 22 February 2017.

35 On Afghanistan, see Human Rights Watch, 'No Safe Place', *Insurgent Attacks on Civilians in Afghanistan*, 8 May 2018, <www.hrw.org/report/2018/05/08/no-safeplace/insurgent-attacks-civilians-afghanistan>, 1–2, 7, 27–35; UNHCR, *UNHCR Eligibility Guidelines for Afghanistan*, 30 August 2018, HCR/EG/AFG/18/02, 12, where UNHCR notes that, as of 31 January 2018, the Taliban was reported to control or contest 43.7% of all districts in Afghanistan (citing Special Inspector General for Afghanistan Reconstruction (SIGAR), Quarterly Report to the United States Congress, 30 April 2018). On Iraq, see for instance, Human Rights Watch, *Annual Report 2017: Iraq*, <www.hrw.org/world-report/2018/country-chapters/iraq>.

36 UNHCR, *UNHCR Eligibility Guidelines for Afghanistan*, 30 August 2018 HCR/EG/AFG/18/02, 39. UNHCR has not updated its Eligibility Guidelines for Iraq since 2012. However, it did make a similar statement in relation to Iraq in its 2012 Eligibility Guidelines: see UNHCR, 'Eligibility Guidelines for Assessing the International Protection Needs of Iraqi Asylum-Seekers', 31 May 2012, HCR/EG/IRQ/12/03, 13: 'the current situation in Iraq does not warrant cessation of refugee status on the basis of Article 1C(5) of the 1951 Convention'. This is significant, as some states were seeking to apply Article 1C(5) in relation to refugees from Iraq during this period.

and Afghanistan and other post-conflict societies which have not yet reached a situation of transparent governance, stability and security.

These features of cessation are important, as the individualised application of Article 1C(5) has received less academic analysis than other provisions of the Refugee Convention, such as the refugee definition in Article 1A(2) and the exclusion clauses under Article 1F.[37] This comparative lack of attention has primarily been due to the lack of state practice relating to the provision. Some commentators have discussed certain aspects of the cessation clauses, such as the need for changes to be 'fundamental, stable and durable',[38] and the 'compelling circumstances' exception to cessation.[39] Hathaway and Foster, in particular, have set out a compelling critique of current state practice and jurisprudence on Article 1C(5) in their 2014 text.[40] Similarly, there has been some analysis of Article 11(1)(e), the cessation provision of the EU Qualification Directive.[41] However, very little analysis has been produced in relation to the way in which Article 1C(5) interacts with time-limited visa regimes[42] or the interpretation which should be given to the ceased circumstances cessation provisions set out in Article 11(1)(e) of the EU Qualification Directive.[43]

Given this background, I now turn to discuss the aims and structure of this book and the interpretative framework which I will use to examine cessation.

37 Apart from the work of the author, there are only a relatively small number of academic papers focusing on the individualised application of Article 1C(5), see for example, J. Fitzpatrick, 'The End of Protection: Standards for Cessation of Refugee Status and Withdrawal of Temporary Protection' (1999) 13 *Georgetown Immigration Law Journal* 343; J. Fitzpatrick and R. Bonoan, 'Cessation of Refugee Protection', Chapter 8 in E. Feller, V. Türk, and F. Nicholson (eds.), *Refugee Protection in International Law: UNHCR's Global Consultations on International Protection* (Cambridge University Press, 2003), 491–544; J.R. Tarwater, 'Analysis and Case Studies of the "Ceased Circumstances" Cessation Clause of the 1951 Refugee Convention' (2001) 15(3) *Georgetown Immigration Law Journal* 563; M.E. Cwik, 'Forced to Flee and Forced to Repatriate: How the Cessation Clause of Article 1C(5) and (6) of the 1951 Refugee Convention Operates in International Law and Practice' (2011) 44(3) *Vanderbilt Journal of Transnational Law* 711; Goodwin-Gill and McAdam, above n 29, 139–49.

38 Hathaway and Foster, above n 30, 479; Goodwin-Gill and McAdam, above n 29, 142–3; J.C. Hathaway, *The Rights of Refugees under International Law* (Cambridge University Press, 2005), 922–35.

39 Hathaway and Foster, above n 30, 490–4; D. Milner, 'Exemption from Cessation of Refugee Status in the Second Sentence of Article 1C(5)/(6) of the 1951 Refugee Convention' (2004) 16(1) *International Journal of Refugee Law* 91.

40 Hathaway and Foster, above n 30, 476–90.

41 E.g. R. Errera, 'Cessation and Assessment of New Circumstances: A Comment on *Abdulla*, CJEU, 2 March 2010' (2011) 23(3) *International Journal of Refugee Law* 521.

42 There is a brief discussion of this issue in A. Edwards, 'Tampering with Refugee Protection: The Case of Australia' (2003) 15(2) *International Journal of Refugee Law* 192, 206–07. See also the author's published work on Article 1C(5): M. O'Sullivan, 'Before the High Court: *Minister for Immigration v QAAH*: Cessation of Refugee Status' (2006) 28(2) *Sydney Law Review* 359; M. O'Sullivan, 'Withdrawing Protection under Article 1C(5) of the 1951 Convention: Lessons from Australia' (2008) 20(4) *International Journal of Refugee Law* 586.

43 See however Errera, above n 41.

Aims and structure of book

The basis for my analysis of state practice of cessation is the 1951 Refugee Convention and the EU Qualification Directive. My method utilises primarily a doctrinal research approach, with an emphasis on comparative analysis. The book also undertakes reform-oriented research and analysis in that it seeks to expose problems associated with the current application of cessation by states and puts forward recommendations as to how cessation may be applied in order to better align it with a 'good faith' interpretation of the 1951 Refugee Convention.[44] In doing so, it will consider how best to calibrate the cessation standards so they are not only consistent with the terms of the Refugee Convention but also pragmatic and workable by states. It also situates cessation in the context of other areas of refugee law, drawing links to debates on the meaning of protection, non-state actors of protection, complementary protection[45] and the return of asylum seekers to situations of armed conflict. This raises the issue of whether a more consistent approach and holistic interpretation should be taken of 'safety' and 'protection' across international refugee law.

This book focuses on the application by *states* of the cessation clause of the 1951 Refugee Convention in relation to *individually recognised refugees*. However, I will also compare individual cessation with the issuing of group-based declarations of cessation by UNHCR.[46] It is also important to flag that this book focuses on cessation of *refugee status*. In practice, cessation is also applicable to *complementary protection*. Due to various reasons, this book is focused on cessation as it applies only to the refugee definition, but I note that the analysis set out in this text can also be applied to complementary protection.

Finally, this book is not merely a doctrinal study of the law on cessation (although it focuses on this). Where necessary, I have referred to key studies from international relations and political science. For instance, in Chapter 5 on non-state actors of protection, I place emphasis on writings from non-law disciplines (e.g. on the concept of failed states) and work on political community and the concept of 'refugeehood'. I take the view that the inclusion of such scholarship is vital to understanding not only the legal context but also the geo-political context in which cessation operates.

44 Article 31(1) of the Vienna Convention on the Law of Treaties provides that 'A treaty shall be interpreted in good faith in accordance with the ordinary meaning to be given to the terms of the treaty in their context and in the light of its object and purpose': Vienna Convention on the Law of Treaties, done at Vienna on 23 May 1969, entered into force on 27 January 1980, United Nations, Treaty Series, vol. 1155, p. 331.

45 I note that this book focuses on time-limited visas and Article 1C as set out in the 1951 Refugee Convention. However, similar cessation provisions apply to complementary protection in most states: see e.g. EU Qualification Directive, above n 3, Article 16.

46 For instance, UNHCR and the Government of Rwanda announced on 7 October 2011 that UNHCR will recommend to states that they invoke cessation in relation to Rwanda by 31 December 2011, effective on 30 June 2012: see 'UNHCR/Government of Rwanda Joint Communiqué', 7 October 2011, <http://reliefweb.int/sites/reliefweb.int/files/reliefweb_pdf/node-451476.pdf?>.

Relevant interpretative principles

As an international treaty, the general principles governing interpretation of the 1951 Refugee Convention are set out in the Vienna Convention on the Law of Treaties (VCLT).[47] Article 31 of the VCLT provides 'General Rules of Interpretation' and states that a treaty:

> shall be interpreted in good faith in accordance with the ordinary meaning to be given to the terms of the treaty in their context and in the light of its objects and purpose.[48]

Article 31(2) and (3) then permit consideration of extraneous material to the treaty, comprising interpretative agreements between the parties, subsequent practice and relevant rules of international law.[49] The term 'context' for the purpose of the interpretation of a treaty is defined by Article 31(2) as comprising, in addition to the text (including its preamble and annexes):

> a any agreement relating to the treaty which was made between all the parties in connection with the conclusion of the treaty;
> b any instrument which was made by one or more parties in connection with the conclusion of the treaty and accepted by the other parties as an instrument related to the treaty.[50]

Articles 31(3) and 32 of the VCLT then provide further detail as to which types of additional material shall be considered. These include subsequent agreement and practice of the parties,[51] relevant rules of international law[52] and supplementary means of interpretation, including the preparatory work of the treaty and the circumstances of its conclusion.[53] Ancillary sources of interpretation which

47 Vienna Convention on the Law of Treaties, 23 May 1969, 155 UNTS 331 (hereinafter Vienna Convention on the Law of Treaties).

48 Ibid, Article 31. See also Article 26 of the Vienna Convention on the Law of Treaties which states that '[e]very treaty in force is binding upon the parties to it and must be performed by them in good faith'. The case law on 'good faith' is discussed by J. McAdam, 'Interpretation of the 1951 Convention', in A. Zimmermann (ed.), *The 1951 Convention Relating to the Status of Refugees and Its 1967 Protocol: A Commentary* (Oxford University Press, 2011), 93–5.

49 Vienna Convention on the Law of Treaties, above n 47, Article 31(2)–(3).

50 See Ibid, Article 31(2).

51 Ibid, Articles 31(3)(a) and (b). Article 31(3) provides: 'There shall be taken into account, together with the context: (a) any subsequent agreement between the parties regarding the interpretation of the treaty or the application of its provisions; (b) any subsequent practice in the application of the treaty which establishes the agreement of the parties regarding its interpretation'.

52 Vienna Convention on the Law of Treaties, above n 47, Article 31(3)(c).

53 Ibid, Article 32: 'Recourse may be had to supplementary means of interpretation, including the preparatory work of the treaty and the circumstances of its conclusion, in order to confirm the meaning resulting from the application of article 31, or to determine the

have been recognised by courts as relevant extrinsic materials in interpreting the Refugee Convention include the *travaux préparatoires* to the Convention and the UNHCR Handbook.[54] Some courts have also referred to UNHCR Executive Committee (Ex Com) Conclusions, UNHCR Guidelines and academic commentary.[55] This is relevant to cessation, as UNHCR has issued guidelines on the interpretation of cessation and has made *amicus curiae* submissions and other representations in litigation on cessation. It has also issued country guidance documents on the applicability of cessation to Iraq and Afghanistan. Despite this, many aspects of UNHCR's views have not been endorsed by the states which have applied Article 1C(5) to date.[56]

In relation to the obligation to interpret the Refugee Convention in 'good faith' provided in Article 31 of the VCLT, Hathaway and Foster note that two critical insights follow from that overarching duty:

> First, those interpreting the Convention must seek to promote the Convention's **effectiveness**. . . . Second, and related, the duty of good faith requires an effort to ensure that the treaty can continue to function within its **present social reality and contemporary legal context**.[57]

Article 32 of the VCLT also provides for reliance on 'supplementary means of interpretation' and specifically permits reference to the drafting history of a treaty.[58]

As to 'subsequent practice' of a treaty, provided for in Article 31(3) of the VCLT,[59] it is generally agreed that this includes legislation and case law.[60] As Jane McAdam notes, '[t]he weight to be accorded to State practice depends on its extent, uniformity, and consistency, as well as which States are involved'.[61] As will be discussed in Chapter 6 of this book, subsequent state practice has been important in

---

meaning when the interpretation according to article 31: (a) leaves the meaning ambiguous or obscure; or (b) leads to a result which is manifestly absurd or unreasonable'.

54 See *Applicant A v Minister for Immigration and Ethnic Affairs* (1997) 190 CLR 225, 231 (Brennan CJ) (*Applicant A*): 'The form in which a treaty is drafted, the subject to which it relates, the mischief that it addresses, the history of its negotiation and comparison with earlier or amending instruments relating to the same subject may warrant consideration in arriving at the true interpretation of its text'. See also *R v Secretary of State for the Home Department, Ex parte Adan* [1999] 3 W.L.R. 1274 1296 (Court of Appeal, Laws LJ): 'While the Handbook is not by any means itself a source of law, many signatory States have accepted the guidance which on their behalf the UNHCR was asked to provide, and in those circumstances it constitutes in our judgment, good evidence of what has come to be international practice within Art 31(3)(b) of the Vienna Convention'.

55 See McAdam, above n 48, 112–5.

56 Discussed in Chapter 4.

57 Hathaway and Foster, above n 30, 6 [footnotes omitted, emphasis in original].

58 Vienna Convention on the Law of Treaties, above n 47, Article 32.

59 Ibid, Article 31(3)(b) 'any subsequent practice in the application of the treaty which establishes the agreement of the parties regarding its interpretation'.

60 See McAdam, above n 48, 96.

61 Ibid 96–7.

interpreting the proviso to Article 1C(5), which sets out an exception to cessation where there are compelling reasons arising out of past persecution.[62] In relation to this exception, the English Court of Appeal in the 2002 case of *Hoxha*[63] noted that where the Convention sets out a clear provision, it is necessary to demonstrate 'very convincing evidence of a widespread and general practice of the international community'.[64] The court emphasised that Article 31(3)(b) of the VCLT requires the subsequent practice to establish the *agreement* of the parties regarding the interpretation and suggested the standard was similar to that required for customary international law.[65] It also stressed that the state practice must be done in 'recognition of a legal obligation to do so' or 'to the adoption of a particular interpretation of the 1951 Convention' rather than 'for admirable humanitarian reasons'.[66]

Interpretative relevance of human rights law

The influence of international human rights law on refugee law is important in the context of this book because the return of a former refugee to a country will clearly raise a number of human rights issues – both in terms of the human rights standards in the country of origin and in terms of any human rights claims which the refugee may have by virtue of establishing links to the asylum host state (via duration of stay, marriage, children, economic links, etc.) (discussed in Chapter 7). Here I note that human rights principles have been applied to the definition of a refugee by many states (e.g. to assist in interpreting the meaning of 'persecution'), and there is no reason such principles should not also be applied to other constituent parts of the Refugee Convention, including Article 1C.[67]

The human rights purposes of the Refugee Convention are clearly set out in the preambular paragraphs of the Convention which refer to the principle 'that human beings shall enjoy fundamental rights and freedoms without discrimination'[68] and

62 Refugee Convention, above n 2, Article 1C(5) provides that it 'shall not apply to a refugee falling under section A(1) of this Article who is able to invoke compelling reasons arising out of previous persecution for refusing to avail himself of the protection of the country of nationality'.

63 *R (on appn of Hoxha) v Secretary of State for the Home Department* [2002] EWCA Civ 1403, [2002] All ER (D) 182 (*Hoxha*).

64 *Hoxha* [47]: 'Where one has clear and express language imposing a restriction upon the scope of a particular provision, as is the case with the proviso to Article 1C(5), it must require very convincing evidence of a widespread and general practice of the international community to establish that that restriction is no longer to be applied as a matter of international law'.

65 *Hoxha* [44]: 'It is to be observed that Article 31.3(b) requires the subsequent practice to establish the agreement of the parties regarding the interpretation. That reflects again the approach adopted in customary international law as was established in the case of *The Temple of Preah Vihear* [1962] ICJ Reports page 33'.

66 *Hoxha* [45].

67 Thank you to Cathryn Costello for raising this in response to my presentation on cessation and integration to the 2018 Refugee Law Initiative Conference, University of London.

68 Refugee Convention, above n 2, Preambular paragraph 1: 'Considering that the Charter of the United Nations and the Universal Declaration of Human Rights approved on 10 December

the interest of the UN in affording 'refugees the widest possible exercise of these fundamental rights and freedoms'.[69] This is important, as the VCLT recognises that the language of a treaty's preamble can provide insight into the 'object and purpose' of the treaty, against which the operative provisions of the treaty should be interpreted.[70] This is echoed by UNHCR, courts and commentators who have also underlined the need to take a purposive rather than literal interpretation of the Refugee Convention[71] and to take a holistic approach to interpretation of the Convention when analysing its constituent articles.[72] Thus, UNHCR and courts have emphasised the need to interpret the Convention in light of its reference to 'fundamental human rights'.[73] The UNHCR's Executive Committee states that:

1948 by the General Assembly have affirmed the principle that human beings shall enjoy fundamental rights and freedoms without discrimination'.

69 Refugee Convention, above n 2, Preamble, second paragraph: 'Considering that the United Nations has, on various occasions, manifested its profound concern for refugees and endeavoured to assure refugees the widest possible exercise of these fundamental rights and freedoms'.

70 Vienna Convention on the Law of Treaties, above n 47, Article 31(1).

71 See McAdam, above n 48, 83–86; *Applicant A*; New Zealand Refugee Status Appeals Authority, *Refugee Appeal No. 70366/96*; and the UK House of Lords, *Horvath v. Secretary of State for the Home Department* [2001] 1 AC 489, 508 (Lord Clyde). In *Horvath*, Lord Clyde stated that '[w]hile the language of the article has to be respected, any pre-occupation with the precise words may fail to meet the broad intent of the Convention'. See also the House of Lords in *Adan v Secretary of State for the Home Department* [1999] 1 AC 293 (House of Lords) 305 (*Adan* House of Lords 1999), where Lord Lloyd recognises the importance of an holistic and purposive interpretation but emphasises the importance of the language used: 'It follows that one is more likely to arrive at the true construction of article 1A(2) by seeking a meaning which makes sense in the light of the Convention as a whole, and the purposes which the framers of the Convention were seeking to achieve, rather than by concentrating exclusively on the language. A broad approach is what is needed, rather than a narrow linguistic approach. But having said that, the starting point must be the language itself'.

72 See UNHCR, 'The International Protection of Refugees: Interpreting Article 1 of the 1951 Convention Relating to the Status of Refugees' (2001) 20(3) *Refugee Survey Quarterly* 78; and V. Türk and F. Nicholson, 'Refugee Protection in International Law: An Overall Perspective', in E. Feller, V. Türk, and F. Nicholson (eds.), *Refugee Protection in International Law: UNHCR's Global Consultations on International Protection* (Cambridge University Press, 2003), 42–3; *Januzi (FC) v Secretary of State for the Home Department* [2006] UKHL 5, [4]. In *Applicant A*, 231 (Brennan CJ): explained that 'the holistic approach to interpretation may require a consideration of both the text and the object and purpose of the treaty in order to ascertain its true meaning'.

73 See e.g. the High Court of Australia in *Applicant A*, 247–8 where Dawson J states that 'The humanitarian aims of the Convention are apparent from its preamble'. His Honour notes that the first, second and third preamble refer to fundamental human rights. However, he then notes that preamble 4 and 5 refer to the need for states to share the burden and avoid refugees becoming a cause of tension between states. In this respect, he notes that the humanitarian scope of the Convention is limited. On the issue of the objects and purposes of the Convention, see McAdam, above n 48, 91–3; and H. Battjes, *European Asylum Law and International Law* (Martinus Nijhoff, 2006), 460.

> the modern duty of protection . . . goes beyond simply respecting the norms of refugee law; it includes also the obligation to 'take all necessary measures to ensure that refugees are effectively protected . . . in compliance with their obligations under international human rights and humanitarian law instruments bearing directly on refugee protection'.[74]

A number of common law courts have held that the human rights purposes of the Refugee Convention provides the background against which interpretation of individual provisions of the Convention should take place.[75] For instance, the Supreme Court of Canada has stated that:

> the Refugee Convention itself expresses 'a profound concern for refugees,' and its principal purpose is to 'assure refugees the widest possible exercise of fundamental rights and freedoms'.[76]

Commentators, however, disagree as to the exact relationship between human rights law and refugee law and the weight which should be applied to the former. On one hand, James Hathaway has stated that 'the advancement of human rights is at the core of refugee law's object and purpose'.[77] David Cantor, on the other hand, has urged some caution, stating that the weight to the given to the mention of human rights in the preamble should not be overstated.[78] As he notes, 'the totality of the Convention's operative provisions are also based on a language and rationale distinct from that of human rights'.[79] In particular, Cantor argues that the 'manner in which the UNHCR Handbook integrates international human rights law into its interpretative analysis seems somewhat haphazard'.[80] He points to the fact that whilst the UNHCR Handbook uses human rights standards to illustrate certain elements of Article 1A(2), such as the meaning of 'being persecuted', their role in relation to other parts of Article 1A(2) is 'not specified'.[81] I would add to this by pointing out that the focus has very much been on using human rights law only in relation to *Article 1A(2)* and no other aspects of the refugee definition – particularly Article 1C – and further

74 UNHCR Executive Committee Conclusion No. 81, 'General Conclusion on International Protection' (1997), para. (e); Hathaway, above n 38, 119–20.

75 Discussed in M. Foster, *International Refugee Law and Socio-Economic Rights: Refuge from Deprivation* (Cambridge University Press, 2007), 44.

76 *Suresh v. Canada* [2002] 1 SCR 3 (Can. SC, Jan. 11, 2002).

77 Hathaway, *Rights of Refugees*, above n 2, 11.

78 D. Cantor, 'Defining Refugees: Persecution, Surrogacy and the Human Rights Paradigm', in B. Burson and D. Cantor, *Human Rights and the Refugee Definition: Comparative Legal Practice and Theory* (Brill, 2016), 373: 'questions remain as to the weight to be attributed to the mention of human rights in the preamble'.

79 Ibid.

80 Ibid 352.

81 Ibid 352–3.

consideration must be given to how human rights should inform those other provisions of the Convention.

Structure

This book commences with the concept of temporary protection – its development from a group to an individualised mechanism – before going on to examine in detail the meaning of key aspects of Article 1C(5). Chapter 2 discusses the way in which cessation fits into the concept of protection under refugee law. Here I introduce the notion of protection for duration of risk (via temporary protection and time-limited visas) and provide an overview of some of the ways in which cessation intersects with other key aspects of refugee law. In Chapter 3, I discuss the content and function of Article 1C(5) and the primary interpretative issues which have arisen in relation to Article 1C(5). Here I examine the differences between cessation and recognition of refugee status (that is, whether Article 1C(5) is simply the 'mirror image' of Article 1A(2)) and the concept of persecution and protection. Importantly, Chapter 3 explains the basis of 'effective protection', which is the central legal concept utilised in this thesis. It examines whether the test for cessation should be the absence of a well-founded fear of persecution or the presence of affirmative 'effective protection' (the latter of which encapsulates such factors as the existence of human rights, a stable security situation and a functioning legal and justice system). In doing so, I focus my analysis on the relationship between recognition and cessation of refugee status.

In Chapter 4, I discuss the standard of proof for 'changed circumstances', and, in particular, how circumstances can be said to have changed where there is a situation of armed conflict within a country. I then proceed in Chapter 5 to examine the relationship between cessation and protection in relation to the question of non-state actors of protection. In Chapter 5, I analyse the interplay between cessation and Article 7 of the EU Qualification Directive, which explicitly recognises non-state bodies as actors of protection.[82] I do so by reference to the theoretical concept of refugeehood as representing a break in the bond between citizen and state. This follows on from the work of Atle Grahl-Madsen and Andrew Shacknove who have described refugeehood as a situation where the normal mutual bond of trust, loyalty, protection and assistance between an individual and the government of his home country has been broken.[83] This informs my approach to non-state actors as agents of protection.

This then leads into a discussion of the onus of proof and the relevance of past persecution in Chapter 6 and the way in which a refugee's integrative links in an asylum host state should be considered a part of the cessation decision, in Chapter 7. In this latter chapter, I make clear recommendations as to how cessation

82 EU Qualification Directive, above n 3, Article 7.

83 A. Grahl-Madsen, *The Status of Refugees in International Law* (A.W. Sijthoff-Leyden, Vol. 1, 1966), 78–9; A. Shacknove, 'Who Is a Refugee?' (1985) 95 *Ethics* 274–84, 275. Discussed in Chapter 5.

can be applied fairly to those refugees who have resided in an asylum host state for long periods.

In the concluding chapter, the book considers the implications that increased state utilisation of Article 1C(5) may have for the development of international refugee law more generally. This underlines one of the purposes of this book – to not only present an in-depth study of cessation of refugee status but also to highlight some trends in the way that states interpret the Refugee Convention to highlight some broader issues about the future of refugee protection globally.

2 Protection for the duration of risk, temporary residence and naturalisation

Introduction

One difficult question raised by the granting of only time-limited visas to refugees is how this practice relates to our legal understanding of key notions such as residence, protection, citizenship and cessation. This is an important question, as whilst a time-limited visa of 3 or 5 years duration may be justified as acceptable for covering the duration of risk, the legal situation becomes muddied when that period of residence stretches to 5 or 10 years and those refugees effectively become part of the host state's community.

This chapter therefore examines the way in which cessation fits in with the broader issues in refugee law, in particular, the meaning of protection. It focuses on the notion that protection is a tool to cover the duration of risk only; it traces the development of 'temporary protection' in group and individual situations; and then it discusses the way in which cessation interacts with integration, naturalisation and citizenship. The latter themes are then picked up in Chapter 7, which discusses the considerations which should apply when a state seeks to apply Article 1C(5) to a long-term resident refugee as part of a return decision.

Historical background – group-based temporary protection and cessation

In the period following World War II, the emphasis of refugee protection was on two types of durable solutions: integration in the country of asylum and resettlement.[1] As a result of the Cold War, asylum states developed an 'exilic bias'[2] in

1 See S. Kneebone, 'Introduction: Refugees and Asylum Seekers in the International Context: Rights and Realities', in S. Kneebone (ed.), *Refugees, Asylum Seekers and the Rule of Law: Comparative Perspectives* (Cambridge University Press, 2009), 17.

2 That is, states permitted access to immigration streams and residency. The term 'exilic basis' is used by T.A. Aleinikoff, 'State Centred Refugee Law: From Resettlement to Containment' (1992–93) 14(1) *Michigan Journal of International Law* 120, 121, 125; G.J.L. Coles, 'The Human Rights Approach to the Solution of the Refugee Problem: A Theoretical and Practical Enquiry', in A.E. Nash (ed.), *Human Rights and the Protection of Refugees under International Law* (Institute for Research on Public Policy, Nova Scotia, 1988), 195, 209.

their treatment of refugees due to self-interest and political strategy.[3] Integration was particularly common in Europe during this Cold War period.[4] Although some states continue to utilise resettlement as part of their refugee policy,[5] increasingly states have moved away from integration and resettlement towards a restrictive approach to refugee flows which encompasses measures such as containment, push-backs, detention and various forms of temporary protection.

Whilst it is outside the realm of this book to canvass the entire history of temporary protection, it is useful by way of background to highlight a number of salient features from the past use of temporary protection by states and UNHCR. As noted in the Introduction to this book, the focus of my analysis is on cessation arising from individualised 'temporary protection' (via time-limited visas or residence permits),[6] rather than on the broader use of 'temporary protection' given to asylum seekers on a group basis.[7] Whilst this is the case, it is necessary by way of background to discuss the practice of UNHCR and states in relation to temporary protection and group-based cessation so as to place the issue of individualised cessation in an historical and legal perspective.[8]

In examining the development and contemporary practice of temporary protection, I note that there is no 'one' type of group-based temporary protection. Rather, states have utilised the concept for differing reasons, and grant vastly differing rights and benefits to protected persons. This section is intended simply to briefly canvass some aspects of state practice using examples from two regions: Africa and the former Yugoslavia. These regions have been chosen because a significant number of group cessation declarations have been made in relation to Africa, and the granting of temporary protection to those refugees who fled the crisis in the former Yugoslavia in the 1990s shaped the contemporary use of both group and individualised temporary protection in the European Union.

3 See e.g. F. Crepeau and L. Holland, 'Temporary Protection, Continuing Insecurity: A Regime Replacing Convention Protection of Refugees in Violation of International Law' (1997) 12 *Canadian Journal of Law and Society* 239, 240.

4 J. van Selm, *Refugee Protection in Europe: Lessons of the Yugoslav Crisis* (Martinus Nijhoff/Kluwer, 1998), 244.

5 As UNHCR notes, the United States is the world's top resettlement country, with Australia, Canada and the Nordic countries also providing a 'sizeable' number of places annually: UNHCR, 'Resettlement: A New Beginning in a Third Country', <www.unhcr.org/pages/4a16b1676.html>.

6 That is, via time-limited visas such as temporary protection visas (Australia) or temporary residence permits (EU).

7 Accordingly, the 'group cessation' determinations made by UNHCR are referred to in this book, but not discussed in great detail. A more detailed discussion of these determinations can be found in J. Fitzpatrick and R. Bonoan, 'Cessation of Refugee Protection', in E. Feller, V. Turk, and F. Nicholson (eds.), *Refugee Protection in International Law: UNHCR's Global Consultations on International Protection* (Cambridge University Press, 2003), 499–512.

8 Historically, cessation began to first be applied (from 1973 onwards) in relation to groups of asylum seekers, whereas its application to individually recognised refugees is more recent (2003 onwards).

Temporary protection in Africa

Group-based temporary protection is utilised extensively in Africa. The nature of the persecution from which refugees tend to flee in Africa (arising from long-standing religious, ethnic and political conflict, and in some cases, acts of genocide) has tended to produce situations of mass influx. Many of these conflicts have been of a long-standing nature, leading to Africa having a substantial number of what UNHCR categorises as 'protracted refugee situations'.[9] The number of refugee flows in Africa is large: ranging between 5.89 million in 1990[10] to 2.2 million at the end of 2010.[11] According to UNHCR's 2017 statistics, sub-Saharan Africa was host to 6.3 million refugees – almost one-third of the world's refugee population.[12] This has made individually based refugee determination difficult to undertake. Therefore, there has been a tendency in Africa to use *prima facie* refugee status determinations and the granting of only temporary rather than permanent protection.[13]

Of relevance here is the 1969 Convention Governing the Specific Aspects of Refugee Problems in Africa (OAU Convention), which explicitly sets out a provision dealing with temporary protection. Article 2(5) of that Convention states that:

> Where a refugee has not received the right to reside in any country of asylum, he may be granted temporary residence in any country of asylum in which he first presented himself as a refugee pending arrangement for his resettlement in accordance with the preceding paragraph.[14]

In terms of the status and rights granted to beneficiaries of group-based protection in Africa, practiced has varied. Controversially, many African host states have

9 As Jeff Crisp, writing as a member of the UNHCR's Evaluation and Policy Analysis Unit, notes: 'by far the majority of these [protracted refugee situations] are to be found in Africa'. J. Crisp, 'No Solution in Sight: The Problem of Protracted Refugee Situations in Africa', *New Issues in Refugee Research Working Paper No. 75*, UNHCR, January 2003, 1–2, <www.unhcr.org/research/RESEARCH/3e2d66c34.pdf>. See also UNHCR Ex Com, *Protracted Refugee Situations*, UN Doc. EC/54/SC/CRP.14, 10 June 2004.

10 UNHCR, *State of the World's Refugees 2000*, Annex 3, 310, <www.unhcr.org/3ebf9ba62.html>.

11 UNHCR, *Global Trends 2010*, 9, <www.unhcr.org/4dfa11499.html>.

12 UNHCR, *Global Trends 2017*, 13, <www.unhcr.org/5b27be547.pdf>.

13 See M. O'Sullivan, 'Human Security and the Protection of Refugees in Africa', in A. Abass (ed.), *Protecting Human Security in Africa* (Oxford University Press, 2010), 160, citing various UNHCR sources. For instance, during the Libyan uprising, Guido Ambroso notes that Libyan refugees were protected generously by Tunisia and Egypt, but sub-Saharan Africans were treated much differently: 'The same was not true for sub-Saharan Africans, who were ordered to stay in the Shousha and Salloum camps and could not go any further as neither Tunisia nor Egypt was prepared to allow them to enjoy full asylum on their territory but only temporary protection in the two camps': G. Ambroso, 'Bordering on a Crisis' (June 2012) 39 *Forced Migration Review* 6.

14 Convention Governing the Specific Aspects of Refugee Problems in Africa, 10 September 1969, entered into force 20 June 1974, 1001 UNTS 45, 48 (hereinafter OAU Convention).

dealt with mass influxes by housing large numbers of refugees in closed refugee camps for extended periods, rather than allowing local integration.[15] Such refugees have limited legal rights in that they tend not to have residence rights in the country of asylum or any right to work.[16] These elements have contributed to security concerns both within camps and in the regions concerned. This situation is exacerbated by the fact that African refugees face great difficulty in obtaining access to countries outside Africa in order to claim refugee status, due to the strict border controls and restrictive refugee policies of many asylum host states (particularly those European nations which are geographically close to Africa).[17] These restrictions have placed pressure on African states to repatriate refugees. Although the OAU Convention obliges member states to respect the 'essentially voluntary character of repatriation',[18] the voluntariness of certain repatriations in the African region has been questioned by some commentators and non-governmental organisations.[19]

The development of temporary protection in Europe in the 1990s – the former Yugoslavia

Another example of the use of temporary protection, and one which has been highly influential on refugee policies in Europe, is the response to the crisis in the former Yugoslavia in the 1990s. This crisis is said to have caused the flow of approximately 1.8 million refugees and displaced persons,[20] many of whom fled to Europe. Thus, it has been said that '[t]he wars of dissolution in the Former Yugoslavia from 1991 to 1995 created a refugee crisis on a scale unseen in Europe since the end of the second World War'.[21] Until this time, the regular and widespread practice of European states was to give recognised refugees permanent

15 The Executive Committee of UNHCR (Ex Com) states: 'in times of crisis, the granting of asylum to large numbers of prima facie refugees is often premised on their being confined to camps.' See UNHCR Ex Com, *Protracted Refugee Situations*, UN Doc. EC/54/SC/CRP.14, 10 June 2004 [9].

16 Crisp, above n 9, 11–12.

17 See e.g. Amnesty International, 'Spain: The Southern Border: The State Turns Its Back on the Human Rights of Refugees and Immigrants', AI Index: EUR 41/008/2005, 20 June 2005; Amnesty International, 'Libya: Totally Inadequate Response by EU States to Refugees Stuck in Limbo', 19 September 2011, <www. amnesty.org>.

18 OAU Convention, Article 5: the 'essentially voluntary character of repatriation shall be respected in all cases and no refugee shall be repatriated against his will'.

19 For instance, Jeff Crisp points out that information collected by the US Committee for Refugees suggests that in Africa 'at least 12 major repatriation movements took place under duress during 1998, involving seven different countries of asylum': J. Crisp, 'Africa's Refugees: Patterns, Problems and Policy Challenges', *New Issues in Refugee Research, Working Paper No. 28*, UNHCR Evaluation and Policy Analysis Unit, Geneva, August 2000, 16.

20 UNHCR, *A Comprehensive Response to the Humanitarian Crisis in the Former Yugoslavia*, 24 July 1992, HCR/IMFY/1992/2 [1], <www.unhcr.org/refworld/docid/438ec8aa2.html>.

21 D. Sopf, 'Temporary Protection in Europe after 1990: The "Right to Remain" of Genuine Convention Refugees' (2001) 6 *Washington University Journal of Law and Policy* 109, 110.

residence.[22] However, during the Yugoslav crisis, temporary protection began to be utilised on a widespread scale by European countries. One problem which arose in this context was that the numbers of refugees from the former Yugoslav residing in European countries varied enormously, and the burden was viewed as not being shared equally. For instance, statistics show that as of March 1997, Germany and Croatia bore a large 'burden' of protecting refugees from Bosnia-Herzegovina with 345,000 present in Germany and 288,000 in Croatia. In contrast, there were only 15,000 such refugees present in France, 8,430 in Italy and 6,000 in the United Kingdom.[23]

There are a number of important features of the response by Europe to the Yugoslav crisis which I wish to highlight. The first is that many European states characterised the conflicts in the former Yugoslavia as 'civil wars', which meant that asylum seekers from the region were primarily viewed as requiring humanitarian protection and as falling outside the scope of the 1951 Refugee Convention.[24] Such persons were generally not legally recognised as Convention refugees but were simply granted authorisation for a temporary stay,[25] with most spending more than 5 years under temporary protection in various European states.[26] This is despite the fact that a large number of people who fled from the Former Yugoslavia to Europe were in fact considered to be 'genuine 1951 Convention refugees'.[27] As Joan Fitzpatrick has noted:

> The pressures of rapidly increasing asylum caseloads during the late 1980s and early 1990s in northern states attracted policy makers to temporary protection as a strategy to circumvent the highly contested arena of refugee status determination.[28]

22 See ibid 110, where Sopf notes that up until the Yugoslav crisis, 'the host countries [in Europe] provided stable shelter for those refugees, and their status as 1951 Convention refugees regularly led to permanent integration into a new society'.

23 UNHCR, *The State of the World's Refugees 1997–98: A Humanitarian Agenda* (1997), figure 5.6.

24 Convention relating to the Status of Refugees, Geneva, 28 July 1951, in force 22 April 1954, 1989 UNTS 137, supplemented by the Protocol relating to the Status of Refugees, New York, 31 January 1967, in force 4 October 1967, 19 UST 6223, 6257 (hereinafter Refugee Convention). This point is discussed in Sopf, above n 21, 111.

25 M. Barutciski, 'EU States and the Refugee Crisis in the Former the Yugoslavia' (1994) 14(3) *Refuge* 32, 34.

26 Sopf, above n 21, 156.

27 Ibid 140, citing G.S. Goodwin-Gill, *The Refugee in International Law* (Oxford University Press, 2nd ed., 1996), 19–20.

28 J. Fitzpatrick, 'Temporary Protection of Refugees: Elements of a Formalized Regime' (2000) 94(2) *The American Journal of International Law* 279, 280 (hereinafter Fitzpatrick, 'Formalised Regime'), citing her earlier article, 'Flight from Asylum: Trends toward Temporary "Refuge" and Local Responses to Forced Migration' 35 (1994) *Virginia Journal of International Law* 27–40.

Second, European state practice in this period emphasised return to the country of origin, rather than permanent settlement.[29] For instance, Germany gave temporary protection to approximately 320,000 Bosnian asylum seekers and encouraged the majority of those temporary protection beneficiaries to be repatriated.[30] (However, the commentary on this is somewhat contradictory, as other reports suggest that most EU states appear to have ultimately granted these refugees permanent status or residency.)[31]

Group-based temporary protection appealed to EU states for a number of reasons, including the fact that (unlike refugee status) it could be withdrawn without the need to go through a formal cessation process.[32] This was problematic in the Yugoslav crisis era, as state practice on the ending of temporary protection varied considerably across European jurisdictions. For instance, Koser and Black note:

> there has been no conformity on the question of how to end 'temporary protection'. Some member states have transferred individuals to status entitling them to permanent residence, others to refugee status, and Germany has shifted the status downwards. Some member states have ended "temporary protection" for all Bosnians, others have drawn distinctions. Where distinctions have been drawn, they have often been on the basis of different combinations of criteria. If "temporary protection" is to be a meaningful status, there is surely a need to determine how the status is concluded.[33]

29 Discussed in D. Sopf, above n 21, 132.

30 According to UNHCR figures, of the 320,000 Bosnian asylum seekers given temporary protection by Germany, 200,000 were voluntarily repatriated, 26,000 were resettled (mainly to the United States) and 2,900 were deported: see UNHCR, *The World: Germany*, <www.unhcr.ch/world/euro/germany>, cited in Fitzpatrick, 'Formalised Regime', above n 28, 299. Fitzpatrick notes that reliable statistics on repatriation by recognised refugees are not available (at 299).

31 K. Koser and R. Black, 'Limits to Harmonization: The "Temporary Protection" of Refugees in the European Union' (1999) 37 *International Migration* 521, 528–9. Koser and Black also note that 'outside of Germany, which attempted to return Bosnians, 'the predominant solution for Bosnians has been local integration. It needs to be stressed, however, that this was not the solution towards which "temporary protection" was originally oriented' (at 534).

32 Ibid 526–7: 'First, by granting "temporary protection" *en masse* to Bosnians, normal asylum procedures were circumvented, so that no additional strain was added to the asylum system. Second, public support could be maintained by stressing the temporary nature of the status, and by conveying the Bosnian displacement as a matter of protection, rather than a disguised form of economic migration. Third, repatriation was considered an easier and less disruptive solution than is often the case for refugees, as no formal process had to be initiated to withdraw status'.

33 Ibid 535. They also note: 'What lies at the heart of all these issues is the question of what is temporary about "temporary protection". Is it a temporary sojourn in a host country, or is it a precursor to more permanent protection? One of the most important lessons from the

The experience of the Yugoslav crisis is relevant to this book, as it was an important turning point for protection policies in Europe and set the scene for the contemporary use of time-limited residence permits in the EU. In particular, it influenced the drafting of the various asylum directives developed as part of the CEAS: specifically, the provisions on temporary residence permits under the EU Qualification Directive[34] and standards under the EU Temporary Protection Directive.[35] The problem is that temporary protection, which was originally designed as interim means of managing a 'mass influx' of asylum seekers has become the norm for both groups *and* individual, recognised refugees and therefore is no longer limited as an *exceptional* measure. This raises the issue of how cessation procedures should be calibrated to ensure that cessation is undertaken according to not only the terms of Article 1C(5) but also the objects and purposes of the Refugee Convention.

State practice – time-limited visas and cessation for individually recognised refugees

Temporary protection and residency

One significant question in cessation is whether Article 1C(5) operates to end both the protection given to a refugee via refugee status *and* also the residency status of that person. Here it is important to recognise that state practice on this very central point differs markedly across jurisdictions.

For instance, the Australian TPV regime is distinctive in that those these visas incorporate both a *protection* and a *residence* component: the visa constitutes recognition by the Australian government that the person is a 'refugee' within the meaning of Article 1A(2) of the Refugee Convention. Secondly, it grants that person lawful authority to remain in Australia.[36] Thus, it conflated protection and residency components into one visa. This is an unusual and important feature of TPVs, as temporary residence permits in other jurisdictions (such as the EU)

Bosnian experience is that it does not make sense to orientate the status towards a single solution' (536).

34 *Directive 2011/95/EU of The European Parliament and of The Council of 13 December 2011 on standards for the qualification of third-country nationals or stateless persons as beneficiaries of international protection, for a uniform status for refugees or for persons eligible for subsidiary protection, and for the content of the protection granted (recast)* [2011] L 337/9 (hereinafter 2011 EU Qualification Directive).

35 *EU Council Directive 2001/55/EC of 20 July 2001 on minimum standards for giving temporary protection in the event of a mass influx of displaced persons and on measures promoting a balance of efforts between member states in receiving such persons and bearing the consequences thereof* (2001) OJ L212/12 (hereinafter EU Temporary Protection Directive).

36 The dual nature of the grant of a TPV was explicitly recognised by the Department of Immigration in its submission to the High Court in *Minister for Immigration and Multicultural Affairs v QAAH of 2004* [2006] HCA 53; (2007) 19(2) *International Journal of Refugee Law* 293 *(QAAH)*: see Minister for Immigration and Multicultural and Indigenous Affairs, 'Appellant's Outline of Submissions', 1 June 2006 [16].

separate refugee status from residence.[37] The dual role of the TPV also means that upon expiry of the visa, the refugee loses both domestic refugee status *and* residence rights. In the previous incarnation of Australian TPVs (1999–2008), this created complications, as there was no scope in either the Migration Act or Migration Regulations for a TPV to be converted into a permanent protection visa.[38] Rather, the procedural regime established under the Migration Regulations required that the holder of a TPV lodge a *fresh application* for a permanent protection visa in order to remain in Australia as a refugee.[39] This 'fresh application' procedure was decisive in the leading Australian case on cessation – *QAAH* (discussed in Chapter 3 in this book). Current Australian practice is even more restrictive – with TPV holders now unable to apply for permanent protection visas at all.

The Australian TPV regime is also illustrative of the tendency of time-limited protection permits to result in less protection than permanent status. In terms of the rights which accrued to holders of TPVs in Australia, such persons are able to access a number of benefits, such as work rights, access to the public medical system and social security benefits.[40] However, they cannot access a number of rights and services that are otherwise offered to refugees holding permanent protection visas. For instance, TPV holders do not have rights to refugee family reunion schemes, access to English language tuition or accommodation support. In the previous TPV regime (1999–2008), TPV holders were not given travel documents or a right to re-enter Australia.[41] The inability of refugees to

37 This means that revocation of refugee status does not necessarily also result in revocation of a former refugee's residence permit.

38 Contrast this to the requirements set out in the EU Qualification Directive which *do* appear to allow for renewability of refugee status and residence permits: 2011 EU Qualification Directive, above n 34, Articles 14 and 24.

39 Migration Regulations 1994, Schedule 2, Item 866.21. This regulation does not explicitly say 'a fresh application must be lodged', but this is the effect of the provision.

40 Department of Immigration (Australia) Fact Sheet, 'Temporary Protection Visas', 10 December 2014:

> A TPV will allow you to work and have access to Medicare, social security benefits (Centrelink), job matching and short-term counselling for torture or trauma where required. Minors will have access to education. Once you are granted a TPV, you can apply to travel outside of Australia. Travel will only be allowed if you can demonstrate compassionate or compelling circumstances. You will need to get permission in writing to travel. You will not be allowed to travel to the country from which you sought protection. We will give you more information on how to apply for permission to travel if you are granted a TPV. If you are granted a TPV, you will not be able to sponsor family members for a visa through the Australian Humanitarian or Family Migration Programmes.

41 Refugee Council of Australia, 'Position Paper on Australia's Use of Temporary Protection Visas for Convention Refugees', September 2003, 9–11, <www.refugeecouncil.org.au/docs/resources/ppapers/pp-tvp-sep03.pdf>; A. Edwards, 'Tampering with Refugee Protection: The Case of Australia' (2003) 15(2) *International Journal of Refugee Law* 192, 206–07. Under the present TPV regime, a TPV holder can apply to travel outside of Australia

obtain travel documents arguably breaches Article 28 of the Refugee Convention, and a ban on family reunion is inconsistent with international human rights law standards.[42] Such limitations were established as part of a broader policy of deterrence by Australia in response to a perceived misuse of the refugee system. Consequently, the use of TPVs in Australia has attracted a substantial amount of criticism from UNHCR[43] and from both domestic and international NGOs.[44] One of the main concerns raised by commentators was the uncertainty and instability caused to refugees' lives by such visas.[45]

In contrast, the use of temporary residence permits for refugees in the EU is rather different than that of TPVs in Australia. The provision of individualised temporary protection permits is set out in Article 24(1) of the EU Qualification Directive, which obliges Member States to issue a 3-year residence permit to refugees '[a]s soon as possible after their status has been granted'. The Directive states that such permits 'must be valid for at least three years and renewable unless compelling reasons of national security or public order otherwise require'.[46] Most EU Member States implement Article 24 of the Qualification Directive into national law by providing 3-year temporary residence permits for recognised refugees.[47] However, this state practice is somewhat uneven: others only grant 2-year permits,[48] whilst others give a 5-year 'leave to remain'.[49]

---

but travel will only be allowed if the applicant can demonstrate compassionate or compelling circumstances and s/he will need to get permission in writing to travel.

42 See discussion in Edwards, above n 41, 204–07.

43 UNHCR submission to the Senate Legal and Constitutional References Committee regarding the Inquiry into the Administration and Operation of the Migration Act 1958, UNHCR Regional Office, Canberra, 28 July 2005 [18], <www.unhcr.org.au/pdfs/AdministrationandOperationMigAct.pdf>.

44 Human Rights Watch, *Commentary on Australia's Temporary Protection Visas for Refugees*, May 2003, New York, <www.hrw.org>; Amnesty International Australia Submission to the Senate Legal & Constitutional References Committee regarding the Inquiry Into the Administration and Operation of the Migration Act 1958 August 2005, <www.aph.gov.au/Senate/committee/legcon_ctte/migration/submissions/sub191.pdf>; Refugee Council of Australia, 'Position Paper', above n 41.

45 See e.g. Refugee Council of Australia, 'Position Paper', above n 41; Edwards, above n 41, 200.

46 2011 EU Qualification Directive, above n 34, Article 24(1). Article 24(2) then sets out similar provisions for family members.

47 For instance, in Germany, refugees are granted a 3-year residence permit (Section 25(2), Residence Act). Prior to expiry of that permit, the immigration authorities are required to reassess the refugee's continuing need for protection. Similarly, in the Netherlands, the Aliens Act 2000 provides a 3-year temporary residence permit for recognised refugees, which can be revoked if the government finds that conditions in the home country have improved sufficiently: see Aliens Act 2000 (Complete Revision of the Aliens Act) [Netherlands], 1 April 2001, §§ 26–29, <www.unhcr.org/refworld/docid/3b5fd9491.html>.

48 Italy grants only 2-year residence permits to recognized refugees: Exiles 10, Chapter 7: Asylum: Italy 172, <www.exiles10.org/IMG/pdf/asylum_italy.pdf>.

49 The UK gives recognised refugees an initial grant of 5 years' limited leave: UK Immigration Rules, paragraphs 330 and 335, <www.gov.uk/guidance/immigration-rules/immigration-rules-part-11-asylum>.

The introduction of temporary residence permits in the EU is significant, as the domestic law in all EU Member States had previously provided for the granting of permanent residence for recognised refugees.[50]

Importantly, the granting of a temporary residence permit by an EU Member State is made as a separate decision which follows on from the granting of refugee status. That is, an EU residence permit is granted for residence purposes and, whilst it follows from recognition of refugee status, it involves separate criteria and is considered a separate decision.[51] This is in contrast to the unusual structure of temporary protection visas under the Australian system, which encompass both a residence and refugee protection status. This has significant repercussions for cessation decisions in the EU. Under the Australian TPV regime, cessation of refugee status brought about a revocation of both refugee status and 'residence' or lawful permission to remain. In comparison, a cessation decision in the EU context revokes a person's refugee status but does not automatically affect that person's residence permit. In the EU, a separate decision must be made to revoke a residence permit.

One question which arises here is how those on temporary residence permits can apply for permanent residency and whether in doing so they must 'reprove' their refugee status. This is significant because the granting of permanent residence generally means any change in conditions in the country of origin are no longer relevant.[52] There are two issues which must be considered here – the renewability of temporary residence permits and the procedure which occurs upon application for permanent residency.

Renewability of temporary residence permits

The EU Qualification Directive is silent on the obligation of states to grant permanent residency to refugees. Article 24(1) of the Qualification Directive states that the temporary residency permits set out in that article are 'renewable' and does not state at what point an asylum host state must grant permanent residence to a refugee. The fact that temporary residence permits are 'renewable' means that holders of such permits can be on 'rolling' temporary permits, which may continue indefinitely, and as such they may not be necessarily translated into permanent residence permits, unless refugees meet the requirements of the EC Long

50 For instance, in the UK, prior to 2005, recognised refugees were given indefinite leave to remain. Similarly, the law and practice in the Netherlands was to grant indefinite residence permits to recognised refugees.

51 See e.g. the practice of Germany, discussed in Chapter 4.

52 Although note that there was a proposal in the Canadian Bill C-31 for cessation due to changed circumstances to be applied to refugees holding permanent residence. This was subsequently deleted from the bill: see Protecting Canada's Immigration System Act 2012. See also Citizenship and Immigration Canada, 'News Release: Amendments to the Protecting Canada's Immigration System Act', 9 May 2012, <www.cic.gc.ca/english/department/media/releases/2012/2012-05-09.asp>.

Residence Directive.[53] This is reflected in the different state practice on duration of residence permits discussed previously.

Procedure for Application for Permanent Residency

UNHCR has taken the view that 'in order to take into account the special position of refugees, permanent residence should be granted to them at the latest at the end of the three year residence period established by the Qualification Directive'.[54] Under the EC Long Residence Directive, refugees can now apply in EU Member States for a long-term residence permit if certain residency conditions are satisfied.[55] Under Article 4 of that Directive, EU Member States are required to grant long-term resident status to third-country nationals, including refugees, who 'have resided legally and continuously within its territory for five years immediately prior to the submission of the relevant application'.[56] EU Member States differ on this issue, with some permitting access to permanent residency after 5 years of lawful residence,[57] and some after 4 years.[58] In contrast,

53 *Directive 2011/51/EU of the European Parliament and of the Council of 11 May 2011 amending Council Directive 2003/109/EC to extend its scope to beneficiaries of international protection* [2011] OJ L 132/1 (hereinafter 2011 Long Residence Directive).

54 UNHCR, 'Note on the Integration of Refugees in the European Union', 2007 [20].

55 2011 Long Residence Directive, above n 53. Previously, refugees were expressly excluded from the Directive, but it was amended in 2011 to permit inclusion of refugees and those holding subsidiary protection status. Amended Article 4 of that Directive sets out special provisions relating to calculation of the periods of residence for refugees and those holding subsidiary protection:

> Regarding persons to whom international protection has been granted, at least half of the period between the date of the lodging of the application for international protection on the basis of which that international protection was granted and the date of the grant of the residence permit referred to in Article 24 of Directive 2004/83/EC, or the whole of that period if it exceeds 18 months, shall be taken into account in the calculation of the period referred to in paragraph 1.

56 2011 Long Residence Directive, Article 3, amending Article 4 of the 2003 Long Residence Directive. Note that this requirement is conditional on the applicant having sufficient economic resources and to have integrated to a certain extent in the EU Member State: 2003 Long Residence Directive, Article 5.

57 See e.g. UK: at the end of the 5 years limited leave, subject to the outcome of any review and to the policies in place at the time, a refugee will be eligible to seek indefinite leave to remain (a permanent residence status): see UK Asylum Policy Instruction, 'Refugee Leave', <www.ukba.homeoffice.gov.uk/sitecontent/documents/policyandlaw/asylumpolicyinstructions/>. See also Germany, where settlement permits are issued if a foreigner has possessed a residence permit for 5 years and meets the additional requirements, which include a secure income, no criminal record and adequate command of the German language: see German Federal Office for Migration and Refugees, 'Residence in Germany', <www.bamf.de/EN/Willkommen/Aufenthalt/aufenthalt-node.html>.

58 E.g. Sweden, see website of Migrationsverket (Swedish Migration Agency): <www.migrationsverket.se/English/Private-individuals/Becoming-a-Swedish-citizen/Citizenship-for-adults/Time-in-Sweden.html>.

under legislation in the United States, persons granted refugee status may apply for lawful permanent residence (via a Green Card) 1 year following a grant of asylum.[59] Similarly, in Canada, most refugees are granted permanent residence upon recognition of refugee status.[60] However, the current version of the Canadian Immigration and Refugee Act does allow for the granting of both permanent *and* temporary residence permits to refugees.[61]

As to the burden of proof on refugees applying for permanent residency, EU countries do not appear to require refugees holding a temporary residence permit to *re-establish* their refugee status in order to remain permanently in the country of asylum. Although refugees may be required to apply for a permanent residence status or permit in order to stay permanently in the asylum host state,[62] this does not require the refugee to then *reprove* their refugee status. Instead, the authorities must show that cessation under Article 1C(5) has occurred, and in such cases, the onus is on state authorities to demonstrate that the requirements for cessation of refugee status have been met.[63] In contrast, under Australian law, the holder of a TPV was required to lodge a *fresh application* for a permanent protection visa in order to remain in Australia as a refugee[64] and to reprove they were a refugee under Article 1A(2) of the Refugee Convention.[65]

A further question which arises in relation to temporary residence permits in the EU is why they have not attracted the level of criticism which was directed against TPVs in Australia. As discussed earlier, the use of TPVs in Australia has been extensively and heavily criticised by UNHCR,[66] academic commentators[67] and non-governmental organisations.[68] In comparison, the use of temporary resi-

59 Immigration and Nationality Act (United States) 8 USC 1159, s. 209.

60 The only exception to this is that certain refugees who have arrived by boat ('designated foreign nationals') are precluded from applying for permanent residence for five years: Immigration and Refugee Protection Act (Canada) SC 2001, c. 27, s 11.

61 Immigration and Refugee Protection Act (Canada), SC 2001, c. 27, s 95.

62 For instance, in the event that the Home Office finds that the applicant is a refugee, they will be granted refugee status and given a 5-year temporary residence permit (called 'limited leave to remain'). Near the end of this term such applicants may apply for permanent settlement, that is, 'indefinite leave to remain' in the UK.

63 For instance, Article 11(2) of the EU Qualification Directive places the onus of proof on Member States: 'Member States are to have regard to whether the change of circumstances is of such a significant and non-temporary nature that the refugee's fear of persecution can no longer be regarded as well-founded': EU Qualification Directive, above n 34, Article 11(2). This is discussed further in Chapter 4 of this book.

64 Migration Regulations 1994, Schedule 2, Item 866.21. This regulation does not explicitly state that 'a fresh application must be lodged', but this is the effect of the provision.

65 *QAAH* [38].

66 UNCHR Submission to the Senate Legal and Constitutional References Committee Inquiry into the Administration and Operation of the Migration Act 1958, 2005 [17], <www.unhcr.org.au/pdfs/AdministrationandOperationMigAct.pdf>.

67 See e.g. Edwards, above n 41.

68 Human Rights Watch, *Commentary on Australia's Temporary Protection Visas for Refugees*, May 2003, New York; Amnesty International Australia, 'Submission to the Senate Legal and Constitutional References Committee Regarding the Inquiry into the Administration and

dence permits for recognised refugees in the EU and the provisions of Article 24 of the Qualification Directive has not been met with the same level of opposition. Indeed, there is very little or no criticism of EU temporary residence permits in the literature.[69] This is rather puzzling given that the two schemes have the same aim – to make refugee status under the 1951 Convention only temporary in nature. However, this may be explained by certain differences between the two schemes. First, there is no restriction on the rights granted to holders of temporary residence permits (unlike the Australian TPV regime which limits family reunion). Second, in contrast to Australia, cessation of refugee status in the EU does not necessarily lead to expiry of the person's residence permit (as these components are kept separate in the EU procedures).

A further reason for the criticism of TPVs in Australia is that the cessation or expiry of a TPV in Australia leaves refugees open to deportation, unless they are successful in appealing to the Minister for Immigration for exercise of his or her personal, discretionary powers to substitute a new decision.[70] This has been considered problematic as, until comparatively recently, there was no formal complementary protection avenue available under Australian law. This has now been addressed via the entry into force of the Australian Complementary Protection Act in 2011.[71] As a result, Section 36(2) of the Migration Act now provides that a protection visa is to be granted not only to non-citizens to whom Australia has protection obligations but also to non-citizens with respect to whom:

> the Minister is satisfied Australia has protection obligations because the Minister has substantial grounds for believing that, as a necessary and foreseeable consequence of the non-citizen being removed from Australia to a receiving country, there is a real risk that the non-citizen will suffer ***significant harm***.[72]

Operation of the Migration Act 1958', August 2005, <www.aph.gov.au/Senate/committee/legcon_ctte/migration/submissions/sub191.pdf>.

69 Instead, the criticism of the Qualification Directive has mostly been directed at the provisions relating to subsidiary protection, internal flight alternative and exclusion: see *UNHCR Comments on the European Commission's proposal for a Directive of the European Parliament and of the Council on minimum standards for the qualification and status of third country nationals or stateless persons as beneficiaries of international protection and the content of the protection granted* (COM(2009)551, 21 October 2009), July 2010, <www.unhcr.org/4c5037f99.pdf> (hereinafter UNHCR Comments 2011 Recast); ECRE, 'Comments on the Recast Qualification Directive', March 2010, <www.statewatch.org/news/2010/mar/eu-ecre-qual-dir.pdf>.

70 Migration Act 1958 (Cth), s 417.

71 Migration Amendment (Complementary Protection) Act 2011 (Cth). This was assented to by Parliament and commenced on 14 October 2011.

72 Migration Act 1958 (Cth), Section 36(2)(aa) (emphasis added). 'Significant harm' is defined in subsection 36(2A) to cover situations where the 'non-citizen' will be arbitrarily deprived of his or her life; will be subjected to the death penalty; will be subjected to torture, cruel or inhuman treatment or punishment, or degrading treatment or punishment. See discussion of complementary protection as it relates to situations of armed conflict in Chapter 4 of this book.

Unlike the situation during the TPV period in Australia, ceased refugees are able to apply for complementary protection under legislation in EU Member States.[73]

Given the preceding summary of key state practice, I will now go on to consider the legal rationale for temporary protection and the use of time-limited visas.

Analysis – the legal rationale for temporary protection

There are a number of differences between the legal basis and operation of group and individualised temporary protection. Temporary protection as used in group situations is defined and justified as a compromise measure which allows for a minimum level of protection to be given to asylum seekers in 'mass influx situations'[74] where individual status determination is not possible.[75] It is often viewed as a discretionary, humanitarian concept which provides basic protection to those fleeing harm.[76] In this regard, temporary protection is directed at preventing the return of refugees for a period of time and does not necessarily entitle protected persons to a full range of associated rights, such as the right to work and freedom of movement.[77] In this way, it is different from the notion of the core principle of protection in the 1951 Refugee Convention under which refugees must demonstrate an individualised threat of persecution and are, upon recognition, given a formal legal status. As part of the conferral of refugee status, states are obliged to provide recognised refugees the suite of 'acquired rights' under Articles 3–34 of the Convention. Another difference between the two forms of temporary protection is that group-based temporary protection has often been used to provide protection to those fleeing situations of armed conflict, whereas this is not usually recognised as the basis for individualised refugee status under Article 1A(2) of the 1951 Convention (unless there is a persecutory

73 The grounds for complementary protection (which is 'subsidiary protection' in the EU) are set out in Article 15 of the 2011 EU Qualification Directive, above n 34.

74 This is defined by UNHCR as 'the arrival across an international border of persons seeking protection in such numbers and at such a rate as to render individual determination of their asylum claims impracticable': UNHCR, *UNHCR Guidelines on the Application in Mass Influx Situations of the Exclusion Clauses of Article 1F of the 1951 Convention Relating to the Status of Refugees*, Protection Policy and Legal Advice Section Department of International Protection, February 2006 [1].

75 UNHCR Executive Committee (Ex Com) Conclusion No. 19 (XXXI) 'Temporary Refuge' 16 October 1980 [(i)]; UNHCR Ex Com Conclusion No. 22 (1981) [II A (1)]; UNHCR, 'Note on International Protection', UN Doc A/AC.96/815 (1993) [25]; UN High Commissioner for Refugees, 'Note on International Protection', UN Doc A/AC.96/830 (1994) [50].

76 See e.g. van Selm, above n 4, 249; Fitzpatrick, 'Formalised Regime', above n 28, 280.

77 For instance, UNHCR has stated that 'since it [temporary protection] is conceived as an emergency protection measure of hopefully short duration, a more limited range of rights and benefits are offered in the initial stage than would customarily be accorded to refugees granted asylum under the 1951 Convention and the 1967 Protocol: UNHCR, 'Note on International Protection', U.N. Doc. A/AC.96/830 (1994), 22–24 [46].

element to that harm).[78] As Joan Fitzpatrick has noted, temporary protection 'can form part of a strategy to de-legalize refugee protection and to relocate it in the realm of politics and humanitarian assistance'.[79]

In this way, it may be argued that temporary protection does not lead to membership of the asylum state polity. Indeed, Matthew E. Price distinguishes temporary protection from asylum, noting that '[a]sylum confers a *political* good – *membership*',[80] whereas:

> recipients of temporary protection are given permission to remain in the country for a predetermined period of time, which can be extended at the discretion of the executive, and, in most countries, are ineligible to adjust their status to legal permanent residence regardless of their length of stay.[81]

Price further notes that temporary protection should be available for those who lack protection of their basic rights, 'while asylum should be reserved for those exposed to serious harm because they *lack political membership*'.[82]

This is a significant conceptual point, because the issue of political membership and refugeehood is one which also arises in relation to cessation and protection by non-state actors, as discussed in Chapter 5 of this book.

This leads me to the next legal issue: the scope of individualised temporary residence for recognised refugees.

Individualised temporary residence – protection for the duration of risk?

On a conceptual level, there is a debate about whether refugee protection should in fact be temporary at all, or whether it should at some point result in permanent residence in the asylum host state. In situations involving *groups*, the use of short-term protection is usually justified as an exceptional measure necessary to protect those fleeing as part of a mass influx. This is the basis upon which UNHCR[83] and some academic commentators[84] have supported it. However, where no such exceptional circumstances exist (e.g. no mass influx), the use of individualised

78 See further discussion of this in Chapter 4 of this book.

79 Fitzpatrick, 'Formalised Regime', above n 28, 281.

80 M.E. Price, 'Persecution Complex: Justifying Asylum Law's Preference for Persecuted People' (2006) 47 *Harvard International Law Journal* 413, 431 (emphasis in original).

81 Ibid 431. This reflects the importance of the status-granting function of asylum host states.

82 Ibid 431 (emphasis added).

83 UNHCR Ex Com Conclusion No. 19 (XI) 'Temporary Refuge', 16 October 1980 [(i)]; UNHCR Ex Com Conclusion No. 22 (1981) [II A (1)]; UNHCR, 'Note on International Protection', UN Doc A/AC.96/815, (1993) [25]; UNHCR, 'Note on International Protection', A/AC.96/830 (1994) [50].

84 See van Selm, above n 4, 241: 'many of the displacement situations of the post-Cold war period may be best dealt with by the granting of temporary protection, in line with the minimum protection guaranteed by *non refoulement*, and in keeping with the notion of burden sharing'.

temporary protection mechanisms as the means of dealing with recognised refugees under the 1951 Refugee Convention is arguably more contestable. There are several reasons for this, which I will now discuss, including the interpretation of Article 1C as justifying temporary protection, the significance of Articles 3–34 of the Refugee Convention (particularly Article 34) and the issue of integration.

The 1951 Convention does not explicitly refer to temporary protection, nor does it set out the precise legal or residence status that should be accorded to persons recognised as refugees under domestic law. However, many commentators argue that the presence of cessation in the Refugee Convention implies that protection under the Convention is not necessarily permanent in nature, and therefore may be temporary.[85] The concept that protection under the Convention is temporary only has been echoed by some courts.[86] However, when such an argument is made it tends to be stated as an obvious consequence of the presence of a cessation clause in the Convention, without sufficient reasoning as to the legal basis for such a claim, and the limits of such an argument. One limit on this justification is that not *all* types of individualised 'temporary protection' can be justified by reference to Article 1C. Whilst Article 1C clearly permits states to cease refugee status under certain conditions, it is not the only provision of the Convention which is relevant to temporary protection. In justifying the use of temporary protection, *all provisions* of the Convention should be considered, namely, Articles 3–34 of the Refugee Convention.[87]

This has the following implications for the legal support of temporary protection based on Article 1C. First, Article 1C does not support use of time-limited visas or permits which give holders lesser rights than those to which they are entitled under Articles 3–34 of the Refugee Convention. Secondly, Article 1C does not support what Castillo and Hathaway neatly describe as the 'indefinite warehousing of refugees'.[88] That is, the existence of Article 1C does not justify the use of open-ended temporary protection which does not require state authorities to grant permanent status after a defined period or which cannot be translated at some point to permanent protection, with its attendant opening of avenues

85 See e.g. M. Kjaerum, 'Temporary Protection in Europe in the 1990s' (1994) 6 *International Journal of Refugee Law* 444, 445–6: 'The 1951 Geneva Convention reflects the temporary nature of refugee status in the cessation clauses of article 1C, especially paragraph 5'. See also Fitzpatrick and Bonoan, above n 7, 492; J.C. Hathaway, *The Law of Refugee Status* (Butterworths, Canada, 1991), 5; M.A. Castillo and J.C. Hathaway, 'Temporary Protection', in J.C. Hathaway (ed.), *Reconceiving International Refugee Law* (Martinus Nijhoff, The Hague, 1997), 2.

86 For instance, the UK House of Lords has stated that '[r]efugee status is a temporary status for as long as the risk of persecution remains': *R. v. Secretary of State for the Home Department, ex parte Yogathas* [2003] 1 A.C. 920 954 (Lord Scott). See also UK Court of Appeal in *Saad v. Secretary of State for the Home Department* [2001] EWCA Civ 2008: 'It would be enough to satisfy the Convention if the Secretary of State were to grant refugees temporary leave to remain for so long as their refugee status persisted'.

87 This has been recognised by the Federal Court of Canada in *Minister for Immigration v Bermuda*, 2016 FCA (Canada) 131, [22].

88 Castillo and Hathaway, above n 85, 17.

for naturalisation and citizenship.[89] For instance, it arguably does not justify the use of time-limited visas to be granted on a continually renewable basis with no avenue for permanency. This is a question of immediate practical relevance, because such a situation applies to those refugees holding TPVs in Australia who are only eligible to receive 'rolling' 3-year visas and are not permitted to apply for permanent protection visas.

A maximum period of individual temporary residence?

The preceding discussion raises the question as to whether there is a maximum period of 'temporary' protection after which a state party to the Convention is obliged to make that status permanent. Goodwin-Gill has argued that a presumption of permanent residence may arise in relation to individual refugees (as opposed to those coming as part of a 'mass influx'). He states:

> the fact of being a refugee in the sense of the 1951 Convention/1967 Protocol may properly give rise to a *presumption or expectation* that asylum in the sense of a local, lasting solution will be forthcoming. As a matter of principle, that presumption should only be rebutted by evidence clearly indicating the personal acceptability of the refugee.[90]

Thus, it may be important for states to have a clear policy which sets out a maximum period for time-limited protection for recognised refugees. This is so because it may become necessary to render a refugee's residence permanent if the situation in the country of origin is protracted in nature (which reduces the likelihood of return of refugees). The development of protracted refugee situations often occurs in cases involving armed conflict, as illustrated by the ongoing security, conflict and human rights problems in Iraq and Afghanistan.[91] The problem of addressing protracted conflicts is addressed by Joanne van Selm, who supports a form of temporary protection under certain conditions,[92] but suggests that if a conflict in the country of origin is 'enduring' then there is an obligation upon the asylum host state to give the protected person a more permanent solution via 'integration':

> Temporary protection should be seen as a phase in state-individual and state-state relations which ceases once return becomes possible, once resettlement

89 See e.g. state practice in Canada where legislation now precludes certain refugees ('designated foreign nationals') from applying for permanent residence for 5 years: *Bill C31*, Section 5, amending Section 11 of the Immigration and Refugee Protection Act (Canada).

90 G. Goodwin-Gill, *The Refugee in International Law* (Oxford University Press, 2nd ed., 1996), 197 (emphasis added).

91 As discussed in the Introduction to this book.

92 van Selm, above n 4, 241: 'many of the displacement situations of the post-Cold war period may be best dealt with by the granting of temporary protection, in line with the minimum protection guaranteed by non refoulement, and in keeping with the notion of burden sharing'. She adds later that '[t]he aim of protection is to maintain the right to life' (at 245).

> with permanent integration is offered or once integration in the protective state becomes the only viable medium-to-long-term alternative because a conflict is enduring.[93]

A number of commentators (specifically, Fitzpatrick[94] and Castillo and Hathaway[95]) have stated that temporary protection should come to an end within 5 years. Castillo and Hathaway justify the use of such a 'cut-off point' as follows:

> Because it is impossible to guarantee that conflicts will be solved within a reasonable period of time, a cut-off point has to be established at which temporary protection yields to a permanent solution. From the perspective of our commitment to a genuinely humane regime of temporary protection, it would not be reasonable to allow a 'temporary' protection regime to force refugees to wait indefinitely for safety to be restored in their country of origin in order to secure a permanent status, and to rebuild their lives for the long-term. A maximum duration for permanent protection, defined in flexible terms, ensures that it cannot become an excuse for the indefinite warehousing of refugees.[96]

The reference by Castillo and Hathaway to the resolution of conflicts is important, as most of the group-based temporary protection situations and many of the individual uses of temporary protection arise from civil conflict situations.[97]

Linking cessation and integration – Article 34 of the Refugee Convention

In discussing the temporariness and permanency of refugee protection, consideration must also be given to the fact that time-limited visas affect the integration of refugees in the asylum host state. This is of significant interest, given the increasingly high thresholds set out by states for the acquisition of citizenship by foreign nationals, including language proficiency and citizenship tests.

I acknowledge that states have a central interest in controlling membership of their societies via the granting of nationality/citizenship and may take measures to keep asylum seekers and refugees out of this system of community recognition

93 van Selm, above n 4, 244.

94 Joan Fitzpatrick states: 'Despite a lack of changed circumstances, temporary protection should also "cease" (to be replaced by a more secure form of protection) after a lapse of no more than five years. This principle arises from a recognition of the human need for stability and a chance to rebuild life following trauma': J. Fitzpatrick, 'The End of Protection: Legal Standards for Cessation of Refugee Status and Withdrawal of Temporary Protection' (1999) 13(3) *Georgetown Immigration Law Journal* 343, 372 (Fitzpatrick, 'End of Protection').

95 Castillo and Hathaway, above n 85, 17.

96 Ibid 17.

97 See e.g. the use of temporary protection in Africa and the EU response to conflict in the former Yugoslavia, discussed later in this chapter.

and integration.[98] However, Articles 3–34 of the Refugee Convention encourage the naturalisation and assimilation of refugees.[99] In this context, the use of cessation under Article 1C as a justification for individualised temporary protection must be weighed against Article 34 of the Convention which calls upon state signatories to 'as far as possible facilitate the assimilation and naturalization of refugees'.[100] Indeed, it is arguable that temporary protection visas and time-limited residence permits for refugees, which may prevent assimilation and naturalisation of refugees, conflict with this obligation.

The strength of Article 34 as requiring states to grant permanent residence and citizenship is contested. UNHCR has emphasised the importance of secure legal residence status for the integration and psychological health of refugees and underlined the importance of Article 34:

> In UNHCR's view secure legal residence is of utmost importance to the successful integration of refugees and other persons with international protection. Secure residential status has a psychological impact which is conducive to integration. It enables beneficiaries of international protection to focus unequivocally on a future and to work towards integration in their host communities on an equal basis with other legally residing third country nationals. This premise is emphasized in Article 34 of the 1951 Convention.[101]

Academic opinion as to whether states are *bound* to assimilate and naturalise refugees pursuant to Article 34 differs somewhat. On one hand, James Hathaway describes the terms of Article 34 as 'largely one of principle rather than formally binding'.[102] Similarly, David Cantor notes that Article 34 encourages host states

98 For instance, Susan Kneebone notes: 'The Australian Government thus defines refugees as non-citizens who are outside our "imagined community" and who can be excluded from our legal system': S. Kneebone, 'The Rights of Strangers Refugees, Citizenship and Nationality: What Is the Basis of Protection?' (2004) 10(2) *Australian Journal of Human Rights* 16. See also the writings of moral philosopher Joseph Carens, who refers to 'the community's control over membership': J. Carens, 'Refugees and the Limits of Obligation' (1992) 6(1) *Public Affairs Quarterly* 31, 35.

99 Articles 3–34 of the Refugee Convention set out rights which are linked to lawfulness of residence and attachment to the host states: Refugee Convention, above n 24.

100 Refugee Convention, above n 24, Article 34. It also states: 'They shall in particular make every effort to expedite naturalization proceedings and to reduce as far as possible the charges and costs of such proceedings'.

101 UNHCR, 'Response to Home Office Border Agency Consultation: The Path to Citizenship: Next Steps in Reforming the Immigration System', May 2008, 1, <www.unhcr.org.uk/fileadmin/user_upload/pdf/080516ResponsetoHomeOfficeBorderAgencyconsultationoncitizenship.pdf>.

102 See J.C. Hathaway, *The Rights of Refugees under International Law* (Cambridge University Press, 2005), 983. Hathaway also states: 'Refugee status does not give rise to an entitlement to access citizenship, even after the passage of a long period of time. But the Refugee Convention does commit governments to assisting refugees to access whatever opportunities for naturalization may exist under the host state's general laws' (at 990).

to consider naturalisation, but does not require this.[103] In contrast, Frelick has underscored the importance of the provision given its geographical location in the Convention:

> By placing the call for naturalization directly after the non-refoulement guarantee (Articles 33 and 34), the Convention's drafters indicated what they saw as non-refoulement's corollary principle – that while not returning a refugee is a mandatory minimum, it is not sufficient as a solution to the refugee's plight; that, indeed, a solution entails permanent protection, and that such protection is best achieved through naturalization (for refugees not able or willing to return).[104]

Others, such as Reinhard Marx, acknowledge the non-binding nature of the words used in Article 34 but emphasise its significance nonetheless. Marx notes that Article 34 'takes the form of a recommendation'.[105] However, he then goes on to state that 'it is incumbent upon contracting States, at the very least, to provide a good faith justification for the formal or *de facto* exclusion of refugees from naturalisation proceedings'[106] and that the Convention 'does commit governments to assisting refugees to access whatever opportunities for naturalisation may exist under the domestic law of the State of sojourn'.[107]

What does this mean for cessation? I acknowledge that the call for states to facilitate naturalisation and assimilation of refugees in Article 34 is limited by the words 'as far as possible'.[108] Thus, Article 34 does not *require* states to grant recognised refugees permanent protection status or permanent residence. However, when viewed in the context of the Refugee Convention as a whole, and the object and purpose of the Convention, it is arguable that the Convention *does* recognise that states should attempt to grant refugees some form of lasting protection and

103 D. Cantor, 'Defining Refugees: Persecution, Surrogacy and the Human Rights Paradigm', in B. Burson and D. Cantor, *Human Rights and the Refugee Definition: Comparative Legal Practice and Theory* (Brill, 2016), 365.

104 B. Frelick, 'Secure and Durable Asylum: Article 34 of the Refugee Convention', in US Committee for Refugees, *World Refugee Survey 2001*, 42, as cited in Hathaway, above n 102, 302 (footnote 304). James Hathaway responds that 'while Frelick's argument is plausible, the travaux record neither a preference for naturalization over other alternative solutions (repatriation, reestablishment, or resettlement), nor any discussion suggesting that the physical placement of Art. 34 after the non-refoulement obligation was meant to signal its corollary nature': Hathaway, above n 102, 983 (footnote 304).

105 R. Marx, 'Article 34', in A. Zimmermann (ed.), *The 1951 Convention Relating to the Status of Refugees and Its 1967 Protocol: A Commentary* (Oxford University Press, 2011), 1451. See also Paul Weis: 'Article 34 is in the form of a recommendation. It contains, nevertheless, the obligation to facilitate the assimilation and naturalization of refugees as far as possible': P. Weis, *The Refugee Convention, 1951: The Travaux Préparatoires Analysed* (Cambridge University Press, 1995), 352.

106 Marx, above n 105, 1452.

107 Ibid.

108 Refugee Convention, above n 24, Article 34.

security to refugees without constant review of status. Such an interpretation also accords with the aim of providing refugees with a durable solution to their plight[109] and with the structure of rights and benefits which accrue to refugees under Articles 3–34. These 'accrued' or 'acquired' rights in Articles 3–34 are relevant, as they are linked to the level of attachment that refugees have to the asylum host state. This means that the rights and benefits provided to refugees under the Convention have different levels of applicability depending on the nature of the refugee's sojourn or residence in the country: the more integrated and greater recognised a refugee becomes, the more rights that refugee must be granted under the Convention.[110] The fact that the Convention sets out a suite of rights which are commensurate with integration and legal acceptance in the asylum host state (and which are, for the most part, similar to rights and benefits given to citizens and permanent residents), supports the notion that the Convention places great importance on a level of integration, stability and security of residence. As UNHCR has itself pointed out:

> The rights attached to refugee status under the 1951 Convention (Articles 2 to 34) contribute to integration, in particular provisions on access to education, the labour market and to social assistance as well as certain civil liberties.[111]

The issues of integration and the acquired rights set out in Articles 3–34 of the Convention also become important in interpreting Article 1C(5) itself. In particular, the fact that cessation results in the *withdrawal of acquired rights* set out in the Convention supports the main argument in this book that protection for

109 UNHCR has repeatedly emphasised the need to find 'durable solutions' to refugee flows. See e.g. UNHCR, *Agenda for Protection* (3rd ed.), October 2003, Goal 5, 73–81; UNHCR Framework for Durable Solutions for Refugees and Persons of Concern, May 2003, <www.unhcr.org/3f1408764.html>. See also UNHCR Ex Com Conclusion No. 33 (XXXV) (1984) [k]; UNHCR Ex Com Conclusion No. 36 (XXXVI) (1985) [b]; UNHCR Ex Com Conclusion No. 79 (XLVII)(1996) [b]; UNHCR Ex Com Conclusion No. 90 (LII) (2001): Conclusion on International Protection, [j].

110 This ranges from presence in the jurisdiction of the state, to presence in the territory, lawful presence and lawful stay.

111 UNHCR, 'UNHCR Statement on the "Ceased Circumstances" Clause of the EU Qualification Directive' (2008), 6–7, footnote 35, <www.unhcr.org/refworld/docid/48a2f0782.html> (hereinafter UNHCR Cessation Statement 2008). See also D. Sopf: 'Once a claimant's status as a 1951 Convention refugee has been determined, the *United Nations High Commissioner for Refugees (UNHCR) Handbook* implies a certain duration and stability of that status': Sopf, above n 21, 124. He notes further, 'This strict approach towards the determination of refugee status eminates (sic) from the need to provide refugees with the assurance that their status will not be subject to constant review in light of temporary changes – not of fundamental character – in the situation prevailing in their country of origin' (at 124).

the purpose of cessation is effective protection, rather than a narrowly defined test of protection against persecution only.[112]

The foregoing discussion suggests that acceptance of the use of *group* temporary protection does not necessarily translate to acceptance of *individually based* temporary protection for recognised refugees. This is particularly so because group-based temporary protection is a humanitarian, discretionary response which is designed to be restricted to a mass influx of displaced persons. Although there is provision in the Refugee Convention for refugee status to be ceased under Article 1C, care must be taken in utilising the concept of temporary protection – a mechanism designed as an exceptional measure to be utilised in situations of mass influx – to the situation of individually recognised refugees where no such exceptional measures exist. This also means that cessation of such individualised temporary protection must be carried out with due caution and utilising strict criteria.

Conclusions

The preceding discussion has demonstrated that there are a number of differences between group temporary protection and individualised time-limited permits which will have implications for the way cessation is applied to each category. One significant difference is that time-limited visas are not utilised in mass-influx situations. That is, they are not utilised where the asylum determination system is regarded as being unable to cope. For instance, Australia's stated rationale for its use of temporary protection visas is for deterrent purposes rather than due to an inability to cope with a mass influx. Additionally, as recognised refugees, holders of time-limited visas are entitled to the catalogue of acquired rights set out in Articles 3–34 of the Refugee Convention. Some time-limited visas, however, may not necessarily grant the full catalogue of those rights, as is seen by the operation of the Australian TPV regime. Similarly to those under group temporary protection, the entitlements granted to recipients of 'time-limited' protection and residence visas may also be less than those granted to recipients of permanent protection or residence.[113]

Further, some time-limited permits (such as temporary residence permits in the EU) can lead to integration via permanent residency and citizenship.[114] In contrast, group-based temporary protection tends to be undertaken by states on the understanding that asylum seekers will be returned to their country of origin. It is therefore open-ended in nature, and can be protracted, with no legal

112 See discussion in Chapters 3 and 4 in this book.

113 For instance, under the Australian temporary protection visa system as it operated between 1999 and 2008, visa holders did not have a right to travel documents: see discussion in Edwards, above n 41, 204–05.

114 See discussion of the EU Long Residence Directive above.

obligation on host states to provide asylum seekers/refugees with permanent residence or protection.

Such individualised, temporary protection becomes of concern where there is no obligation on states to eventually grant a permanent status to affected refugees, or where, as was the case in Australia, visa holders are given less rights than those of refugees granted permanent protection.

Temporary protection was originally approved by UNHCR and since has been codified in documents such as the EU Directive on Temporary Protection, as an exceptional measure which is to be used in situations of mass influx.[115] However, as a routine procedure to be used in relation to individually recognised refugees, it is more problematic, given that recognised refugees under the Convention are entitled to a suite of acquired rights under Articles 3–34 and states are obliged to facilitate naturalisation and assimilation of such refugees pursuant to Article 34. It is also of concern given the 'need to respect a basic degree of stability for individual refugees' – a point which has been recognised in the UNHCR Global Consultations on International Protection, and in the subsequent 2003 Cessation Guidelines.[116] These arguments must be considered in the interpretation of Article 1C(5) of the Convention and they support the main contention of this book: that protection for the purpose of cessation is effective protection, and not merely protection against persecution.

In the light of this background on the development of temporary protection and the use of cessation, I now turn to discuss the content and function of Article 1C(5) of the Refugee Convention and interpretative questions which have arisen in relation to that clause.

115 EU Directive on Temporary Protection, above n 35, Article 2(a) defines temporary protection as: 'A procedure of exceptional character to provide, in the event of mass influx of displaced persons from third countries who are unable to return to their country of origin, immediate and temporary protection to such persons, in particular if there is also a risk that the asylum system will be unable to process this influx without adverse effects on its efficient operation, in the interests of the persons concerned and other persons requesting protection'.

116 'Summary Conclusions on Cessation of Refugee Status, Global Consultations on International Protection, Lisbon Expert Roundtable', May 2001 [17], reproduced in E. Feller, et al. (eds.), *Refugee Protection in International Law: UNHCR's Global Consultations on International Prostection* (Cambridge University Press, 2003), 548. This statement is cited in UNHCR, 'Guidelines on International Protection: Cessation of Refugee Status under Article 1C(5) and (6) of the 1951 Convention relating to the Status of Refugees (HCR/GIP/03/03)', 10 February 2003, 3.

3 The content and function of Article 1C(5)

Absence of persecution or effective protection?*

Introduction

The ending of refugee status via application of the 'ceased circumstances' cessation clause set out in Article 1C(5) of the 1951 Refugee Convention[1] poses a number of difficult interpretative questions. One of the main legal issues is how cessation interacts with the recognition of refugee status under Article 1A(2) and with the central concepts of 'persecution' and 'protection' in that definition (and more broadly under the Convention).

Article 1C(5) applies in principle in cases where a well-founded fear of persecution has already been found to exist, and refugee status has been granted on that basis (with the concomitant accrual of rights under Articles 3–34 of the Convention). It is also generally recognised that for cessation to operate, changes in the country must be 'fundamental, stable and durable'.[2] This raises a question: does cessation of refugee status and return of that person to their country of nationality require a broader inquiry than absence of persecution? In assessing cessation, is there an argument for looking more broadly at the availability of 'effective

* Parts of this chapter were previously published in M. O'Sullivan, 'Withdrawing Protection under Article 1C(5) of the 1951 Convention: Lessons from Australia' (2008) 20(4) *International Journal of Refugee Law* 586–610.

1 Convention Relating to the Status of Refugees, 28 July 1951, 189 U.N.T.S. 150 (hereinafter Refugee Convention).

2 UNHCR Ex Com, Conclusion No. 65 (1992), (q); UNHCR ExCom, Conclusion No. 69 (1993); UNHCR, *Handbook on Procedures and Criteria for Determining Refugee Status under the 1951 Convention and the 1967 Protocol Relating to the Status of Refugees*, HCR/IP/4/Rev.1, 1979, re-edited, Geneva, January 1992 [135] (hereinafter *UNHCR Handbook*); G. Goodwin-Gill and J. McAdam, *The Refugee in International Law* (Oxford University Press, 3rd ed., 2007), 142–3; J.C. Hathaway, *The Rights of Refugees under International Law* (Cambridge University Press, 2005), 922–35. A slightly different version of this test, requiring 'significant and non-temporary' change is set in Article 11(2) of the EU Qualification Directive and some European national jurisdictions: see e.g. *Directive 2011/95/EU of The European Parliament and of The Council of 13 December 2011 on standards for the qualification of third-country nationals or stateless persons as beneficiaries of international protection, for a uniform status for refugees or for persons eligible for subsidiary protection, and for the content of the protection granted (recast)*, [2011] L 337/9 (hereinafter 2011 EU Qualification Directive), Article 11(2); UK Immigration Rules, para 339A.

protection' in the country of origin, encompassing criteria such as human rights protections, adherence to the rule of law and the absence of armed conflict? (these latter questions are addressed in Chapter 4).

In order to answer the legal questions just raised and analyse this jurisprudence, it is necessary to understand why Article 1C(5) was inserted into the Convention, its role and function and its interaction with other key provisions of the Convention. Thus, this chapter discusses the purpose and function of Article 1C(5), its drafting history and development. I start by canvassing the general principles to be used in interpreting the Convention as a whole and its drafting history. I then go on to examine the role of Article 1C(5) in the Refugee Convention. Specifically, I compare Article 1C(5) to other relevant provisions in the 1951 Refugee Convention, such as the other cessation clauses in Article 1C(1)–(4), the refugee definition in Article 1A(2), the *non-refoulement* principle in Article 33 and the 'acquired rights' set out in Articles 3–34. This provides important background for the analysis of the three case studies which form the core of this chapter, which are:

1 The decisions of UK courts in *Adan*,[3] *Hoxha*[4] and *MA (Somalia)*;[5]
2 The High Court of Australia case of *QAAH v. Minister of Immigration*;[6] and
3 European case law, namely, the decision of the German Federal Administrative Court in *BVerwG 10 C 33.07*[7] and the referral of questions arising to the Court of Justice for the European Union (CJEU) in *Abdulla and others v. Federal Republic of Germany*.[8]

This discussion will particularly focus on how Article 1C interacts with the core concepts of persecution and protection in the refugee definition in Article 1A(2). In so doing, it establishes the basis for the main argument of this book: that the test for cessation is not merely absence of persecution but a wider concept of 'effective protection'. This argument is then developed in subsequent chapters which deal with standard and onus of proof and non-state actors of protection.

3 *R v. Secretary of State for the Home Department, Ex parte Adan; R v. Secretary of State for the Home Department Ex parte Aitseguer* [2001] 2 A.C. 477 (*Adan*).
4 *Hoxha v Secretary of State for the Home Department* [2002] EWCA Civ 1403 (England and Wales Court of Appeal) (*Hoxha*, Court of Appeal) and *In re B (FC) (Appellant) (2002). Regina v. Special Adjudicator, Ex parte Hoxha* (FC), [2005] UKHL 19 (House of Lords), 10 March 2005 (*Hoxha*, House of Lords).
5 *The Secretary of State for the Home Department v MA (Somalia)* [2018] EWCA Civ 994, 17 April 2018 (*MA Somalia*).
6 *Minister for Immigration and Multicultural and Indigenous Affairs v QAAH of 2004* [2006] HCA 53 (*QAAH*).
7 *Bundesverwaltungsgericht, BVerwG 10 C 33.07*, 7 February 2008, <www.refworld.org/cgi-bin/texis/vtx/rwmain?docid=48e4ed9d2> (*BVerwG C 33.07*).
8 *Salahadin Abdulla and Others v. Bundesrepublik Deutschland*, C-175/08; C-176/08; C-178/08 & C-179/08, Court of Justice of the European Union, 2 March 2010, <www.refworld.org/cases,ECJ,4b8e6ea22.html> (*Abdulla*).

The purpose and function of Article 1C

The *travaux préparatoires* of the 1951 Convention and Article 1C(5)

The text of Article 1C of the Refugee Convention had its genesis in UN General Assembly Resolution 429(V), which set out the draft 1951 Convention. The draft cessation clauses are similar in most respects to the final version of Article 1C. Indeed, Article 1B(1)–(4) of the draft 1951 Convention are identical to the current Article 1C(1)–(4). However, there are differences in relation to Article 1C(5)–(6). The draft cessation clause Article 1B provided:

> B. The present Convention shall cease to apply to any person falling under the term of section A if:
>
> . . .
>
> (5) He can no longer, because the circumstances in connexion with which he has been recognised as a refugee have ceased to exist, *claim grounds other than those of personal convenience* for continuing to refuse to avail himself of the protection of the country of his nationality. *Reasons of a purely economic character may not be invoked*; or
>
> (6) Being a person who has no nationality, he can no longer, because the circumstances in connexion with which he has been recognized as a refugee have ceased to exist and he is able to return to the country of his former habitual residence, claim grounds *other than those of personal convenience* for continuing to refuse to return to that country.[9]

There are three points to note about this draft. First, it states that cessation applies where the refugee can no longer claim 'grounds *other than those of personal convenience* for continuing to refuse to avail himself of the protection of the country of his nationality'.[10] This wording is identical to Paragraph 6A(ii)(e) of the UNHCR Statute[11] and was also incorporated into the definition of a refugee in

9 Conference of Plenipotentiaries, UN Doc. A/CONF.2/1 (1951), 5 (emphasis added). See also UN General Assembly Resolution 429 (V) of 14 December 1950. Prior to the Conference of Plenipotentiaries, the cessation clauses received little or no discussion in the preparatory debates held in the UN in 1950: see Goodwin-Gill and McAdam, above n 2, 142 (footnote 40).

10 The phrase had its original genesis in Article I(2) of the 1938 Convention: see A. Grahl-Mad sen, *The Status of Refugees in International Law* (A.W. Sijthoff-Leyden, The Netherlands, Vol. 1, 1966), 400. The concept of 'grounds of personal convenience' is discussed by Grahl-Madsen at 407–08.

11 Paragraph 6A (ii)(e) of the UNHCR Statute states: 'He can no longer, because the circumstances in connection with which he has been recognized as a refugee have ceased to exist, claim grounds other than those of personal convenience for continuing to refuse to avail himself of the protection of the country of his nationality. Reasons of a purely economic character may not be invoked'.

Article 1A of the draft 1951 Convention.[12] However, the 'personal convenience' qualification is not set out in the present day Article 1C(5). During negotiations at the Conference of Plenipotentiaries, the phrase raised the concern of the Swedish delegation, which viewed it as a negative and vague formula.[13] The Israeli delegation therefore suggested the use of a compelling reasons exception, which is discussed in Chapter 6 of this book.[14]

The second point to note about the draft cessation clause is that it states that '[r]easons *of a purely economic character may not be invoked*'.[15] This was based on Paragraph 6A(e) of the UNHCR Statute.[16] Similar words had been utilised in the Constitution of the International Refugee Organisation (IRO Constitution).[17] However, this phrase was deleted from the final version of Article 1C(5) and (6). This is significant given that there is a current debate about whether cessation applies where a person faces economic hardship in the form of restrictions on basic livelihood in the country of origin.[18] In this context, it is now accepted by some that refugee status may be granted on the basis of denial of social and economic rights where such amounts to 'being persecuted' within the meaning of Article 1A(2) of the 1951 Convention.[19]

A final point to note about the draft cessation clause attached to UN General Assembly Resolution 429(V) is that it did not contain the 'compelling reasons' proviso which is set out in the present day Article 1C(5) and (6). That proviso was included as a result of debate during the Conference of Plenipotentiaries. When the issue of drafting a proviso to Articles 1C(5) and (6) arose in the Conference of Plenipotentiaries, the Israeli delegation proposed that it should be termed quite broadly to include 'compelling family reasons' as per the

12 The 1946 Constitution of the International Refugee Organisation also encapsulated this idea: see United Nations, *Constitution of the International Refugee Organisation*, 15 December 1946, United Nations, Treaty Series, vol. 18, p. 3 (hereinafter IRO Constitution).

13 Statement of Robinson (Israel), Conference of Plenipotentiaries, UN Doc. A/CONF.2/SR.23 (1951), 20–21, summarising the Swedish view.

14 Ibid.

15 The term 'reasons of a purely economic character' is discussed by Grahl-Madsen, above n 10, 409–10.

16 This provides that 'reasons of a purely economic character may not be invoked'.

17 IRO Constitution, above n 12, Annex I General Principles para. 1(e): 'It should be the concern of the Organization to ensure that its assistance is not exploited by persons . . . unwilling to return . . . or by persons who intend to settle in other countries for purely economic reasons'.

18 UNHCR, 'Statement on the "Ceased Circumstances" Clause of the EC Qualification Directive' (2008), 8, 14, <www.unhcr.org/refworld/docid/48a2f0782.html> (hereinafter UNHCR Cessation Statement 2008) and discussed at Chapter 4 of this book.

19 See M. Foster, *International Refugee Law and Socio-Economic Rights: Refuge from Deprivation* (Cambridge University Press, 2007), 87–155. Note also that Section 91R(2)(d) of the Australian Migration Act (Cth) 1958 recognises that 'significant economic hardship that threatens a person's capacity to subsist' may amount to 'serious harm' for the purpose of determining whether there has been persecution within the meaning of Article 1A(2) of the 1951 Convention.

IRO Constitution.[20] This wording was questioned by the French delegation in debates,[21] in response to which the Israeli representative explained that:

> 'compelling family reasons' were meant to cover, for example, the case of an aged woman refugee in France who had no members of her family still living in the land where she had formerly suffered persecution, and to which she would therefore have no desire to return.[22]

During the Conference of Plenipotentiaries the phrase 'compelling family reasons' was deleted from the draft and instead the draft was amended to refer simply to 'compelling reasons arising out of previous persecution', which is now set out in the final version of Article 1C(5).[23] Importantly, the proviso was phrased so as to be limited to Article 1A(1) (that is, pre-1951 refugees), which has caused great difficulties in adopting a modern-day interpretation of the provision.[24] A brief discussion during the drafting process suggests that the proviso was limited in this way due to the concerns of states as to the uncertainty of obligations arising under the 1951 Convention if it were not so restricted.[25] When the 1967

20 The suggested wording was: 'Provided that this paragraph shall not apply to refugees falling under section A/1/ of this Article who are able to invoke compelling family reasons, or reasons arising out of previous persecutions for refusing to avail themselves of the protection of the country of nationality': see Conference of Plenipotentiaries, UN Doc. A/CONF.2/81 (1951). Israel also proposed an identical redraft to stateless persons under the then Article 1 B (now Article 1C(6): Conference of Plenipotentiaries, UN Doc. A/CONF.2/82/Rev.1 (1951).

21 The French representative asked: 'What exactly did the Israeli representative mean by the words "compelling family reasons" used in his amendments? Could the family attachment which a refugee might have contracted in his country of residence be regarded as compelling reasons? And was separation from his family to be regarded for that purpose as a compelling family reason?', Statement of Rochefort (France), Conference of Plenipotentiaries, UN Doc. A/CONF.2/SR.28 (1951), 11.

22 Statement of Robinson (Israel), Conference of Plenipotentiaries, UN Doc. A/CONF.2/SR.28 (1951), 11. The French representative replied that 'in that case the words "for reasons other than personal convenience" should be deleted from sub-para. A(2) of article 1. He was not convinced that compelling family reasons provided sufficient justification'. Statement of Rochefort (France), Conference of Plenipotentiaries, UN Doc. A/CONF.2/SR.28 (1951), 11.

23 During the 28th Meeting of the Conference of Plenipotentiaries, Petrén (Sweden) 'suggested that the word "compelling" should be inserted before the words "reasons arising out of" in the Israeli amendments to sub-paras. B(5) and (6) (A/CONF.2/81, A/CONF.2/82/Rev.1)', Statement of Petrén (Sweden), Conference of Plenipotentiaries, UN Doc. A/CONF.2/SR.28 (1951), 10. Robinson (Israel) accepted the Swedish suggestion, see Statement of Robinson (Israel), Conference of Plenipotentiaries, UN Doc. A/CONF.2/SR.28 (1951), 10.

24 See discussion of the compelling reasons exception to cessation in Chapter 6 of this book.

25 'In the matter of the practical difficulty arising out of the uncertainty of the obligations to be assumed by Governments, the Israeli delegation's suggestion was that refugees falling under sub-paragraph (1) of paragraph A of article 1, where to all intents and purposes the obligations were known, should alone be referred to', Statement of Robinson (Israel), Conference of Plenipotentiaries, UN Doc. A/CONF.2/SR.23 (1951), 20, summarising the Swedish view.

Protocol was ratified and the temporal limitation relating to 1951 was deleted from Article 1A(2),[26] there was no decision to delete the reference to pre-1951 refugees from the compelling reasons proviso in Article 1C(5) and (6).[27]

The *travaux préparatoires* of the 1951 Refugee Convention provide very little definitive guidance on Article 1C(5), as it is unclear from the minutes of the proceedings from the Conference of Plenipotentiaries why certain terms were used in the clause and how they were understood to operate.[28] Therefore, apart from some discussion of the compelling reasons proviso, the *travaux préparatoires* of the 1951 Convention do not shed a great deal of light on the meaning to be attributed to Article 1C(5) by the 1951 Convention founders. An isolated reference to it was made by the representative of France, Mr Rochefort, who noted that if an applicant's home country 'reverted to a democratic regime', the obligation to assist should not fall upon the asylum state.[29] He emphasised that France did not wish to be under an obligation to continue to provide assistance to refugees who could seek the protection of their country of origin.[30] However, he did note that '[i]t would be an inhuman act to withdraw from them the right to assistance unless they were assured of receiving it from their country of origin'.[31]

The first United Nations High Commissioner for Refugees, G.J. van Heuven Goedhart, speaking to the conference of plenipotentiaries, stated that refugee status should:

> *not be granted for a day longer than was absolutely necessary*, and should come to an end (or, possibly, should never even come into existence) if, in accordance with the terms of the Conventions or the Statute, a person had the status of de facto citizenship, that is to say, if he really had the rights and obligations of a citizen of a given country.[32]

26 The definition of a refugee under Article 1A(2) of the 1951 Convention was originally limited to those who 'As a result of events occurring before 1 January 1951' held a well-founded fear of persecution on a 1951 Convention ground.

27 See *In re B (FC) (Appellant) (2002) Regina v Special Adjudicator ex parte Hoxha (FC)* [2005] 1 W.L.R. 1063 [69] (Brown LJ) (*Hoxha*, House of Lords): 'The failure in 1967 to amend it, as it could so easily have been amended simply by deleting the "(1)" from the reference to "section A (1)", seems to me eloquent of the continuing intention of the contracting parties to confine the benefit of the proviso to the diminishing number of statutory refugees who would otherwise have remained vulnerable to the loss of their Convention rights under the cessation clause'.

28 For instance, very little is said about the standard to be met for a 'change in circumstances'. On this point, see Goodwin-Gill and McAdam, above n 2, 142 (footnote 40).

29 Statement of Rochefort (France), Conference of Plenipotentiaries, UN Doc. A/CONF.2/SR.28 (1951), 13.

30 Ibid 14.

31 Ibid.

32 G.J. van Heuven Goedhart, Conference of Plenipotentiaries on the Status of Refugees and Stateless Persons: Summary Record of the Twenty-Third Meeting, 26 November 1951 (emphasis added). This statement is cited by UNHCR in UNHCR, 'Note on the Cessation Clauses', EC/47/SC/CRP.30, 30 May 1997 [4].

This statement has been cited by some commentators in support of the use of temporary protection and Article 1C.[33] However, the relevance of the preceding to Article 1C(5) is limited, given that van Heuven Goedhart's comments appear to relate to the wording of the current Article 1E of the Convention rather than to Article 1C.[34]

Thus, as Goodwin-Gill and McAdam note, '[a]part from isolated references to the restoration of democracy, the *travaux préparatoires* do not deal with how or when change of circumstances should result in cessation of refugee status'.[35] In any case, one might question the wisdom of placing too much importance on the *travaux préparatoires* given the need to interpret the Convention as a living instrument.[36] Indeed, Elihu Lauterpacht and Daniel Bethlehem have cautioned that:

> The *travaux préparatoires* of the 1951 Convention must, therefore, for the purposes of the interpretation of the Convention, be approached with care. The world of 1950–51 in which the Convention was negotiated was considerably different from the present day circumstances in which the Convention falls to be applied.[37]

Jane McAdam has also noted that the *travaux* are 'often an incomplete or inaccurate record of treaty negotiations and accordingly should be approached cautiously'.[38] Hathaway and Foster also note that the *travaux* is treated as a supplementary means of interpretation in the VCLT. They argue this:

> signals that a treaty's drafting history is not a free-standing interpretative source, but rather a privileged source of *evidence* on the true meaning of a

33 See e.g. J.C. Hathaway, 'The Right of States to Repatriate Former Refugees' (2005) 20 *Ohio State Journal of Dispute Resolution* 175, 205 (footnote 108).

34 Article 1E of the Convention states that the Convention 'shall not apply to a person who is recognized by the competent authorities of the country in which he has taken residence as having the rights and obligations which are attached to the possession of the nationality of that country'.

35 Goodwin-Gill and McAdam, above n 2, 142 (footnote 40).

36 Various national courts have highlighted the need to interpret the Refugee Convention as a 'living instrument': see e.g. *Adan* [2001] 2 A.C. 477, 500 (House of Lords, per Laws LJ); *Sepet v Secretary of State for the Home Department* [2003] 1 W.L.R. 856, 862 (House of Lords, per Bingham LJ, with whom Steyn, Hutton and Rodger LJ agreed). In Canada, the Supreme Court held in Suresh that 'international conventions must be interpreted in the light of current conditions': *Suresh v Canada* (Minister of Citizenship and Immigration) [2002] 1 SCR 3, 87. See also discussion by Jane McAdam in A. Zimmermann (ed.), *The 1951 Convention Relating to the Status of Refugees and Its 1967 Protocol: A Commentary* (Oxford University Press, 2011), 104.

37 E. Lauterpacht and D. Bethlehem, 'The Scope and Content of the Principle of *Non-Refoulement*: Opinion', in E. Feller, V. Türk, and F. Nicholson (eds.), *Refugee Protection in International Law: UNHCR's Global Consultations on International Protection* (Cambridge University Press, 2003), 106.

38 McAdam, above n 36, 101. See also her discussion of the approach taken by courts to the *travaux* at 102–03.

> treaty's text construed purposively, in context, and with a view to ensuring its effectiveness.[39]

They acknowledge that 'reference to the drafting history often provides vital insight into the rationale and intended purpose of elements of the refugee definition'.[40] However, they caution against over-reliance on it.[41]

Against this background, it may be that little guidance can be gleaned from the *travaux* as to Article 1C(5). What is noteworthy is the reference to a change in country conditions to a democratic regime. Thus, this again suggests that a significant change in circumstances in the country of origin is required – a fundamental political and legal change. In the light of the preceding, I now turn to discuss the way in which Article 1C(5) interacts with other parts of the Refugee Convention.

The function of Article 1C

The function of Article 1C of the 1951 Convention is to set out the conditions under which a person who has been *formally recognised* or *determined* to be a refugee (within the meaning of Article 1A of the 1951 Convention)[42] ceases to be a refugee. Therefore, the meaning of the act of *recognition* of refugee status and the interaction between Article 1C and other provisions in the Refugee Convention (particularly Article 1A) are of central importance.

In interpreting Article 1C(5), which is the focus of this book, it should also be noted that Article 1C of the Convention sets out provisions for cessation of refugee status on the basis of six recognised bases. The first four subclauses of Article 1C, Article 1C(1)–(4), have a common link in that they operate due to changes in the individual or personal circumstances of the refugee and generally come into play due to a particular act by a refugee.[43] In comparison, the grounds for cessation set out in Article 1C(5) and (6)[44] are based on a change in circumstances in

39 J.C. Hathaway and M. Foster, *The Law of Refugee Status* (Cambridge University Press, 2nd ed., 2014), 7 [footnotes omitted, emphasis in original].

40 Hathaway and Foster, above n 39, 11.

41 Ibid, arguing that the *travaux* should not be given weight 'disproportionate to their probative value' and that they should not be 'used in a cut-and-paste fashion to dictate object and purpose'. They also note that '[a]t the end of the day, of course, such historical intentions must be reconciled to more general human rights goals, mandating an interpretation of the refugee definition that ensures that the Convention is seen "as a living thing, adopted by civilised countries for a humanitarian end which is constant in motive but mutable in form"': Hathaway and Foster, above n 39, 11.

42 In practice, given the temporal limitation of Article 1A(1), this relates only to Article 1A(2).

43 That is, due to (1) voluntary re-availment of national protection, (2) voluntary reacquisition of nationality, (3) acquisition of a new nationality or (4) voluntarily re-establishment in the country of origin.

44 Article 1C (5) deals with applicants with a nationality and Article 1C(6) with applicants who have no nationality (so called stateless persons).

the applicant's country and are not premised on any act by the applicant. This distinction between the two groups of clauses in Article 1C has been recognised by UNHCR, which notes that the first four of the six clauses 'reflect a change in the situation that has been brought about by [the refugee] himself' whilst the last two are 'based on the consideration that international protection is no longer justified on account of changes in the country where persecution was feared, because the reasons for a person becoming a refugee have ceased to exist'.[45]

In analysing the interaction between Article 1C(5) and other provisions in the Refugee Convention, I begin by discussing its place in relation to Article 1 as a whole, and Article 1C. I then turn to examine in detail its interaction with Article 1A(2), the concepts of persecution and protection, and the scope of Articles 3–34 of the Convention.

Article 1C(5) in the context of Article 1 as a whole

The placing of Article 1C(5) in relation to the refugee definition and the terms utilised in that clause are significant. Article 1C forms part of Article 1 in Chapter 1 (General Provisions) of the 1951 Convention, which sets out the definition of the term 'refugee'. Thus, Article 1C is part of the *definitional* section of the 1951 Convention. There are a number of other things to note about the wording of Article 1C(5) as it relates to the refugee definition under Article 1 of the Convention. Firstly, Article 1C(5) begins with the words 'This Convention *shall* cease to apply'.[46] Thus, Article 1C is expressed in mandatory terms: it provides that the 1951 Convention 'shall cease' rather than 'may' cease to apply.[47] Secondly, Article 1C(5) explicitly applies where the 'circumstances in connection with which he has been *recognised* as a refugee have ceased to exist'.[48] It is therefore generally understood that Article 1C applies to only those persons who have been formally *determined* to be a refugee.[49] For instance, Lord Brown in *Hoxha* notes:

> The words 'the circumstances in connection with which he has been recognised as a refugee' could hardly be clearer. They expressly postulate that the

45 *UNHCR Handbook*, above n 2, [114]–[115]. Provision for cessation of refugee status is also made in regional asylum instruments. Article 1.4 of the 1969 OAU Convention has similar wording to the Convention's cessation clauses. However, it does not have the 'compelling circumstances' proviso. Article 11 of the EU Qualification Directive also sets out a cessation clause similar in many respects to that of Article 1C(5) of the Convention.

46 Refugee Convention, above n 1, Article 1C(5) (emphasis added).

47 Note that Article 1A of the 1951 Convention is also expressed mandatorily, i.e. it says 'the term "refugee" shall apply to any person who . . .'.

48 Refugee Convention, above n 1, Article 1C(5) (emphasis added).

49 See *UNHCR Handbook*, above n 2, [112]: 'Once a person's status as a refugee has been determined, it is maintained unless he comes within the terms of one of the cessation clauses'. Paragraph 28 of the *UNHCR Handbook* clearly suppose that there will be a formal determination of refugee status: 'A person is a refugee within the meaning of the 1951 Convention as soon as he fulfils the criteria contained in the definition. This would necessarily occur prior to the time at which his refugee status is *formally determined*' (emphasis added).

> person concerned 'has been *recognised* as a refugee', not that he 'became' or 'was' a refugee.[50]

Such an interpretation is supported by UNHCR, which refers to Article 1C as applying to 'determined' or 'formally recognised' refugees.[51] Some academic commentators also support this interpretation. For instance, Fitzpatrick and Bonoan note that '[t]he term cessation should be restricted to the termination of status of recognised refugees'.[52]

In relation to the role of cessation in Article 1 of the Convention, Article 1C is to be contrasted with that of the exclusion clauses in Article 1F. Article 1C states that the Convention 'shall *cease* to apply' where the requirements of the clause are met.[53] In contrast, Article 1F begins 'provisions of this Convention shall *not* apply' to affected persons.[54] Article 1C therefore does not operate as an *exclusion* provision. This is particularly so because, as noted earlier, cessation is limited to those persons already *recognised* as refugees.[55] As a result, UNHCR and academic commentators have cautioned against the mixing of cessation and exclusion-type offences.[56]

In this regard, I also note that it is widely understood that cessation is different to *cancellation* of refugee status, which applies where it is found that the person should not have been recognised as a refugee in the first place.[57] UNHCR has stated that cancellation must be distinguished from cessation,[58] and some state

50 *Hoxha*, House of Lords, [62] (Brown LJ; emphasis added). In this case, the House of Lords held that the appellants were unable to avail themselves of the compelling reasons proviso in Article 1C(5) because they did not come within the first part of Article 1C(5), that is, they were not regarded as having been 'recognised' as refugees within the meaning of Article 1C(5) (even if they may have previously fulfilled the Article 1A(2) criteria at some earlier point in time).

51 UNHCR, '*Xhevdet Hoxha v. Special Adjudicator and B v. Immigration Appeal Tribunal*, and the United Nations High Commissioner for Refugees (Intervener): Case for the Intervener', 2005, [9.7], <www.unhcr.org/cgi-bin/texis/vtx/refworld/rwmain?docid=423ec5724>.

52 J. Fitzpatrick and R. Bonoan, 'Cessation of Refugee Protection', Chapter 8 in E. Feller, V. Türk, and F. Nicholson (eds.), *Refugee Protection in International Law: UNHCR's Global Consultations on International Protection* (Cambridge University Press, 2003), 531.

53 Refugee Convention, above n 1, Article 1C(5) (emphasis added).

54 Ibid, Article 1F (emphasis added).

55 *Hoxha*, House of Lords, [62] (Brown LJ).

56 J. Fitzpatrick, 'Current Issues in Cessation of Protection under Article 1 C of the 1951 Convention and Article I.4 of the 1969 OAU Convention', UNHCR Background Paper for Expert Roundtable Discussion on Cessation (2001), [13], [42]–[45], [68], [86]–[91]. See also UNHCR, *UNHCR Annotated Comments on the EC Council Directive 2004/83/EC of 29 April 2004*, 28 January 2005, 30–31, <www.unhcr.org/cgi-bin/texis/vtx/refworld/rwmain?docid=4200d8354>.

57 On cancellation, see *UNHCR Handbook*, above n 2, [117]; S. Kapferer, 'Cancellation of Refugee Status', UNHCR Legal and Protection Policy Research Series, March 2003, <www.unhcr.org/refworld/pdfid/3f4de8a74.pdf>.

58 See e.g. *UNHCR Handbook*, above n 2, [117]; UNHCR Guidelines on International Protection: Cessation of Refugee Status under Article 1C(5) and (6) of the 1951 Convention relating to the Status of Refugees, 10 February 2003, [1] (hereinafter UNHCR Cessation Guidelines 2003) [4]; Kapferer, above n 57, [5].

parties to the Refugee Convention also recognise that these concepts must be differentiated.[59]

Article 1C(1)–(4)

Article 1C(1)–(4) of the Refugee Convention provides that the Convention shall cease to apply to any person falling under the terms of Section 1A if:

1 He has voluntarily re-availed himself of the protection of the country of his nationality; or
2 Having lost his nationality, he has voluntarily re-acquired it; or
3 He has acquired a new nationality, and enjoys the protection of the country of his new nationality; or
4 He has voluntarily re-established himself in the country which he left or outside which he remained owing to fear of persecution.[60]

The operation of Article 1C(1)–(4) has been discussed in some detail elsewhere[61] and will not be analysed in depth for the purpose of this book, which is focused on Article 1C(5) of the Refugee Convention. However, it is important to summarise the key points about interpretation of Article 1C(1)–(4) and to flag some aspects that are relevant to this book, with a focus on the meaning of protection in those subclauses.

In relation to the meaning of protection, it is accepted that Article 1C(1)–(4) must be interpreted by taking the criteria of voluntariness, intent and effective protection into account. For instance, the UNHCR Summary Conclusions from the Expert Roundtable, 2001 Global Consultations stated:

> Cessation based on changes in personal circumstances should be assessed under the criteria of voluntariness, intent, and effective protection, which should not be applied in a formalistic manner.[62]

More specifically, in the context of Article 1C(1), which deals with voluntarily re-availment of the protection of the country of nationality, UNHCR has emphasised the need for the refugee to actually ***obtain effective protection***. The UNHCR Handbook states that there are three requirements for Article 1C(1) of the Convention, one of which is that the refugee must intend to ***and actually obtain***

59 See e.g. UK Border Agency, 'Cancellation, Cessation & Revocation of Refugee Status', 18 December 2008, 6, <www.ukba.homeoffice.gov.uk>.

60 Refugee Convention, above n 1, Articles 1C(1)–(4).

61 See S. Kneebone and M. O'Sullivan, 'Article 1C', in A. Zimmermann (ed.), *The 1951 Convention Relating to the Status of Refugees and Its 1967 Protocol: A Commentary* (Oxford University Press, 2011).

62 UNHCR Lisbon Roundtable Meeting of Experts, Summary Conclusions, May 2001, published in E. Feller et al. (eds.), *Refugee Protection in International Law: UNHCR's Global Consultations on International Protection* (Cambridge University Press, 2003), 550 [25].

protection.[63] Fitzpatrick and Bonoan point out that whilst voluntariness depends on subjective intention, the paramount issue is whether 'effective protection' is in fact available.[64] The requirement that the refugee must actually *obtain* protection is important, as UNHCR and academic commentators have also underlined the need for refugees to obtain the restoration of protection under the operation of Article 1C(5).[65]

What then amounts to 'protection' in the context of Article 1C? Grahl-Madsen states that the physical presence of the refugee in the country of his nationality is not sufficient. Rather, the test is one of the 'normalization of the relationship' between the refugee and his country.[66] Similar arguments as to the normalisation of the relationship between refugee and state have been made by commentators in relation to the other subclauses of Article 1C, that is, Article 1C(2)–(4). For instance, in relation to Article 1C(2), which deals with reacquisition of nationality, Grahl-Madsen states that reacquisition of nationality is evidence of re-availment of protection of the country of his nationality, or 'normalization of relations'.[67] This emphasis on the 'normalisation of relations' between citizen and state supports the argument that cessation does not merely require protection against persecution but also a wider notion of effective protection that encompasses elements such as the rule of law, judicial and administrative infrastructure, human rights protections and the absence of armed conflict.[68] It also supports the argument that non-state bodies cannot be recognised as actors of protection for the purpose of refugee law (as discussed in detail in Chapter 5 of this book).

Similar arguments apply to Article 1C(3) of the Refugee Convention, which provides that refugee status may cease where the refugee has acquired a new nationality and enjoys the protection of the country of his new nationality.[69] This clause is important because it explicitly states that cessation in relation to acquisition of a new nationality only applies where the refugee 'enjoys the protection of the country of his new nationality'. Accordingly, Fitzpatrick and Bonoan have stated that Article 1C(3) refers to enjoyment of 'effective protection', which

63 *UNHCR Handbook*, above n 2, [116]: '(a) voluntariness: the refugee must act voluntarily; (b) intention: the refugee must intend by his action to re-avail himself of the protection of the country of his nationality; (c) re-availment: the refugee must actually obtain protection'. This has been described as an 'appropriate analytical framework for the consideration of such cases, identifying three essential factors for analysis of cases arising under Article 1C(1): *voluntariness*, *intent*, and *actual re-availment*': see Fitzpatrick and Bonoan, above n 52, 524. See also J.C. Hathaway, *The Law of Refugee Status* (Butterworths, 1991), 193–6.

64 Fitzpatrick and Bonoan, above n 52, 525.

65 UNHCR Cessation Statement 2008, above n 18, 14; Goodwin-Gill and McAdam, above n 2, 140; Hathaway, *Rights of Refugees*, above n 2, 922, 927.

66 Grahl-Madsen, above n 10, 384.

67 Ibid 393. See Hathaway, *Law of Refugee Status*, above n 63, 196–7, where he discusses this as 'normalization of relations between the refugee and her state of origin'.

68 On this, see UNHCR Cessation Statement 2008, above n 18, 8, 14.

69 Refugee Convention, above n 1, Article 1C(3).

means more than absence of fear of persecution.[70] Goodwin-Gill and McAdam say in relation to Article 1C(3):

> The new nationality must be effective, in that at least the fundamental incidents of nationality should be recognised, including the right of return and residence in the State.[71]

Significantly, some commentators suggest that where there is automatic acquisition of nationality, Article 1C(3) has a similar operation to the 'ceased circumstances' clauses under Article 1C(5) and (6) of the Convention. For instance, Fitzpatrick and Bonoan suggest that as the circumstances in which Article 1C(3) applies include automatic acquisition of nationality, then 'effective protection' requires assessment of whether the changes are 'fundamental, durable and effective'.[72]

Thus, it appears there is a strong case for arguing that the test in Article 1C(1)–(4) of the Convention involves not merely protection against persecution (that is, the mirror of Article 1A(2)) but a broader notion of 'effective protection'.[73] This is, indeed what the author and Susan Kneebone concluded in a commentary on these subclauses of Article 1C:

> it therefore seems reasonable to conclude that 'protection' in the context of Art. 1C, paras 1 and 4 means 'effective protection' rather than mere absence of fear of persecution.[74]

This interpretation of Article 1C(1)–(4) supports the main argument of this book: that 'protection' for the purposes of Article 1C(5) requires the establishment of 'effective protection' in the country of origin, not merely the absence of persecution. Indeed, there is greater justification for imposing a wider test of 'effective protection' for Article 1C(5), given that it is based on a change in circumstances in the country of origin rather than on some voluntary act of the individual refugee.

Next I turn to examine the role of Article 1C in relation to the refugee definition in Article 1A(2) and the meaning of 'persecution' and 'protection' in this context.

Cessation and recognition of refugee status – a mirror image?

An issue which is related to the preceding discussion about Articles 1A(2) and 1C(5) is the difference between international 'recognition' of refugee status and

70 Fitzpatrick and Bonoan, above n 52, 527.

71 Goodwin-Gill and McAdam, above n 2, 138.

72 Fitzpatrick and Bonoan, above n 52, 527: 'In assessing whether the refugee will enjoy protection in a successor State, status determination officials should inquire whether the nationality law reflects political change that is fundamental, durable, and effective'.

73 Kneebone and O'Sullivan, above n 61, 523.

74 Ibid.

domestic 'protection'.[75] One of the main questions litigated in various national and regional courts has been whether Article 1C(5) is the mirror image of Article 1A(2). This becomes very important in terms of the legal test to be applied for cessation due to changed circumstances, as it dictates whether the test is one of absence of persecution only, or a more robust 'effective protection' test.

The provisions of Article 1A(2) and 1C(5)

Article 1A(2) of the Refugee Convention sets out the definition of a refugee. This, along with the *non-refoulement* principle in Article 33, is a key provision of the Refugee Convention.[76] Article 1A(2) defines a 'refugee' as a person who:

> owing to well-founded fear of being persecuted for reasons of race, religion, nationality, membership of a particular social group or political opinion, is outside the country of his nationality and is unable or, owing to such fear, is unwilling to avail himself of the protection of that country; or who, not having a nationality and being outside the country of his former habitual residence as a result of such events, is unable or, owing to such fear, is unwilling to return to it.

There are some similarities between Articles 1A(2) and 1C. For instance, several parts of Article 1C use the same terms as the refugee definition in Article 1A(2), such as 'fear', 'protection', 'country of his nationality', 'country of his former habitual residence'. The two provisions are also inextricably linked by the fact that cessation applies to refugees recognised to be such under Article 1A(2) of the Convention. However, there are a number of differences between the two provisions which support my argument that the criteria for cessation is different to that of recognition. These include differences in the wording of the two provisions, their function and purpose, and how they have been interpreted by state parties and UNHCR.

The first issue is the interaction between the concepts of a 'well-founded fear' and 'state protection'. To be recognised as a refugee under the 1951 Refugee Convention a person must establish that s/he has a well-founded fear of persecution and that s/he is unable or, by reason of such fear, unwilling to avail him or herself of the protection of the country of his or her nationality.[77] The definition

75 I use the term 'protection' here to denote the act of protecting a refugee from return to their country of origin (in line with prohibition against *non-refoulement*) and the granting of associated rights, such as the right to work, health care and other socio-economic rights.

76 Although as I note elsewhere in this book, the other 'acquired rights' set out in Articles 3–34 of the Refugee Convention are also important.

77 Refugee Convention, above n 1 (emphasis added). This test is broadly replicated in Article 2(c) of the EU Qualification Directive: Article 2(c) of the EU Qualification Directive, like Article 1A(2) of the Refugee Convention refers to an applicant's ability to seek the protection of the 'country of nationality'.

of a refugee is therefore made up of two broad components which are interrelated concepts: firstly, a well-founded fear of persecution and, secondly, a lack of state protection.[78]

There are several points to note about the interpretation of persecution in the context of cessation. Firstly, persecution is generally regarded as forward looking in nature.[79] That is, an applicant for refugee status must show a *current* well-founded fear of persecution for a Convention reason. For instance, in the House of Lords decision in *Adan*, Lord Lloyd (with whom all other Lords agreed) noted that Article 1A(1) of the Refugee Convention deals with historic persecution, that is, those persons who qualified as refugees under previous refugee instruments, whilst Article 1A(2) is concerned with current fear of persecution.[80] Some courts have pointed to the use of the present tense in Article 1A(2), which refers to '*is* outside' and '*is* unwilling, in support of this interpretation.[81] There were strong arguments made during the drafting of the 1951 Convention for past persecution to be a ground for refugee status under Article 1A(2). However, this view did not prevail.[82]

The fact that assessment of a well-founded fear under Article 1A(2) is forward looking has particular implications for the use of cessation under Article 1C(5). It has been used by some courts to hold that, because a refugee must show a current fear of persecution, once a refugee no longer holds such a fear, they cease to be a refugee under the Convention.[83] Thus, the House of Lords in *Adan*, held that because of this, Article 1C(5) 'would *take effect naturally* when owing to the change of circumstance the refugee ceases to have a fear of current persecution'.[84] This approach is critiqued later in this chapter. I also note here that many jurisdictions recognise that experience of persecution by a person in the past should be considered when adjudicating upon the chance that persecution may again occur in the future.[85]

The second aspect of the refugee definition which is relevant here is that Article 1A(2) is *individualistic* in nature. That is, in order to obtain refugee status

78 Goodwin-Gill and McAdam, above n 2, 92: 'Fear of persecution and lack of protection are themselves interrelated elements as Article 1A(2) of the 1951 Convention makes clear'.

79 See e.g. Hathaway, *Law of Refugee Status*, above n 63, 69, 75, 87–88; *Hoxha*, House of Lords, [12] (Lord Hope).

80 *Adan* (House of Lords 1999), 306 (Lloyd LJ).

81 The use of the present tense in Article 1A(2) has been noted by many courts: see e.g. the UK House of Lords in *Adan* (House of Lords 1999), 305 (per Lord Lloyd). See also the High Court of Australia in *QAAH*.

82 See Hathaway, *Law of Refugee Status*, above n 63, 68.

83 See *Adan* (House of Lords, 1999), and the High Court of Australian in *QAAH*.

84 *Adan* (House of Lords 1999), 306 (Lloyd LJ).

85 See e.g. Lord Slynn of the UK House of Lords in *Adan* who noted that '[t]he existence of what has been called a historic fear is not sufficient in itself, although it may constitute important evidence to justify a claim of a current, well-founded fear': *Adan* (House of Lords, 1999), 301 (Lord Slynn of Hadley). See also Baroness Hale in *Hoxha*, House of Lords, [29]. The way in which past persecution should be considered in cessation decisions is examined in detail in Chapter 6 of this book.

under Article 1A(2), a person must show that he or she holds a well-founded fear, not simply that they are part of a group that holds such a fear.[86] Article 1C(5) is also individual in nature, in that it must be shown that the *particular refugee* can no longer continue to refuse to avail him or herself of the protection of the country of his nationality.[87] However, as I argue later, there are aspects to Article 1C(5) which mean it focuses more on general country conditions than is the case with Article 1A(2). These differences include the particular function of cessation in withdrawing refugee status, the fact that Article 1C(5) is centred on *change* in country conditions and the wider reference in the clause to the '*circumstances in connection*' with recognition of refugee status.

The third aspect of the refugee definition is that a refugee must have a well-founded fear of persecution *for reasons of* race, religion, nationality, membership of a particular social group or political opinion.[88] Due to the words persecution 'for reasons of' in Article 1A(2), it is understood that there is a nexus requirement in Article 1A(2) between persecution and the need for protection.[89] This is important because the nexus requirement and the individualised nature of the refugee definition are the main legal issues that courts have focused upon in denying refugee status to persons facing harm in the context of armed conflict and other situations of violence.[90] The function of the nexus requirement has also been contested and has led to different views as to how Article 1A(2) operates in the context of non-state bodies.[91]

This then leads me to the next interpretative issue: is the test for cessation an absence of a well-founded fear or is it necessary to demonstrate the presence of affirmative protection?

The core inquiry: absence of well-founded fear or presence of affirmative protection?

The legal effect of recognition of refugee status

In order to analyse the ending of refugee protection, we must first discuss the legal effect of a *domestic* grant of refugee status on refugee status at international law. If

86 In this case, the refugee would be assessed as a *prima facie* refugee under a group determination procedure. This was discussed briefly in Chapter 1 of this book.

87 Refugee Convention, above n 1, Article 1C(5).

88 Ibid, Article 1A(2).

89 This raises the issue whether the nexus refers to the standard of well-founded fear of persecution or to the link between the state and the persecution. See discussion by S. Kneebone, 'Moving Beyond the State: Refugees, Accountability and Protection', Chapter 11, in S. Kneebone (ed.), *The Refugees Convention 50 Years On: Globalisation and International Law* (Ashgate, 2003), 280–1.

90 See discussion in V. Holzer, 'The 1951 Refugee Convention and the Protection of People Fleeing Armed Conflict and Other Situations of Violence', UNHCR Legal and Protection Policy Research Series, September 2012, PPLA/2012/05, 23–8.

91 Non-state actors of protection are discussed in Chapter 5 of this book.

one begins with the words of Article 1C(5) itself, it is significant to note that the article explicitly states that the Convention shall cease to apply to a person who falls under the definition of a refugee under Article 1A if he 'can no longer, because the circumstances in connexion with which he has been *recognised* as a refugee have ceased to exist'.[92] As discussed in Chapter 2 of this book,[93] the wording of Article 1C(5) therefore suggests that it is designed to apply only to those persons who have been 'recognised' as refugees. Such an interpretation is supported by UNHCR,[94] some academic commentators[95] and certain jurisprudence.[96] Following on from this, it is generally accepted that 'recognition' in the context of Article 1C(5) refers to those persons determined as a refugee under the Convention by way of a *domestic* decision by a contracting state.[97] However, it is also generally accepted that recognition of refugee status is *declaratory* only.[98] That is, an applicant became a refugee upon fleeing his or her country for a Convention, and later domestic recognition of refugee status by a host state simply *declares* that person to be a refugee. In this respect, the domestic grant of refugee status by an asylum state is merely acknowledging an *existing* refugee status under international law.

Consequently, it appears quite clear that when states recognise a person as a refugee (for example, by the grant of a protection visa in Australia) such a decision is simply domestic recognition of a status that *already exists at international law*.[99] Thus, it is incorrect to say (as the majority of the High Court in *QAAH* held) that an applicant who has held a TPV and who has therefore been 'recognised' as a refugee under both Australian domestic law and the Convention, must

92 Refugee Convention, above n 1, Article 1C(5) (emphasis added).

93 See Chapter 2 of this book.

94 UNHCR, '*Hoxha v. Special Adjudicator and B v. Immigration Appeal Tribunal*, and the United Nations High Commissioner for Refugees (Intervener): Case for the Intervener', 5 January 2005, [9.7], <www.unhcr.org/cgi-bin/texis/vtx/refworld/rwmain?docid=423ec5724> (hereinafter UNHCR, Amicus in *Hoxha*), citing UNHCR Guidelines on International Protection: Cessation of Refugee Status under Article 1C(5) and (6) of the 1951 Convention relating to the Status of Refugees, 10 February 2003, [1] (hereinafter UNHCR Cessation Guidelines 2003) and the previous guidelines, The Cessation Clauses: Guidelines on their Application, April 1999, [2].

95 See e.g. Fitzpatrick and Bonoan, above n 52, 531: 'The term cessation should be restricted to the termination of status of recognized refugees'.

96 See e.g. *Hoxha*, House of Lords, 1082 (per Brown LJ).

97 See e.g. UNHCR, Amicus in *Hoxha*, above n 94, [9.7].

98 See UNHCR, Amicus in *Hoxha*, above n 94, [9.8]; *UNHCR Handbook*, above n 2, [28]; Goodwin-Gill and McAdam, above n 2, 244; and 2011 EU Qualification Directive, above n 2, Preamble, Clause 14. The Minister for Immigration also explicitly accepted this point in argument before the High Court in *QAAH*, agreeing that 'it is generally accepted that recognition is declaratory only': see Minister for Immigration, Oral Submissions, Transcript, *MIMIA v QAAH of 2004 & Anor; NBGM v MIMA & Anor* [2006] HCATrans 340, 20 June 2006, line 3715, <www.austlii.edu.au/cgi-bin/viewdoc/au/cases/cth/HCA Trans/2006/340.html>.

99 On this point, see M. O'Sullivan, 'Before the High Court: *Minister for Immigration v QAAH*: Cessation of Refugee Status' (2006) 28(2) *Sydney Law Review* 359, 367, 371; and *QAAH*, High Court, [96]–[104] (Kirby J).

demonstrate *afresh* his or her refugee status under Article 1A(2). Rather, in such cases the 'burden' is on the state to demonstrate cessation under Article 1C(5).

This view is supported by UNHCR and academic commentators, who note that once refugee status is granted, that status continues at international law until Article 1C(5) is applied. For instance, the UNHCR Handbook specifically states that '[o]nce a person's status as a refugee has been determined, it is maintained unless he comes within the terms of one of the cessation clauses'[100] The UNHCR position has consistently been that the tests for Articles 1A(2) and 1C(5) are different, and that although both articles involve a similar issue, 'they do not precisely mirror each other'.[101] Indeed, UNCHR stated that:

> Determining that for Article 1C(5) to be applicable one merely needs to negate Article 1A(2) is tantamount to introducing an additional cessation clause which is at odds with the exhaustiveness of those that are contained in the Refugees Convention.[102]

Similarly, Professor Grahl-Madsen has stated:

> It is generally agreed that the enumeration of cessation clauses in Article 1C of the Refugee Convention . . . is exhaustive. In other words, once a person has become a refugee as defined in Article 1 of the Convention . . . he continues to be a refugee until he falls under any of those cessation clauses.[103]

I now turn to the heart of this chapter: the three case studies which reflect some of the problems in differentiating recognition of refugee status from cessation of that status.

Case study 1: the UK

The core approach to the relationship between Article 1A(2) and Article 1C(5) by UK courts was established in two landmark cases: *Adan* (2001) and *Hoxha* (2002) – an approach which has been followed in more recent UK Court of Appeal cases.

In *Adan*, the applicant had attempted to argue that he was not required to show a present fear of persecution in order to meet the definition of refugee set out in Article 1A(2) of the Convention. Rather, the applicant

100 *UNHCR Handbook*, above n 2, [112]. See also UNHCR Cessation Guidelines 2003, above n 58, [1].
101 Ibid [10]–[11].
102 Ibid [12].
103 Grahl-Madsen, above n 10, 369. Hathaway and Foster also agree that '"ceased to exist" is a more demanding standard than risk below a well-founded fear; and the additional requirement of ability to access protection . . . limits cessation to cases in which there is evidence of access to an affirmative relationship with the home country, not simply the absence of a negative': Hathaway and Foster, above n 39, 478.

argued, it was sufficient that he held a fear of persecution when he had left his home country (an 'historic fear') and that he was presently unable to avail himself of his country's protection. This argument failed before the House of Lords. In delivering judgement for the Court, Lord Lloyd[104] discussed the difference between Article 1A(1) and 1A(2) refugees. He noted that Article 1A(1) deals with *historic* persecution, that is, those persons who qualified as refugees under previous refugee instruments, who may argue that they do not come under Article 1C(5) if they can show compelling reasons via the exception to 1C(5).[105] In contrast, his Lordship said, Article 1A(2) is concerned with *current* persecution and thus Article 1C(5) 'would *take effect naturally* when owing to the change of circumstance the refugee ceases to have a fear of current persecution'.[106]

This approach was also echoed in the later House of Lords case of *Hoxha*.[107] In this case, the applicants had attempted to argue that, despite the fact that they had not been determined to be refugees, the 'compelling circumstances' proviso of Article 1C(5) should be applied to them in relation to their claim of persecution under Article 1A(2).[108] The House of Lords held that the appellants were unable to avail themselves of the 'compelling circumstances' protection in Article 1C(5) because they did not come within the first part of Article 1C(5), that is, they were not regarded as having been 'recognised' as refugees within the meaning of 1C(5) (even if they may have previously fulfilled the 1A(2) criteria at some earlier point in time).[109] In this case, Lord Hope, concurring with the observations made by Lord Lloyd in *Adan*, held that 'the cessation provision in Article 1C(5) takes effect naturally when the refugee ceases to have a current well-founded fear'.[110] His Honour added that such an interpretation 'is in symmetry with the definition in Article 1A(2)'.[111]

In contrast, however, Lord Brown in *Hoxha* appears to take a different view of the symmetry issue in that he found that Article 1A(2) and 1C(5) involves a two-stage approach and cannot therefore be seen as the mirror of each other.[112] Indeed, Lord Brown noted in *obiter* that Article 1C(5) operates only when invoked by the state against the refugee:

> The whole scheme of the Convention points irresistibly towards a two-stage rather than a composite approach to 1A(2) and 1C(5). Stage 1,

104 With whom all other Lords agreed.
105 *Adan*, House of Lords (Lloyd LJ).
106 Ibid 306 (Lloyd LJ). The issue of historic persecution in the context of the standard of proof for cessation decisions is discussed in Chapter 6 of this book.
107 *Hoxha*.
108 Ibid 1077 (Brown LJ).
109 *Hoxha*, House of Lords (Lord Nicholls of Birkenhead, Lord Steyn, Lord Hope of Craighead, Baroness Hale of Richmond and Lord Brown of Eaton-under-Heywood).
110 *Hoxha*, House of Lords, 1067 (Hope LJ).
111 Ibid.
112 Ibid 1083 (Brown LJ).

> the formal determination of an asylum-seeker's refugee status, dictates whether a 1A(2) applicant . . . is to be recognized as a refugee. 1C(5), a cessation clause, simply has no application at that stage, indeed no application at any stage unless and until it is invoked by the State against the refugee in order to deprive him of the refugee status previously accorded to him.[113]

As the foregoing illustrates, there was some disagreement between Lord Brown and Lord Hope as to the relationship between Articles 1A(2) and 1C(5). However, the position in the UK on this matter has been clarified in more recent jurisprudence in 2018, where the UK Court of Appeal in *Secretary of State for the Home Department v. MA (Somalia)* held that a cessation decision *is* the mirror image of a decision determining refugee status.[114] In this case Justice Arden explained:

> By that I mean that the grounds for cessation do not go beyond verifying whether the grounds for recognition of refugee status continue to exist. Thus, the relevant question is whether there has been a significant and non-temporary change in circumstances so that the circumstances which caused the person to be a refugee have ceased to apply and there is no other basis on which he would be held to be a refugee. The recognising state does not in addition have to be satisfied that the country of origin has a system of government or an effective legal system for protecting basic human rights, though the absence of such systems may of course lead to the conclusion that a significant and non-temporary change in circumstances has not occurred.[115]

In this case, the Secretary of State considered a country guidance decision on Somalia and decided that the applicant would no longer be at real risk of

113 Ibid 1082 (Brown LJ). Lord Brown's statement was cited and supported by UNHCR in its written submissions to the High Court in *QAAH*, where it stated that Brown LJ's interpretation 'reflects the basic approach which UNHCR would submit is correct': 'Minister for Immigration and Multicultural and Indigenous Affairs v. QAAH of 2004 – Outline of submissions on behalf of the Office of the United Nations High Commissioner for Refugees (as Amicus Curiae)', 8 June 2006, [27], published in (2007) 19(2) *International Journal of Refugee Law* 360–71 (hereinafter UNHCR Amicus in *QAAH*).

114 *Secretary of State for the Home Department v MA (Somalia)* [2018] EWCA Civ 994 (Arden J) (*MA (Somalia)*).

115 *MA (Somalia)*, (Arden J), [2]. Here the applicant was a Somali national. He left his home city, Mogadishu, in 2003 for Yemen. He arrived in the UK and claimed asylum on 16 July 2004. His application was refused on 13 November 2004 but was subsequently allowed on 15 February 2005. On 7 March 2005, he was granted asylum and indefinite leave to remain on the basis of ethnic origin as he belonged to the Reer Hamar clan. The Secretary of State made a decision to cease the respondent's refugee status on the grounds that the fear which led to the grant of refugee status no longer existed.

persecution on account of his ethnicity. In critiquing this decision, I would underline the fundamental point made throughout this book: that cessation is not merely the 'mirror' of Article 1A(2). Therefore, the test for cessation should be one of positive evidence of effective protection – not merely the absence of persecution. In *MA (Somalia)*, the court appears to be suggesting that lack of effective protection (e.g. absence of a legal system) may be considered under cessation as it may provide evidence that a required change has not occurred. However, the court did not frame this as requiring *positive* evidence of the existence of such systems. This may appear at first glance to be a semantic point: some may argue that absence of effective protection is still being considered under the *MA (Somalia)* test, it is merely being considered under the rubric of 'change of circumstances' rather than requiring positive evidence of the existence of protection systems. Although this is undoubtedly a nuanced point, it is an important one given the nature of cessation and the need to demarcate Article 1C(5) from recognition of refugee status under Article 1A(2), which I discuss further in the Conclusions to this chapter.

Case study 2: Australia

In Australia, the Refugee Convention is only indirectly incorporated into Australian domestic law via Section 36(2)(a) of the Migration Act. Section 36(2)(a) states:

> (2) A criterion for a protection visa is that the applicant for the visa is:
>
> (a) a non-citizen in Australia in respect of whom the Minister is satisfied Australia has protection obligations.[116]

Significantly, prior to 2014, Section 36 explicitly referred to the Refugee Convention. As seen in the preceding quote, there is no mention at all of the Refugee Convention. This is due to amendments made in the Migration Act by the Australian Parliament in 2014 to attempt to formulate a particular Australian interpretation of refugee law which is isolated from international influence. This is in contrast with other contracting states to the Convention, such as Canada and the US, which have legislation incorporating Article 1C(5) into domestic law[117] and with the cessation provisions in the

116 Section 36 of the Migration Act (Cth) 1958 was recently amended by the Migration Legislation Amendment (Regional Processing and Other Measures) Act 2012, which changed the term 'a non-citizen in Australia *to whom* the Minister is satisfied' to 'a non-citizen in Australia *in respect of whom* the Minister is satisfied' (emphasis added). This change came into effect on 18 August 2012.

117 Canada: Immigration and Refugee Protection Act 2001, s 108; US: Immigration and Nationality Act, s.208(c)(2)(d).

EU Qualification Directive.[118] This lacuna in Australian legislation has created significant interpretative difficulties for courts in adjudicating on the extent to which the Convention is transposed into Australian domestic law. This is important, because in the leading case on cessation (*QAAH*), the High Court held that 'it is the law of Australia which prevails in case of any conflict between it and the Convention. It is the law of Australia which must first be identified'[119] and that despite the ways in which 'the Convention may be used in construing the Act, it is the words of the Act which govern'.[120]

Article 1C(5) first became a legal issue in Australia in 2003 when the Department of Immigration[121] commenced the processing of applications for permanent protection visas made by the first batch of temporary protection visa holders. Although the department was considering applications made by persons who had already been recognised as refugees (pursuant to Section 36(2) of the Migration Act), it took the view that Article 1A(2) was the central criteria for the granting of a permanent protection visa, rather than Article 1C(5). As a result, the department required applicants to demonstrate afresh that they held a well-founded fear of persecution based on one of the Convention grounds. The department only considered Article 1C(5) as 'one of a number of relevant considerations that will go to determining whether protection obligations continue to be owed and therefore whether the further protection visa is to be granted'.[122] As a result, significant numbers of those refugees who had held a TPV were denied a permanent protection visa by the Department of Immigration.[123] In contrast, the Refugee

118 Article 11 of the Directive 2011/95/EU of The European Parliament and of The Council of 13 December 2011 on standards for the qualification of third-country nationals or stateless persons as beneficiaries of international protection, for a uniform status for refugees or for persons eligible for subsidiary protection, and for the content of the protection granted (recast), [2011] L 337/9 (2011 EU Qualification Directive). The 2011 Directive replaced an earlier version of the Directive signed in 2004: see EU Council Directive on minimum standards for the qualification and status of third country nationals or stateless persons as refugees or as persons who otherwise need international protection and the content of the protection granted, 2004/83/E, [2004] OJ L304/12; (hereinafter 2004 EU Qualification Directive).

119 *QAAH* [33].

120 Ibid [34].

121 The full name of the Department is currently the 'Department of Home Affairs' (DHA): see <www.homeaffairs.gov.au>. It was previously known as the Department of Immigration and Citizenship, and then again, before that, the Department of Immigration and Multicultural Affairs. Reference will be to former names where position papers have been authored under those previous titles.

122 See Department of Immigration, 'Protecting Refugees: Cessation under Article 1C', written for UNHCR Discussion Paper No. 1/2003 [copy with author].

123 Approximately 25% of holders of TPVs were refused a further protection visa by the Department of Immigration: see Australian Senate, 'Questions on Notice: Refugee Determination Process', Senate Hansard 8 February 2006, 215, Question 1344.

Review Tribunal (RRT)[124] – the review body which heard appeals from the department – adopted a different approach in that it applied both Article 1C(5) and Article 1A(2): Article 1C(5) was first applied to establish whether there had been a change in circumstances leading to cessation and, if the applicant had any fresh claims for persecution, the RRT then considered whether the applicant faced a well-founded fear of persecution under Article 1A(2). The decisions of the RRT on applications made by TPV holders differed significantly from that made by the department, with the RRT setting aside a very high percentage of those departmental decisions relating to applications for further protection visas made by applicants from Iraq and Afghanistan.[125] As a result of this difference in approach between the Department of Immigration and the Refugee Review Tribunal, the correct legal position as to the application of Article 1C(5) in Australia was for some time unclear.

Australian High Court litigation – QAAH

These legal questions about recognition of refugee status and the interpretation to be given to Article 1C(5) were considered by the High Court of Australia in the case of *Minister for Immigration and Multicultural Affairs v. QAAH* (*QAAH*).[126]

The primary submission of the Minister for Immigration[127] before the High Court in *QAAH* was that a precise symmetry exists between the tests imposed by Articles 1A(2) and 1C(5) of the Convention. That is, to ask whether the circumstances in connection with which the person has been recognised as a refugee 'have ceased to exist' (Article 1C(5)) is simply to ask whether or not the person continues to have a well-founded fear of persecution.[128] The Minister argued in her submissions that Article 1C(5)

124 The Refugee Review Tribunal is now called the 'Migration and Refugee Division' of the Administrative Appeals Tribunal: see <www.aat.gov.au/migration-and-refugee-division>.

125 For example, in 2005–06 the RRT set aside the departmental decision in 94% of cases involving applications by Afghan nationals for a further protection visa and 97% of applications for further protection visas by Iraqis: see 'Annual Report of the Migration Review Tribunal and Refugee Review Tribunal 2005–06', Commonwealth of Australia, 2006, 21.

126 *Minister for Immigration and Multicultural Affairs v QAAH of 2004* [2006] HCA 53, 231 ALR 340, (2007) 19(2) *International Journal of Refugee Law* 293 (*QAAH*, High Court). The High Court of Australia is the highest court in the Australian judicial system: see <www.highcourt.gov.au>. A case raising similar issues was heard with *QAAH*: *NBGM v the Minister for Immigration and Multicultural Affairs* [2006] HCA 54, 231 ALR 380 (*NBGM*). The High Court in *NBGM* held that the reasoning set out in *QAAH* applied to the facts of *NBGM*: see *NBGM* 380 (Gummow); 397 (Callinan, Heydon and Crennan JJ).

127 The Minister for Immigration at that time was Amanda Vanstone, a member of the Howard Liberal (Conservative) Government.

128 Minister for Immigration, Written Submissions in *QAAH* [25] (copy on file with author). See also Minister for Immigration, Oral submissions, *MIMIA v QAAH of 2004 & Anor;*

thus expresses the 'negative corollary' of Article 1A(2).[129] The Minister also submitted that Article 1C(5) does not need to be invoked in order to have application to a person, rather it operates automatically according to its terms and is relevant whenever the question arises of whether a person is a refugee.[130] Counsel for the Minister of Immigration submitted that the Full Federal Court in *QAAH* was incorrect in holding that recognition of refugee status at international law continues until Article 1C(5) is successfully applied against a refugee.[131] Rather, 'recognition is declaratory as at a point in time'.[132] Thus, the proper question to ask is whether the applicant *continues* to have a well-founded fear of persecution which was recognised to exist at an *earlier* time.[133]

In making her primary submission as to the symmetry between Articles 1A(2) and 1C(5), the Minister referred to statements by the UNHCR Executive Committee outlined in a publication in 2001 where the committee is said to have stated that:

> Cessation of refugee status may be understood as, essentially, the mirror of the reasons for granting such status found in the inclusion elements of Article 1A(2).[134]

Counsel for Applicant QAAH submitted that Article 1A(2) and Article 1C(5) involve 'separate and distinct' tests, so that where the Minister has previously recognised someone as a refugee pursuant to Section 36(2) of the Migration Act and Article 1A(2) of the Refugee Convention, the initial question for the tribunal is whether such obligations have ceased pursuant to Article 1C(5).[135] Counsel for QAAH argued that a person only ceases to be a 'refugee', and therefore ceases to be a person entitled to the protection

---

NBGM v MIMA & Anor [2006] HCATrans 339 (19 June 2006), lines 330–34: 'on the proper construction of Article 1A(2) and Article 1C(5) they express in different words the same substantive requirement and that requirement is to be a refugee a person must have a current well-founded fear of persecution for a Convention reason'.

129 Minister for Immigration, Oral submissions, *MIMIA v QAAH of 2004 & Anor; NBGM v MIMA & Anor [2006] HCATrans 339 (19 June 2006)*, lines 751–53, <www.austlii.edu.au/au/other/HCATrans/2006/339.html>.

130 Minister for Immigration, Written Submissions *QAAH*, above n 128, [15(c)].

131 Minister for Immigration, Oral submission, *MIMIA v QAAH of 2004 & Anor; NBGM v MIMA & Anor [2006] HCATrans 340 (20 June 2006)*, lines 3718–20, <www.austlii.edu.au/au/other/HCATrans/2006/340.html> ('*QAAH* 20 June 2006 Transcript').

132 Ibid lines 3718–20.

133 Ibid lines 3730–35. See also Minister for Immigration, Written submissions *QAAH*, above n 128 [20].

134 Ibid [26].

135 Ibid [25]–[27].

of the Convention under Article 1C(5).[136] Thus, counsel submitted, 'the question to be asked under Article 1C(5) is not the same question as that to be asked under Article 1A(2)'.[137]

Applicant QAAH's counsel raised a quite novel point in oral argument, noting that a number of rights accorded to a recognised refugee under the Convention under Articles 2–34 of the Convention,[138] such as the right to hold property,[139] of association,[140] access to the courts,[141] to work for remuneration[142] and to welfare[143] involved a 'protective' element, thus engaging Australia's protection obligations. It argued that such rights also illustrated that a protection visa was 'more than simply a permission to stay'.[144] This was an important point because the Minister had argued that the grant of a protection visa merely prevents the return or expulsion of a person contrary to Article 33 of the Convention and does not enliven other obligations under the Convention.[145] In particular, she said, it does not confer a certain status on the holder of that visa.[146] The Minister did acknowledge that where a person is accepted as being a refugee pursuant to the Convention and a protection visa is granted, this:

> constitutes both a positive determination that the person is (at that time) a 'refugee' under the Convention and the grant of statutory authority to remain in Australia (the visa).[147]

However, she submitted, when a further protection visa is sought by a person holding a TPV, the Migration Act (Sections 36(2) and 65) require

136 Ibid [34].
137 Ibid [35].
138 Note that Counsel for Applicant QAAH referred to Articles 2–34 rather than Articles 3–34 in this context. I do not view this difference as significant.
139 Refugee Convention, above n 1, Article 13.
140 Ibid, Article 15.
141 Ibid, Article 16.
142 Ibid, Article 17. Note however that Section 41 of the Migration Act 1958 (Cth) permits qualification of this right. For instance, Section 41(2)(b) provides that Regulations can be made to provide that a visa/visas of a specified class are subject to 'a condition imposing restrictions about the work that may be done in Australia by the holder, which, without limiting the generality of this paragraph, may be restrictions on doing: (i) any work; or (ii) work other than specified work; or (iii) work of a specified kind'.
143 Refugee Convention, above n 1, Articles 20–24.
144 *QAAH* 20 June 2006 Transcript, above n 150, at line 3020 (Bret Walker SC, for Applicant QAAH): 'When one looks at all of those, they do not bespeak moment by moment status. They are continuity of residence in a community in a country: rationing, housing, public education, public relief, labour legislation, social security'.
145 *QAAH*, Minister's oral submissions, 19 June 2006, [460]–[480].
146 Ibid [940–42].
147 Minister for Immigration, Written submissions *QAAH*, above n 128, [16].

the decision maker to decide whether the applicant is a refugee on the basis of the circumstances existing ***at the time*** of the decision on that further protection visa.[148] The effect of this approach is that the previous determination that a person is a refugee under the Convention is seen as merely a function of domestic law (that is, as part of the granting of a protection visa). Thus, expiration of a TPV means that a person no longer has an entitlement to remain in Australia as a refugee. I discuss the High Court's ruling on this approach in the next section of this chapter.

The High Court decision in QAAH

In a decision strongly criticised by UNHCR[149] and leading academic commentators,[150] the High Court in *QAAH* held, in a 6–1 majority decision,[151] that Australian domestic law, rather than the Convention, was determinative of the application of Article 1C(5) to holders of temporary protection visas. Thus, the holder of a TPV is not entitled to a further protection visa[152] if they no longer face persecution pursuant to Article 1A(2) of the Convention. That is, rather than applying the cessation criteria under Article 1C(5), the court held that 'it is the law of Australia which prevails in case of any conflict between it and the Convention. It is the law of Australia which must first be identified',[153] and that despite the ways in which 'the Convention may be used in construing the Act, it is the words of the Act which govern'.[154] In doing so, it did not accept the views of UNHCR as outlined in its ***amicus curiae*** submission to the court.[155]

In ***obiter dicta*** comments, the majority held that the use of the words 'no longer', and 'have ceased to exist' in Article 1C(5) 'make it clear that the circumstances from time to time and not merely as a matter of history are the relevant circumstances'.[156] That is, 'that the "status" . . . of a person

148 Ibid [17]–[19].

149 UNHCR Regional Office for Australia, 'New Zealand, Papua New Guinea and the South Pacific', Press Release, 20 November 2006, 1, <www.unhcr.org.au/pdfs/TPVHighCourt.pdf>.

150 See Goodwin Gill and McAdam, above n 2, 140 (footnote 28).

151 *QAAH* (Gummow ACJ, Callinan, Heydon, Crennan JJ (Kirby J dissenting).

152 As stated earlier in this book, under current Australian law, TPV holders are no longer permitted to apply for a permanent protection visa. However, the analysis of the requirement to make a fresh application in this part of the book is still relevant in terms of the procedure utilised for further TPV applications. Moreover, due to the disquiet that has arisen in relation to this permanent protection visa ban, the law may well revert back to the original position in the near future.

153 *QAAH* [33].

154 Ibid [34].

155 UNHCR Amicus in *QAAH*, above n 113.

156 *QAAH* [43] (Gummow J et al).

permitted to reside in an asylum country may change as circumstances in the country which he has left change'.[157] In this respect, the court adopted a very narrow interpretation of the wording of Article 1C(5), noting that:

> the opening words of Art 1C state that the 'Convention shall cease to apply to any person falling under the terms of [Art 1A]' if any of the following paras (1)–(6) apply. Accordingly, the language of Art 1C(5) is unambiguous and compels the same conclusion as the Act.[158]

Additionally, the court accepted the submission of the Minister for Immigration that Article 1C(5) operated 'automatically', that is:

> that the cessation provision operates automatically according to its terms, and need not for its application be triggered by a request for a, or any particular kind of visa, although in practice such a request will ordinarily be the occasion for a visa consideration of a person's right or otherwise to continuing protection.[159]

The minority judge in *QAAH*, Justice Kirby, delivered a very strong dissenting judgement. On the issue of the relationship between Australian domestic law and the Convention, his Honour held that the visa regime established under the Migration Act cannot be used to alter the language and requirements of the Convention,[160] and that the act must be read 'so as to conform to the convention'.[161] His Honour departed from the findings of the majority by concluding that Article 1C(5) did in fact require a separate and distinct test from Article 1A(2),[162] that a decision maker applying Article 1C(5) is required to consider whether any purported change in circumstances is 'fundamental, stable and durable',[163] and that a 'forensic' obligation exists with the asylum authorities applying Article 1C(5) to provide affirmative evidence of the relevant change in circumstances.[164]

157 Ibid [43].
158 Ibid [44].
159 Ibid.
160 Ibid [145] (Kirby J): 'The temporary and permanent visas established by the Act cannot alter, unilaterally, the language and requirements of the convention that forms part of Australian law. Specifically, they cannot change the provisions and structure of the convention in so far as it provides for the cessation of "refugee" status, once that status has been accepted in the case of a person claiming surrogate protection from a country of refuge. Cessation of such status, once granted, is governed by Art 1C(5) of the convention'.
161 *QAAH* [145] (Kirby J) (note: the word 'Convention' is not capitalised in the citation).
162 *QAAH* [99]–[104] (Kirby J).
163 Ibid [122] (Kirby J).
164 Ibid [53] (Kirby J).

Analysis

As a result of the High Court decision, the position under Australian law is that refugees holding temporary protection visas are required to reprove their claim to refugee status under Article 1A(2), rather than the state bearing the burden of establishing cessation of refugee status under Article 1C(5). This has had significant implications for holders of TPVs in Australia given that it is generally more difficult for refugee applicants to prove refugee status under Article 1A(2) than it is for the state to be required to show cessation of refugee status under Article 1C(5). It also raises a number of concerns about the subjugation of the Refugee Convention to Australian domestic law. The approach of the High Court majority devalued the role of the Refugee Convention, as it found that expiry of a TPV leads to cessation of refugee status under international law without any application by the state of Article 1C(5). Rather than considering the operation of the Refugee Convention, the majority in *QAAH* focused on the requirements of the Australian temporary visa system, noting that the effect of the migration legislation was that when a temporary protection visa expires, 'the holder of it must make a fresh application for another visa . . . because otherwise that person would have no entitlement to remain in Australia'.[165] There was thus no acknowledgement that the recognition of a person as a refugee, and the grant of a protection visa on that basis, has any continuing effect in international law. The court held that when the further protection visa comes to be assessed, the relevant criterion is that the applicant is a person to whom Australia *has* protection obligations under the Convention under Section 36 of the Migration Act.[166] The court emphasised that the criteria set out in Section 36 was expressed in the present tense ('has') rather than referring to any previous status (via terms such as 'in the past had' or 'owed').[167] In its *ratio decidendi*, the court therefore gave primacy to the Migration Act rather than to the Convention. Significantly, the court failed to consider whether the interpretation it adopted would place Australia in breach of its international obligations under the Refugee Convention.

The result of the preceding is that whilst it may be correct to find that Article 1C(5) 'takes effect naturally' as part of an *initial* assessment of

165 Ibid [38].

166 Ibid. Note that the High Court was interpreting Section 36(2) as it then was (in 2006). At that time, Section 36 referred to 'a non-citizen in Australia *to whom* the Minister is satisfied'. Section 36 of the Migration Act (Cth) 1958 was recently amended by the Migration Legislation Amendment (Regional Processing and Other Measures) Act 2012 to change this to 'a non-citizen in Australia *in respect of whom* the Minister is satisfied' (emphasis added). This change came into effect on 18 August 2012. It is not significant in of itself, but the difference is noted for accuracy.

167 The issue of past persecution in the context of cessation is discussed in Chapter 6 of this book.

refugee status under *Article 1A(2)*, such an approach cannot be applied to a situation where a person has already been recognised as a refugee under international law through the granting of a temporary protection visa or temporary residence permit. That, is, once a person is recognised as a refugee (via the grant of a temporary protection visa), then Article 1C(5) does *not* operate naturally but must be invoked against that person by the state. Accordingly, the findings in *Hoxha* and *Adan* as to the relationship between Articles 1A(2) and 1C(5) cannot be applied to holders of TPV visas in the Australian context. This is because Australia *does* 'recognise' a person to be a refugee pursuant to the grant of a TPV.[168]

How, then, can one find (as the Australian High Court did) that expiry of *domestic protection* (via expiry of a TPV) leads to expiry of a person's *international recognition* of refugee status? The answer given by the High Court is that the Migration Act and Migration Regulations required TPV holders to lodge a fresh application for a permanent protection visa and the wording of Section 36(2)(a) of the Migration Act requires that the applicant establish a current, well-founded fear of persecution, rather than cessation of a previous or pre-existing status. However, such an approach fails to recognise the declaratory nature of refugee protection discussed earlier. That is, because the grant of a TPV by Australia under Section 36 of the Migration Act is simply domestic recognition of a status that *already exists at international law*, it cannot then be held that expiry of a TPV leads to expiry of refugee status at international law. Thus, the correct legal position relating to Article 1C(5) and TPVs in Australia appears to be that if legislation requires a refugee who has previously held a TPV to lodge a fresh application to obtain a permanent protection visa, that applicant continues to hold the status of refugee at international law, and Australia therefore continues to have protection obligations towards that person unless it successfully applies Article 1C(5) to that refugee. This analysis appears to be supported by Goodwin-Gill and McAdam who have also expressed concern over this aspect of the decision in *QAAH*, stating that:

> the majority of the High Court of Australia misunderstood the centrality of *status* in the Convention scheme of protection; in applying domestic law without regard to international law and practice, they supposed that cessation was somehow automatic and thereby failed to do justice to the individual dimensions of a case involving a subject to Australia's 'temporary protection visa' regime.[169]

168 Migration Act 1958 (Cth), s 36.
169 Goodwin-Gill and McAdam, above n 2, 140 (footnote 28).

Likewise, the sole dissenting judge in *QAAH*, Justice Kirby, who strongly disagreed with the majority of the High Court, also distinguished between domestic protection of refugees and cessation of refugee status at international law:

> *Recognition*, as envisaged by the convention, can only lapse in accordance with one of the cessation grounds set out in Art 1C. *Protection*, on the other hand, may lapse in accordance with the provisions of the Act. Because they are distinct processes, the lapse of *protection* does not necessarily have any causal effect on a person's *recognition* as a refugee. . . . By assuming that the provisions of the Act dealing with the temporariness of *protection* have some operation in relation to the *recognition* (or cessation) of a person's refugee status, the joint reasons confuse the distinct functions of recognition of refugee status, and protection. With respect, this is a serious error of analysis.[170]

Given the preceding, it would seem that a state which requires an applicant who has already been recognised as a refugee pursuant to a domestic refugee determination process to reprove refugee status under Article 1A(2) will act inconsistently with the Refugee Convention. Thus, if one accepts that the effect of a grant of a TPV is that the person is recognised as a refugee at international law, any domestic legislative provisions or administrative procedures of a state cannot be interpreted in a way which breaches a state's obligations under the Convention.[171] In this respect, the High Court's interpretation of Australian domestic law arguably brings Australia in breach of its international obligations under the Convention.

Thus, the correct legal interpretation of Article 1C(5) in the Australian context appears to be the following: if the scheme governing the application process for protection visas is that those on a TPV can only obtain a permanent protection *visa* by lodging a fresh application for that visa, this does not necessarily mean that the criteria governing the granting of that visa also require a de novo consideration of the applicant's case for *protection.* That is, any *procedural requirements* put in place by migration legislation for the application for a protection visa must not be conflated with the *criteria upon which those visas are granted.* Thus, the presumption at law is that a person continues to be a refugee and to be owed protection

170 *QAAH* (Kirby J) (emphasis in original).
171 See Vienna Convention on the Law of Treaties, 23 May 1969, 155 UNTS 331, Article 26 of which states that '[e]very treaty in force is binding upon the parties to it and must be performed by them in good faith'.

obligations by Australia until the decision maker successfully applies one of the cessation clauses to that applicant.

The preceding argument is strengthened by the fact that the act of granting an applicant a TPV is understood to be declaratory of that applicant's status as a refugee under international law. Because of this, any expiration of a TPV or the existence of any procedural requirement in domestic law to apply for a fresh protection visa has no effect on the continuing status of that applicant as a refugee under international law – the protection of which Australia has undertaken by its grant of a protection visa to that person under Section 36(2) of the Migration Act.

Case study 3: the EU Qualification Directive and European state practice

Cessation of refugee status is provided for in Article 11(1)(e) of the EU Qualification Directive, which sets out the following cessation provision:

> 1 A third country national or a stateless person shall cease to be a refugee, if he or she:
>
> . . .
>
> (e) can no longer, because the circumstances in connection with which he or she has been recognised as a refugee have ceased to exist, continue to refuse to avail himself or herself of the protection of the country of nationality;
>
> 2 In considering points (e) and (f) of paragraph 1, Member States shall have regard to whether the change of circumstances is of such a significant and non-temporary nature that the refugee's fear of persecution can no longer be regarded as well-founded.

Broadly speaking, Article 11(1)(e) of the Qualification Directive largely replicates Article 1C(5) of the Refugee Convention, however, with some significant differences.

First, in considering cessation due to a change in circumstances, Article 11(2) of the Directive requires the relevant decision maker to:

> have regard to whether the change of circumstances is of such a significant and non-temporary nature that the refugee's fear of persecution can no longer be regarded as well-founded.[172]

172 2011 Qualification Directive, above n 2, Article 11(2).

This is an important addition to the cessation criteria in the Directive, as such a requirement is not set out in the Refugee Convention. Rather, these criteria reflect UNHCR opinion and academic commentary on cessation, which has stated that the standard for changes under Article 1C(5) must be 'fundamental, durable and stable'.[173] In this respect, the Directive makes a positive contribution to international refugee law by reflecting a part of the cessation test which has evolved since the 1951 Refugee Convention was ratified. However, there are a number of aspects to this provision which should be noted.

Case study: Germany

Section 73(1) of the German Asylum Procedures Act transposed a version of Article 11 of the 2004 EU Qualification Directive into German national law.[174] Section 73(1), which was amended in 2007 so as to conform with the 2004 EU Qualification Directive, states that:

> Recognition of entitlement to asylum and refugee status shall be revoked without delay if the conditions on which such recognition is based have ceased to exist.
>
> In particular, this shall be the case if, after the conditions on which his recognition as being entitled to asylum or refugee status is based have ceased to exist, the foreigner can no longer refuse to claim the protection of the country of which he is a citizen, or if he, as a stateless person, is able to return to the country where he had his usual residence. The second sentence shall not apply if the foreigner has compelling reasons, based on earlier persecution, for refusing to return to the country of which he is a citizen, or, if he is a stateless person, in which he had his usual residence.[175]

The German legislation contradicts both the 2004 and 2011 Directive in two important ways. Firstly, it alters the wording of Article 11(1)(e) in a

173 UNHCR, Executive Committee Conclusion No. 65, *General Conclusion on International Protection*, U.N. GAOR, 46th Sess., (q) (1991), *aff'd*, ExCom Conclusion No. 69; Hathaway, *Rights of Refugees*, above n 2, 922–41; Goodwin-Gill and McAdam, above n 2, 143.

174 German Procedures Act, promulgated on 27 July 1993 (Federal Law Gazette I, p. 1361), as amended on 19 August 2007.

175 Asylum Procedures Act, promulgated on 27 July 1993 (Federal Law Gazette I, p. 1361), as amended on 19 August 2007, s. 73(1), emphasis added, <www.unhcr.org/refworld/docid/48e5d6582.html>. The CJEU in *Abdulla* set out the provision also: 'The grant of the right to asylum and of refugee status shall be revoked without delay when the conditions *on which they were based* have ceased to exist. This is particularly the case when, the circumstances which led to that right to asylum or refugee status being granted to him having ceased to exist, the foreign national can no longer continue to refuse to avail himself of the protection of his country of nationality': *Abdulla*, above n 9, [28] (emphasis added).

subtle but very significant way by using the phrase 'conditions *on* which such recognition is based' rather than the 'circumstances *in connection with which* he has been recognised as a refugee' (the latter phrase is used in both Articles 1C(5) of the Refugee Convention and 11(1)(e) of the Directive). This is significant because, arguably, the term 'circumstances *in connection* with which' is broader in scope than 'conditions *on* which' such recognition is based. As I argued in Chapter 2, the words 'circumstances in connection' arguably involve broader considerations such as the provision of the rule of law and associated legal infrastructure, human rights protections and a stable security situation, including the absence of armed conflict. I note that this difference may be due to an issue of translation and that neither of the English translations of Section 73 of the German Asylum Procedures Act which are publicly available are 'official translations'. However, notably, the version of the German legislation cited in the judgement of the CJEU in *Abdulla* used the term 'conditions on which' rather than 'circumstances in connection with which'.[176] Thus, it does seem that there may be an issue of difference between the German law and EU Directive here that should be queried.

Secondly, the German act fails to transpose Article 11(2) of the Directive which requires Member States to consider whether the changes are 'significant and non-temporary'.[177]

German legislation obliges the German Federal Office for Migration and Refugees to automatically review, within a period of 3 years, the initial decision which granted a person refugee status, before a decision on a permanent residence permit is made by the local Länder authorities.[178]

176 The CJEU in *Abdulla* set out the provision as follows: 'The grant of the right to asylum and of refugee status shall be revoked without delay when the conditions *on which they were based* have ceased to exist. This is particularly the case when, the circumstances which led to that right to asylum or refugee status being granted to him having ceased to exist, the foreign national can no longer continue to refuse to avail himself of the protection of his country of nationality': *Abdulla*, above n 9, [28] (emphasis added).

177 Although subsequent German Federal Administrative Court jurisprudence has recognised that this is part of the cessation criteria: see *Bundesverwaltungsgericht (Federal Administrative Court, Germany) BVerwG 10 C 25.10* VGH A 9 S 3262/08, 1 June 2011, (2011) 23(4) *International Journal of Refugee Law* 844, 850, where the Court noted that Section 73(1) of the German *Asylum Procedure Act* had to be construed in light of the EU Qualification Directive and that in examining cessation of refugee status based on changed circumstances, 'Member States are to have regard to whether the change of circumstances is of such a significant and non-temporary nature that the refugee's fear of persecution can no longer be regarded as well-founded' as per Article 11(2) of the Directive.

178 Act on the Residence, Economic Activity and Integration of Foreigners in the Federal Territory Residence Act (Germany) (in the version promulgated on 25 February 2008 (Federal Law Gazette I p. 162), last amended by Article 2 (25) of the Act of 22 December 2011 (Federal Law Gazette I p. 3044), Section 26(3) (Residence Act Germany). This should be read in conjunction with Section 73(2a) of the Asylum Procedures Act (Germany), which provides that '[n]o more than three years after the decision becomes non-appealable, it shall

Significantly, after a cessation decision has been made, a decision maker must also ensure that there are no prohibitions on deportation of the ceased refugee under Section 60(2) to (7) of the Residence Act if the authorities wish to return the ceased refugee to their country of origin.[179] Grounds for such prohibitions on deportation include where a person 'will be exposed, as a member of the civilian population, to a substantial individual danger to life or limb as a result of an international or internal armed conflict'.[180]

In this context, it is important to note that revocation of refugee status under German law does not automatically lead to withdrawal of the associated residence permit.[181] This is because under German law, the residence and refugee status components of protection are separated. This is in contrast to the position under the Australian Temporary Protection Regime where that visa serves two purposes: recognition by the Australian government that the person is a 'refugee' under the Convention and the grant to that person of lawful authority to remain in Australia.[182]

The decision in BVerwG 33.07

The case of *BVerwG 33.07* concerned an Iraqi refugee of Kurdish ethnicity and of the Muslim faith. He was granted refugee status in 2001 but later, in 2005, the German Federal Office for Migration and Refugees (the German Federal Office) revoked that status based on a finding of change of circumstances in Iraq arising from the overthrow of Saddam Hussein's regime. On appeal, the first instance appellate court had held that refugee status ceases if the refugee's well-founded fear of persecution (on which recognition was

---

be examined whether the conditions for revocation pursuant to (1) or withdrawal pursuant to (2) exist'. See discussion in European Union, Report by the Commissioner for Human Rights, Mr Thomas Hammarberg, on his visit to Germany 9–11 and 15–20 October 2006, CommDH (2007) 14, 11 July 2007, 35 [126] (hereinafter Hammarberg Report).

179 Residence Act (Germany), as discussed in *BVerwG 10 C 25.10*, [6]. For instance, Section 60(7) of the Residence Act (Germany) provides that 'A foreigner should not be deported to another state in which a substantial concrete danger to his or her life and limb or liberty applies. A foreigner shall not be deported to another state in which he or she will be exposed, as a member of the civilian population, to a substantial individual danger to life or limb as a result of an international or internal armed conflict. Dangers pursuant to sentence 1 or sentence 2 to which the population or the segment of the population to which the foreigner belongs are generally exposed shall receive due consideration in decisions pursuant to Section 60a (1), sentence 1'.

180 Residence Act (Germany), Section 60(7).

181 This is because, unlike the Australian TPV regime, the refugee status and residence aspects are separate legal questions.

182 The dual nature of the grant of a TPV was recognised by the Department of Immigration in its submission to the High Court in *QAAH*: see, Minister for Immigration and Multicultural and Indigenous Affairs, 'Appellant's Outline of Submissions', 1 June 2006, [16], copy available from author.

based) no longer exists, and if the refugee has no reason to fear persecution for other reasons.[183] On appeal to the German Federal Administrative Court, the applicant argued that this decision was in breach of the 2004 EU Qualification Directive and of Article 1C(5) of the Refugee Convention on the basis that those instruments are concerned with a broader meaning of protection that is not limited to protection against persecution within the meaning of Article 1A(2) of the 1951 Convention.[184] Rather, it extends to consideration of the general conditions in the country of origin, such as a state-established order and peace and an existence consistent with human dignity.[185] This therefore raised some of the central questions discussed in this book – whether Article 1C(5) is the 'mirror image' of Article 1A(2) of the Convention and the role of non-state bodies as actors of protection.

The German Federal Administrative Court ordered a stay in this and four other similar cases on cessation as it referred a number of questions on the interpretation of Article 11(1)(e) of the Qualification Directive to the CJEU.[186] These cases shared common facts in that they involved applicants from Iraq whose refugee status had been revoked by German authorities on the basis that they no longer feared persecution due to the overthrow of Saddam Hussein's regime. The proceedings were therefore focused primarily on the interpretation of the cessation provision in Article 11(1)(e) of the 2004 Qualification Directive, although this is relevant to Article 1C(5) of the Refugee Convention upon which it is based and which is similarly worded.

The questions referred to the CJEU

The central question asked of the CJEU by the German Federal Administrative Court concerned the relationship between cessation under Article 11(1)(e) of the 2004 Qualification Directive and recognition of refugee

183 *BVerwG 33.07*, [17].

184 Article 1A(2) provides that the term 'refugee' shall apply to any person who 'owing to a well-founded fear of being persecuted for reasons of race, religion, nationality, membership of a particular social group or political opinion . . . is unable, or owing to such fear, is unwilling to avail himself of the protection of [the country of his nationality]'.

185 *BVerwG 33.07*, [5].

186 The German Federal Administrative Court submitted five identical references for preliminary ruling to the CJEU on 28 April 2008 concerning the interpretation of Article 11(1)(e) Qualification Directive in the following cases: *Case C-179/08, Dler Jamal v. Federal Republic of Germany; Case C-178/08, Ahmed Adem and Hamrin Mosa Rashi v. Federal Republic of Germany; Case C-177/08, Khoshnaw Abdulla v. Federal Republic of Germany; Case C-176/08, Kamil Hasan v. Federal Republic of Germany; Case C-175/08, Aydin Salahadin Abdulla v. Federal Republic of Germany*, OJ 2008 C 197, 3–6. Referrals by national courts to the Court of Justice for the European Union for a preliminary ruling are made under Articles 68 and 234 of the *Treaty Establishing the European Community* [2002] OJ C 325/127.

status under Article 2(c) of that Directive. Specifically, it asked whether Article 11(1)(e) was to be interpreted as meaning that refugee status ceases to exist if the refugee's well-founded fear of persecution (on the basis of which refugee status was granted) no longer exists and he has no other reason to fear persecution under Article 2(c). That is, whether Article 1C(5) is the 'mirror image' of Article 1A(2).

The German Federal Administrative Court then posed related questions that were to be answered in the event that the CJEU held that something more than mere absence of persecution was required for cessation.[187] Matters raised by these other referral questions have been analysed in Chapters 4 to 7 of this book.

Here I discuss the Advisory Opinion on these questions delivered by Advocate General Mazák of the CJEU on 15 September 2009,[188] in addition to the CJEU judgement handed down on *Abdulla* in 2010.

The decision of the CJEU in Abdulla 2010

In *Abdullah*, the CJEU interpreted cessation in Article 11(1)(e) of the Qualification Directive as the mirror of the recognition of refugee status in Article 2(c) of the Directive.[189] The reasoning of the CJEU was that Article 11(1)(e) of the Qualification Directive, like Article 1C(5) of the Geneva Convention, provides that a person ceases to be classified as a refugee when 'he no longer qualifies for refugee status'.[190] It held that the term 'protection' used in Article 11(1)(e) of the Directive therefore refers to protection against acts of persecution:

> In so far as it provides that the national 'can no longer . . . continue to refuse' to avail himself of the protection of his country of origin, Article 11(1)(e) of the Directive implies that the 'protection'

187 *Abdulla*, Referral Questions 2–5.

188 Opinion of Mr. Mazák in Abdulla C-175/08, C-176/08, C-178/08 and C-179/08 Salahadin Abdulla and others, 15 September 2009 (hereinafter AG Mazák Opinion).

189 This interpretation of Article 11 by the CJEU was also cited and approved in subsequent German case law on cessation: see *A v R* 2011, [16]: 'It can further be deduced from the CJEU's judgment that the termination of refugee status because of changes in the country of origin is fundamentally a mirror image of the recognition of that status'.

190 CJEU in *Abdulla*, [65]. See also the court's findings [66]:

> By stating that, because those circumstances 'have ceased to exist', the national 'can no longer . . . continue to refuse to avail himself or herself of the protection of the country of nationality', that article establishes, by its very wording, a causal connection between the change in circumstances and the impossibility for the person concerned to continue to refuse and thus to retain his refugee status, in that his original fear of persecution no longer appears to be well founded.

> in question is the same as that which has up to that point been lacking, namely protection against the acts of persecution envisaged by the Directive.[191]

This is significant, as the CJEU took a similar position to that of the Australian High Court in *QAAH* as to the symmetry between Articles 1C(5) and 1A(2) of the Refugee Convention.[192]

In interpreting cessation in this manner, the CJEU did note that, pursuant to Article 7(2) of the Qualification Directive, the competent authorities must verify that the actor or actors of protection in the country of origin operate *inter alia*, 'an effective legal system for the detection, prosecution and punishment of acts constituting persecution and that the national concerned will have access to such protection'.[193] I note that Article 7(2) reflects one aspect of the 'effective protection' test set out in this book (that is, a functioning legal system) but it is limited to acts of persecution rather than to a broader consideration of factors underlying that persecution and broader changes in the country of origin. In relation to Article 7(2), the CJEU in *Abdulla* said that the authorities may take into account 'the extent to which basic human rights are guaranteed in that country'.[194] This statement of the CJEU is significant, as it refers more broadly to consideration of human rights standards in the country of origin. However, it is notable that the court did not frame it as a mandatory provision. Thus, according to the CJEU approach, evaluation of general human rights standards in the country of origin by states is only a discretionary matter.[195] Further, there is no inclusion of other elements central to 'effective protection', such as provision of a stable security situation and absence of armed conflict.

The position of the CJEU on the relationship between cessation and recognition accords with that of the German Federal Administrative Court and the CJEU Advocate General's opinion in *Abdulla*. The German Federal Administrative Court also took a narrow interpretation of the meaning of 'protection of the country' in Article 1C(5), holding that the term in Article 1C(5) does not differ in meaning from the same words in

191 *Abdulla*, [67]. The court noted further that:

> In that way, the circumstances which demonstrate the country of origin's inability or, conversely, its ability to ensure protection against acts of persecution constitute a crucial element in the assessment which leads to the granting of, or, as the case may be, by means of the opposite conclusion, to the cessation of refugee status: [68].

192 *QAAH*, 352.

193 *Abdulla*, [70].

194 Ibid [71].

195 I note here that this does not affect the 'mirror' approach to interpretation of Article 1C(5) as it relates to Article 1A(2).

Article 1A(2).[196] In doing so, the Federal Administrative Court held that general harm is not a relevant consideration under Article 1C(5).[197] Similarly, in his Advisory Opinion in *Abdulla*, Advocate General Mazák held that cessation does not require that a refugee be protected from the risk of suffering serious harm in his country of nationality,[198] but that protection in Article 1C(5) is narrower, being limited to protection against persecution.[199] Whilst he recognised that the stability of the security situation in a country must be considered, he states this 'should be assessed as an integral part of the availability of protection from persecution' and it must 'be such that a refugee does not face a situation in which he may become eligible for refugee status in the foreseeable future'.[200]

Conclusions

The interpretation of cessation by European judicial bodies, including the German Federal Administrative Court, the CJEU and the CJEU Advocate General, in addition to the UK and Australian courts, is that protection for the purposes of cessation means protection against persecution, that is, that cessation is the 'mirror image' of recognition. However, for the reasons discussed in earlier chapters of this book, it is strongly arguable that cessation of refugee status is not merely the mirror image of recognition under Article 1A(2).

The wording of Article 1C(5) (and its Qualification Directive equivalent) supports this finding, as it states that the Convention will cease where the refugee 'can no longer, because the *circumstances in connection* with which he has been recognised as a refugee have ceased to exist'. Importantly, it does not simply say 'refugee status will cease where the refugee no longer fears persecution in his or her country of nationality'. The term 'circumstances in connection with which' and the nature of the inquiry undertaken in cessation proceedings (which must establish a change in country conditions which goes beyond mere persecutory acts but also encompass broader political issues of stability, security and durability of change) mean that cessation is not merely the mirror of recognition of refugee status. In this regard, I note that other commentators have also emphasised that recognition and cessation decisions should be viewed as separate and distinct processes.[201]

196 *BVerwG 33.07* [23].

197 Ibid [24]: 'general risks (e.g., because of war, natural disasters or poor economic conditions) are not covered by protection under Article 1 A No. 2 of the GRC [1951 Convention], according to the letter and intent of this provision, nor are they covered by Article 1 C No. 5 sentence 1 of the GRC [1951 Convention]. Thus according to Section 73 (1) of the Asylum Procedure Act, there is to be no examination of whether the foreigner can reasonably be expected to return because of general risks in his country of origin'.

198 AG Mazák Opinion, above n 188 [53].

199 Ibid [54], [56].

200 Ibid [62].

201 See e.g. UNHCR Lisbon Roundtable Meeting of Experts, Summary Conclusions, above n 62, 550; Hathaway, 'Rights of Refugees', above n 2, 920.

It is relevant here that AG Mazák of the CJEU recognises that the security situation in the country of origin is relevant, but as part of assessing the existence of a well-founded fear of persecution, not as a separate criteria.[202] Whilst refugee status decision makers do often consider the security situation in a country of origin as part of assessing the well-foundedness of a refugee's fear of persecution, the emphasis in Article 1A(2) and Article 1C(5) on state protection is different. In assessing entitlement to refugee status under Article 1A(2), the criteria is whether the applicant faces a well-founded fear of persecution and is unable or unwilling to return to his or her country of nationality because of that fear. The criteria in Article 1C(5), in comparison, is weighted very much on the existence of a change of circumstances in the country of origin, rather than the fear held by the refugee. It provides that the Refugee Convention may cease to apply to a refugee if the refugee:

> can no longer, *because the circumstances in connection with which he has been recognized as a refugee have ceased to exist*, continue to refuse to avail himself of the protection of the country of his nationality.[203]

As argued previously in relation to the 'mirror image' argument, although a refugee's recognition of refugee status would have involved assessment of his or her well-founded fear of persecution and in that respect, is part of the cessation criteria, the emphasis in Article 1C(5) is the *objective changes* in the country of nationality and the availability of state protection and thus is different to recognition of refugee status under Article 1A(2). As such, assessment of the security situation in a country of origin cannot simply be limited to how that relates to the refugee's well-founded fear of persecution, but must be a separate factor linked to a wider test as to whether there have been sufficient changes in the country of origin, that is, to use the wording of Article 1C(5), whether the '*circumstances in connection with which*' the refugee has been recognised as a refugee have ceased to exist.

Further, if one considers the role of Article 1C(5) in relation to the Convention as a whole, particularly the *non-refoulement* principle in Article 33, and the 'acquired rights' in Articles 3–34 of the Convention, this also supports the use of 'effective protection' as the test for cessation. The argument that there is some 'symmetry' between Articles 1A(2) and 1C(5) is an important one as it can be used (as the High Court of Australia did in *QAAH*) to allow a state to apply Article 1A(2) to cessation cases, rather than Article 1C(5). Despite the comments by certain members of the House of Lords in *Adan* and *Hoxha*, it is highly questionable whether there is any precise symmetry between Article 1A(2) and Article 1C(5). Firstly, as I noted in Chapter 2 of this book, Article 1C expressly states that '[t]his Convention shall cease to apply to any person *falling under the terms of Section A*'.[204] Article 1C(5) then states that the Convention will so cease where the refugee 'can no longer, because the circumstances in connection with *which he has been recognised as*

202 AG Mazák Opinion in *Abdulla*, above n 188, [62].
203 Refugee Convention, above n 1, Article 1C(5) (emphasis added).
204 Ibid, Article 1C (emphasis added).

a refugee have ceased to exist'.[205] The terms of Article 1C therefore indicate that in order for Article 1C(5) to operate, a person must first have been recognised as a refugee under Article 1A(2). This suggests that the Convention contemplates a separation between the stages of recognition of refugee status and that of cessation.

Such a finding is supported by the nature of the questions posed in each provision. That is, even if one accepts that both Articles 1A(2) and 1C(5) involve consideration of a similar issue (that is, an assessment of whether the applicant has a well-founded fear of persecution), the *stages* of assessment involved under each article are quite distinct. Under Article 1A(2) the question asked is: will this person face a real chance of persecution for a Convention reason if returned to his or her country of origin? Under Article 1C(5) the question asked is: have country conditions in the refugee's country of origin changed sufficiently such that he or she no longer has a well-founded fear of the persecution in relation to which he or she was recognised a refugee? This distinction is particularly strong if one accepts that the standard and onus of proof for cessation decisions is different to that of initial determination. As James Hathaway points out:

> While the range of issues to be considered in initially assessing the existence of a well-founded fear and at the cessation stages is similar, Art. 1(C)(5)–(6) nonetheless insists upon a higher standard of scrutiny in the context of adjudicating cessation.[206]

When one compares the jurisprudence of the various states discussed previously, one difference to note is that the Australian High Court focused very much on Australian domestic law and utilised statutory interpretation to interpret the relevant domestic law quite narrowly, which meant TPV holders could not benefit from Article 1C(5) when applying for a permanent protection visa to remain in Australia. In contrast, the German Federal Administrative Court, as a signatory to the EU Qualification Directive was at least required to enact into domestic law the EU equivalent of Article 1C(5).

However, the jurisprudence discussed in this chapter also illustrates some broader issues about the interpretation of the Refugee Convention by state parties. One similarity between the Australian jurisprudence and that of the CJEU is that neither court appeared to take into account the views of UNHCR in interpreting Article 1C(5). UNHCR was permitted to lodge an *amicus curiae* submission in the Australian High Court of *QAAH*. However, it was not referred to in the High Court's judgement in that case. Similarly, the CJEU did not appear to take into account the statement on the cessation issues that were due to be heard in *Abdulla*, which was published in 2008 prior to the CJEU hearing that set of cases.[207]

205 Ibid, Article 1C(5) (emphasis added).
206 Hathaway, 'Rights of Refugees', above n 2, 920 (footnote 20).
207 UNHCR Statement on Cessation 2008, above n 18.

4 'Changed circumstances'

Demonstrating a fundamental, stable and durable change

Introduction

This chapter deals with the standard of proof to be used by states in establishing that there has been a sufficient change in circumstances in a country in order to satisfy the requirements of Article 1C(5).

In discussing this standard, it must be borne in mind that the act of revoking a person's refugee status is a significant one. Due to this, it is strongly arguable that the standard of proof for such revocation should be robust and that due consideration must be given to the context in which cessation often takes place – in countries subject to armed conflict or that have extremely fragile security and political situations. Further, there must be a rethinking of the way in which the judiciary differentiate between refugee status and complementary protection.

The seriousness of cessation is reflected in the fact that there is general agreement by UNHCR and states that the standard of proof for cessation is one of 'fundamental, stable and durable' change[1] (or variants on those criteria).[2] Some

1 UNHCR ExCom, Conclusion No. 65 (1992), (q); UNHCR ExCom, Conclusion No. 69 (1993); UNHCR, *Handbook on Procedures and Criteria for Determining Refugee Status under the 1951 Convention and the 1967 Protocol Relating to the Status of Refugees*, HCR/IP/4/Rev.1, 1979, Reedited, Geneva, January 1992, [135] (hereinafter *UNHCR Handbook*); G. Goodwin-Gill and J. McAdam, *The Refugee in International Law* (Oxford University Press, 3rd ed., 2007), 142–3; J.C. Hathaway, *The Rights of Refugees under International Law* (Cambridge University Press, 2005), 922–35.

2 See *Directive 2011/95/EU of The European Parliament and of The Council of 13 December 2011 on standards for the qualification of third-country nationals or stateless persons as beneficiaries of international protection, for a uniform status for refugees or for persons eligible for subsidiary protection, and for the content of the protection granted (recast)*, [2011] OJ L 337/9 (hereinafter 2011 Qualification Directive), Article 11(2) and Article 14. See also the Norwegian Immigration Appeals Board who say that the change has to have a 'certain degree of permanence': Immigration Appeals Board of Norway (hereinafter Grand board), decisions on Cessation in June 2017, summarised in Immigration Appeals Board, Norway (UNE), 'Grand Board: Cessation of Refugee Status and Revocation of Temporary Residence Permits', <www.une.no/en/sources/stornemndavgjorelser/stornemnd-opphor-av-flyktningstatus/>. The exception to this state practice is the High Court of Australia which has refused to endorse the 'fundamental, stable and durable test' posited by UNHCR, that is: *Minister for Immigration and Multicultural and Indigenous Affairs v QAAH of 2004* [2006] HCA 53 (*QAAH*).

indicators of such change that have been suggested by UNHCR and the UNHCR Executive Committee[3] include democratic elections, significant reforms to the legal and social structure, amnesties, repeal of oppressive laws, dismantling of repressive security forces and general respect for human rights. UNHCR recognises that observance of specific human rights need not be exemplary, but significant improvements and progress towards the development of national institutions to protect human rights are necessary. Significantly, UNHCR has emphasised on a number of occasions that Article 1C(5) can only be applied to a refugee where the protection of his or her country of origin is both effective and available.[4] This is a crucial point in light of the view which has emerged in some jurisdictions that Article 1C(5) is the 'mirror image' of Article 1A(2) and thus requires only the absence of persecution in the country of origin, rather than any broader notion of effective protection encompassing such elements as a stable security situation and absence of violence (as discussed in Chapter 3).

In terms of durability, no precise minimum time frame has been laid down as a definitive guide, but 12 to 18 months has been suggested as indicative of durable change by the UNHCR. The UNHCR itself generally waits for 4 or 5 years to elapse before making a group-based declaration of cessation.[5]

State practice on the standard of proof for cessation indicates that there is substantial agreement on the core of the test (significant, stable, durable). Conceptually, the standard of proof for cessation is linked closely to the legal issues discussed in Chapter 3 about concepts of persecution and protection, in which I have already canvassed the main arguments about the test to be used for cessation. Due to this, and the fact that much commentary has been written on the 'significant, stable, durable' test,[6] I do not propose to revisit the arguments on this core aspect of the standard to be used for a change in circumstances. Rather, I wish to examine a number of case studies which demonstrate how this core standard of proof is complicated by a number of matters. These include:

- Whether Article 1C(5) can be applied if the country of origin continues to suffer from armed conflict;
- How cessation of refugee status interacts with complementary protection status;
- Whether humanitarian principles should be applied, in particular, how cessation of refugee status interacts with human rights protections, particularly those in Article 3 the European Convention on Human Rights; and

3 UNHCR ExCom Conclusion No. 69 (1993).

4 UNHCR, Guidelines on International Protection: Cessation of Refugee Status under Article 1C(5) and (6) of the 1951 Convention relating to the Status of Refugees, HCR/GIP/03/03, 10 February 2003 (hereinafter UNHCR Cessation Guidelines 2003), 15–16; UNHCR, 'UNHCR Statement on the "Ceased Circumstances" Clause of the EC Qualification Directive' (2008), 3, 8, 14, 17, <www.unhcr.org/refworld/docid/48a2f0782.html> (hereinafter UNHCR Cessation Statement 2008).

5 UNHCR, 'Note on the Cessation Clauses', EC/47/SC/CRP.30, 30 May 1997, [21].

6 See e.g. J.C. Hathaway and M. Foster, *The Law of Refugee Status* (Cambridge University Press, 2nd ed., 2014), 479–90.

- Whether partial cessation is sufficient. This raises the legal interaction between cessation and relocation/Internal Flight Alternative (IFA).

I will examine these in turn.

Cessation and armed conflict

The interaction between cessation and armed conflict raises important conceptual questions about the extent to which general country conditions should be considered in cessation decisions which might be different to the test for refugee status in Article 1A(2) of the Convention. This is important, as the refugee definition in Article 1A(2) of the 1951 Refugee Convention is highly individualised in nature. This has traditionally meant that asylum seekers who face a risk of 'generalised violence' from armed conflict do not generally meet the refugee definition unless they can show an individuated or 'differential' risk different to that of the general population.[7] This would seem to pose an obstacle to the inclusion of armed conflict and security considerations in the cessation test. However, the main argument of this book is that *cessation* is not the same as *recognition* of refugee status. Thus, arguably broader considerations apply to cessation criteria, which can include the provision of a stable security situation and absence of civil conflict in the country of origin.

The presence of armed conflict in a country to which a refugee is to be returned is a particularly important feature of the cessation 'landscape', given that Article 1C(5) has been applied primarily to refugees from Iraq, Afghanistan and Somalia – countries which continue to suffer from the effects of civil conflict.[8] More recently, cessation has been applied to Somalia, which is also in a state of armed conflict,[9] although cessation is being applied there on the finding that the security situation in Mogadishu has improved such that it is now safe for refugees.[10]

The individualised nature of the refugee definition and the nexus requirement in Article 1A(2) of the Convention have often led the courts of state parties to the Refugee Convention to find that fear of harm arising from armed conflict or civil war in the country of origin does not give rise to a well-founded fear of

7 See e.g. *Adan v Secretary of State for the Home Department* [1999] AC 293; H. Lambert and T. Farrell, 'The Changing Character of Armed Conflict and the Implications for Refugee Protection Jurisprudence' (2010) 22(2) *International Journal of Refugee Law* 237.

8 See discussion of the current armed conflicts in Iraq and Afghanistan in Geneva Academy of International Humanitarian law and Human Rights, Rule of Law in Armed Conflicts Project, <www.rulac.org/>.

9 This is recognised in many reputable sources, but see e.g. UN Office of the High Commissioner for Human Rights, 'Somalia Conflict Exacting Terrible Toll on Civilians: UN Report Al Shabaab Responsible for Most Civilian Casualties', 11 December 2017, <www.ohchr.org/EN/NewsEvents/Pages/DisplayNews.aspx?NewsID=22520&LangID=E>.

10 See e.g. decisions of the Immigration Appeals Board of Norway (Grand board) in June 2017, above n 2.

persecution. As a result, Hugo Storey has highlighted that there is a 'war flaw' in international refugee law which requires attention:

> Refugee law – and more widely the legal regime governing international protection – has always struggled to deal coherently with claims for international protection by persons fleeing armed conflict; there has always been a 'war-flaw.' In view of the fact that claims of this kind continue to comprise a very significant part of the caseload of decision-makers worldwide, it is high time this was rectified.[11]

These debates raise the question as to whether decision makers adjudicating a 'fundamental, stable and durable' change in the refugee's country of nationality under Article 1C(5) should place weight on any continuing situation of civil conflict in that country. To this end, Fitzpatrick and Bonoan, who wrote a detailed analysis of cessation as part of the 2001 UNHCR Global Consultations, recommended that special guidelines should be drafted in relation to cessation and civil wars. They indicate that changes which may normally satisfy Article 1C(5), may not satisfy it when there is a current conflict or post-conflict situation:

> UNHCR should further develop existing guidelines regarding the application of Article 1C(5) and (6) in cases involving the settlement of civil wars. Efforts by UNHCR to establish a framework of principles for evaluating post-conflict situations implicitly acknowledge that the traditional interpretation of the concept of fundamental change as a transition to democracy is inadequate in such cases.[12]

Volker Türk has also highlighted the link between violence in a state and its ability to protect its citizens:

> Situations of general violence, irrespective of their source, usually engender deteriorating national protection systems, with visibly damaging impacts on social systems and national governance structures. As a result, the fear of being harmed by indiscriminate violence, when such violence is generalized, is usually much broader and is embedded in a fundamental dysfunction of a social, economic and even political system.[13]

The presence of armed conflict in a country to which cessation is being applied is problematic, as it indicates that a returned refugee will be unable to access the

11 H. Storey, 'Armed Conflict in Asylum Law: The "War-Flaw"' (2012) 31(2) *Refugee Survey Quarterly* 1, 2. See a reply to this: J.-F. Durieux, 'Of War, Flows, Laws and Flaws: A Reply to Hugo Storey' (2012) 31(3) *Refugee Survey Quarterly* 161.

12 J. Fitzpatrick and R. Bonoan, 'Cessation of Refugee Protection', Chapter 8 in E. Feller, V. Türk, and F. Nicholson (eds.), *Refugee Protection in International Law: UNHCR's Global Consultations on International Protection* (Cambridge University Press, 2003), 531, 536.

13 V. Türk, 'Protection Gaps in Europe? Persons Fleeing the Indiscriminate Effects of Generalized Violence', 18 January 2011, 4, <www.unhcr.org/refworld/docid/4d37d8402.html>.

necessary state protection against acts of persecution, and that any changes in country conditions are likely to be volatile rather than stable and durable. For instance, UNHCR has recognised this in its 2016 Position on Returns to Iraq:

> The security situation in many parts of central and northern Iraq continues to be highly volatile and unpredictable due to ongoing military offensives and counter-offensives. Parts of northern and central Iraq remain under de facto control of ISIS, which is reported to continue to commit grave and widespread human rights abuses against the population in these area.[14]

UNHCR has also recognised the interconnectedness of circumstances in a country of origin, including the significance of armed conflict:

> Where indeed a 'particular cause of fear of persecution' has been identified, the elimination of that cause carries more weight than a change in other factors. Often, however, circumstances in a country are inter-linked, be these armed conflict, serious violations of human rights, severe discrimination against minorities, or the absence of good governance, with the result that resolution of the one will tend to lead to an improvement in others. All relevant factors must therefore be taken into consideration. An end to hostilities, a complete political change and return to a situation of peace and stability remain the most typical situation in which Article 1C(5) or (6) applies.[15]

Here it is instructive to examine the practice of UNHCR in making generalised declarations of cessation where conflict is ongoing. Unlike the practice of many asylum host states, UNHCR typically requires the resolution of armed conflict prior to the making of cessation declarations.[16]

For instance, UNHCR issued a cessation declaration in relation to Angola which ended group refugee status on 30 June 2012 for people who fled Angola during the country's 1965–75 war of independence and subsequent civil war.[17]

14 UNHCR, 'UNHCR Position on Returns to Iraq', 14 November 2016, [5], <www.refworld.org/docid/58299e694.html>. See also previous guidance from UNHCR, 'UNHCR Eligibility Guidelines for Assessing the International Protection Needs of Iraqi Asylum-Seekers', 31 May 2012, HCR/EG/IRQ/12/03, 6, <www.unhcr.org/refworld/docid/4fc77d522.html>.

15 UNHCR Cessation Guidelines 2003, above n 4, [11].

16 There are numerous examples of this, but some include the UNHCR declaration of cessation in relation to Sudan in 1973, a year after the end of the civil war and the signing of a peace agreement between the government of Sudan and the South Sudan Liberation Movement; UNHCR also issued a declaration of cessation in relation to refugees from Mozambique in December 1996 after the government of Mozambique and the Mozambique National Resistance Movement signed a peace accord in 1992 that brought to end that civil war. Further developments, including the holding of successful elections in 1994 and voluntary repatriation of 1.7 million refugees in 1996 led to the finding of 'fundamental' and 'durable' change warranting application of the ceased circumstances clause: see discussion of many examples in Fitzpatrick and Bonoan, above n 12, 499–500, 507–08.

17 UNHCR, 'News Stories: UNHCR Repatriates Almost 14,000 Angolans; Steps Up Pace of Return Ahead of Deadline', 8 June 2012, <www.unhcr.org/4fd1f16e9.html>.

This declaration was made on the basis that there was peace in Angola, that elections had been held, a new constitution adopted and improvements made in economic and social conditions.[18] In particular, UNHCR placed weight on the formal ending of the civil war in Angola in 2002 and the 'relative peace and tranquility' enjoyed in Angola since that time.[19] It had monitored conditions in Angola for 9 years after the ending of the civil war, finding that cessation had occurred once a significant period of peace had elapsed and after there had been sufficient and relevant improvements in the legal, social and economic conditions in the country.[20]

This is not to say that UNHCR cessation declarations have always been accepted by commentators. For instance, Verdirame and Harrell-Bond raise concerns as to the role played by UNHCR in ceasing temporary protection of pre-1991 Ethiopian refugees, that is, those who had fled the Mengistu regime. They argue that 'UNHCR took this step in 1999 for all Ethiopian refugees from this period in the Horn of Africa and East Africa regions, despite the still repressive human rights situation in Ethiopia'.[21] Yasmeen Siddiqui also notes that 'declarations of cessation have sometimes been made when the situation in the country of origin is still volatile'.[22] However, it does appear that UNHCR places great weight on the ending of armed conflict in declarations of cessation.

Applying this to individualised cessation decisions by states, I argue that an ending of hostilities may not necessarily indicate a 'fundamental, stable and durable' change in circumstances.

Case study: Somalia

The importance of an end of hostilities is a contested notion, particularly when one examines how decision-making bodies have interpreted country information on the security situation in a particular area. This is illustrated

18 UNHCR, *Implementation of the Comprehensive Strategy for the Angolan Refugee Situation, Including UNHCR's Recommendations on the Applicability of the 'Ceased Circumstances' Cessation Clauses*, 15 January 2012, <www.unhcr.org/refworld/pdfid/4f3395972.pdf> (hereinafter UNHCR *Strategy Angola*).

19 Ibid [23]. UNHCR notes '[t]he Angolan civil war ended conclusively with the signing of the Luena Memorandum of Understanding on 4 April 2002 between the Government of the Republic of Angola and the National Union for the Total Independence of Angola (UNITA). Since the Luena agreement of 2002, Angola has enjoyed relative peace and tranquility, with the exception of Cabinda Province where sporadic violence in relation to a secessionist movement has occurred'.

20 Ibid [26].

21 G. Verdirame and B.E. Harrell-Bond, *Rights in Exile: Janus-Faced Humanitarianism* (Berghahn, 2005), 111.

22 Y. Siddiqui, 'Reviewing the Application of the Cessation Clause of the 1951 Convention Relating to the Status of Refugees in Africa', *University of Oxford Working Paper 76*, August 2011, [19]–[22], <www.rsc.ox.ac.uk/publications/working-papers-folder_contents/RSC-workingpaper76.pdf/view>.

by the different approaches taken to the armed conflict in Somalia. In cessation decisions of the Immigration Appeals Board of Norway in 2017, a majority of the Grand Board found that 'significant' changes had taken place in Mogadishu.[23] The majority of the board noted that the main security threats in Mogadishu are terrorist attacks carried out by al-Shabaab, and that these terror threats are aimed at the authorities and representatives of the authorities (including international representatives who support the authorities in Mogadishu) but are not directed at the civilian population. The minority, in contrast, found that a significant and 'permanent' change had *not* occurred, that it was not clear from the country information as to whether al-Shabaab constitutes a risk to the civilian population in Mogadishu and that a significant change must also have taken place in the democratic and human rights situation in the country of origin.[24]

Indeed, I argue that cessation may not be able to be applied in *post-conflict* situations where the state continues to be 'fragile' in nature and where key aspects of state protective infrastructure, such as operative rule of law institutions and basic socio-economic standards do not yet exist. It is relevant to consider the absorptive capacity of *fragile states* to receive refugee returns. The need to exercise caution in returning refugees to fragile states has been highlighted by many UN and NGO organisations, including UNDP who note that '[i]n crisis-affected and fragile situations the rule of law is often profoundly undermined, and injustice and insecurity are allowed to flourish'.[25]

Some may argue that an end of conflict is not in fact required under Article 1C of the Refugee Convention, particularly as harm from armed conflict is usually seen as falling outside the scope of the refugee definition. In answer to that, I would refer to the former discussion in Chapter 3: that is, the Article 1C(5) criteria are not the same as that in Article 1A(2). Further, it is doubtful whether a change can be regarded as 'fundamental, stable and durable' if there is armed conflict in the country of origin.

Here an analogy can be made to the interpretation of 'persecution' and 'protection' utilised in the tests for internal relocation. This is on the basis that the concepts of relocation and cessation are linked, in that they both concern the definition of a refugee under Article 1 of the Refugee Convention and both entail consideration of the adequacy of protection in the

23 Immigration Appeals Board of Norway (Grand board), decisions on Cessation in June 2017, above n 2. It found that '[w]ith the help of AMISOM [the African Union Mission in Somalia], the Somali authorities regained control of the city in 2012, which has led to a gradual improvement in the security situation in Mogadishu, and that al-Shabaab is no longer deemed to constitute a real risk to the appellants'.

24 Ibid.

25 United Nations Development Programme (UNDP), 'Strengthening the Rule of Law in Crisis-Affected and Fragile Situations' (2011), 9.

refugee's country of origin. Indeed, as noted previously, UNHCR and some commentators have already highlighted symmetries between these two concepts and have recommended taking a more integrated approach to their interpretation.[26] Significantly, the UNHCR 2003 Guidelines on Internal Relocation recommend that in a situation of internal armed conflict (which by its nature is volatile), internal relocation should not generally be available:

> In most cases, countries in the grip of armed conflict would not be safe for relocation, especially in the light of shifting armed fronts which could suddenly bring insecurity to an area hitherto considered safe.[27]

Given that protection for the purposes of cessation should not simply be protection against *persecution* but a broader notion of effective protection, and in light of the fact that cessation involves return of *recognised* refugees who have been shown to have had a well-founded fear of persecution, I argue that the existence of armed conflict in a country should militate against the use of cessation by states.

This links to a central argument made in this book: that a more consistent approach and holistic interpretation should be taken of 'safety' and 'protection' across international refugee law. In particular, I submit that a refugee being returned to his or her country of origin under cessation under Article 1C(5) should be considered under similar principles to those applicable to internal relocation, particularly in situations of armed conflict and where the protection is said to be provided by a non-state actor who controls a 'part' of the territory of the country of origin.[28] Thus, it is strongly arguable that a risk of serious harm arising from a situation of armed conflict, for instance, should be considered as part of the 'effective protection' criteria for cessation decisions.

Cessation of refugee status and complementary protection

Following on from the preceding discussion, the next important question is whether the test for cessation of refugee status should be linked to the criteria for complementary protection. That is, should a decision maker applying cessation be required to consider whether that person will be subjected to 'serious harm' upon return. Due to the inclusion of 'indiscriminate violence' in Article 15(c) of the EU Qualification Directive. I will be focusing on the question posed by the German Federal Administrative Court to the CJEU in *Abdulla*. That question is: does

26 UNHCR Cessation Statement 2008, above n 4, 15.

27 UNHCR, Guidelines on International Protection: 'Internal Flight or Relocation Alternative' within the Context of Article 1A(2) of the 1951 Convention and/or 1967 Protocol relating to the Status of Refugees, 2003, [27].

28 The latter is discussed in detail in Chapter 5 of this book.

cessation of refugee status under Article 11(1)(e) of the Qualification Directive require that, in the country of the refugee's nationality, the refugee should not be threatened with serious harm within the meaning of Article 15 of the Directive, which leads to the granting of subsidiary protection under Article 18?

This is largely a question relevant to the EU. It is a question which was not raised in the litigation in the Australian cessation case of *QAAH*, as Australia did not at that time have a formal complementary protection regime, having only introduced this into law in 2011.[29] I also note that the complementary protection ground of 'indiscriminate violence' set out in Article 15(c) of the EU Qualification Directive is not explicitly provided as a complementary protection regimes in other states, such as those in Australia and Canada.[30]

This is a significant question as it reflects a broader debate currently being discussed in international refugee law discourse as to the interaction between refugee status and complementary protection. With the introduction of a formal complementary protection regime in the EU under the Qualification Directive, refugee advocates and decision-making bodies are increasingly utilising complementary protection status when granting protection to applicants, rather than refugee status.[31] As a result, it has become imperative to clearly delineate the functions of refugee status and complementary protection and consider how interpretation of one status may affect interpretation of the other.[32] Thus, care must be taken to ensure that the existence of complementary protection does not dilute or restrict interpretation and application of the refugee definition.[33]

In response to the question of the interaction between cessation and complementary protection, the CJEU correctly notes that the term 'international protection' used in the Qualification Directive governs 'two distinct systems of protection': refugee status and subsidiary protection status.[34] It points out that this separation is reflected in the fact that Article 2(e) of the Directive states that a person eligible for subsidiary protection is one 'who does not qualify as

29 Migration Amendment (Complementary Protection Act) 2011 (Cth).

30 E.g. the Australian Migration Amendment (Complementary Protection) Act (Cth) 2011; Immigration and Refugee Protection Act (Canada).

31 See K. Wouters, 'Protecting People Fleeing Conflict and Generalized Violence: UNHCR's Perspective', *Joint Council of Europe/UNHCR Colloquium on the Role of Regional Human Rights Courts in Interpreting and Enforcing Legal Standards for the Protection of Forcibly Displaced Persons*, Strasbourg, 15–16 June 2011, 1–2.

32 For instance, Jane McAdam states that '[c]omplementary protection does not supplant or compete with the Refugee Convention': J. McAdam, 'Australian Complementary Protection: A Step-by-Step Approach' (2011) 33 *Sydney Law Review* 687, 694.

33 In this regard, Volker Türk has raised concerns about the use of complementary protection at the expense of the Refugee Convention: 'It is a concern for UNHCR that with the emergence of these supplementary legal categories, some refugees who would otherwise fulfil the criteria of the 1951 Convention are being instead subsumed under the broader category': V. Türk, 'Protection Gaps in Europe? Persons Fleeing the Indiscriminate Effects of Generalized Violence', 18 January 2011, 8, <www.unhcr.org/refworld/docid/4d37d8402.html>.

34 Indeed, Article 2(a) of the Directive defines 'international protection' as 'the refugee and subsidiary protection status as defined in (d) and (f)'.

a refugee'.[35] It therefore held that the two regimes were separate and must be interpreted independently:

> Therefore, as there would otherwise be a failure to have regard for the respective domains of the two systems of protection, the cessation of refugee status cannot be made conditional on a finding that a person does not qualify for subsidiary protection status.[36]

The findings of the CJEU in *Abdulla* demonstrate a strict demarcation between refugee status and complementary protection. Whilst it is acknowledged that the criteria for complementary protection must be demarcated to some extent from that of refugee status, in order to recognise the special nature of refugee status and the 1951 Refugee Convention, the complementary protection criteria must not be referred to as a way of limiting the interpretation of the refugee definition. In the context of cessation under Article 1C(5) there is some crossover between refugee status and complementary protection in relation to the existence of serious harm. I therefore argue that serious harm arising from situations such as armed conflict, should be considered in cessation decisions and the fact that this may also be encompassed in complementary protection criteria should not be a bar to a purposive, good faith interpretation of the 1951 Refugee Convention.

The approach of the CJEU is significant here, as this contradicts the stated position of UNHCR, which has held that the presence of a 'real risk of serious harm' under Article 18 of the Qualification Directive *would* exclude the operation of the cessation provision under Article 11(1)(e).[37] In doing so, UNHCR links the definition of 'serious harm' used in the complementary protection provisions of the Directive with the 'significant and non-temporary' criteria for cessation under Article 11(2), particularly in relation to cases of indiscriminate violence:

> Serious harm is defined in Article 15 of the Qualification Directive with reference to the most fundamental rights. If there is a real risk of serious harm in the sense of Article 15, this means that effective protection allowing for a life in safety and dignity is not available. In such a situation, it is also unlikely that significant and non-temporary changes of the type required for cessation will have taken place. Rather, a risk of torture, inhuman or degrading

35 *Salahadin Abdulla and Others v. Bundesrepublik Deutschland*, C-175/08; C-176/08; C-178/08 & C-179/08, Court of Justice of the European Union, 2 March 2010, [78], <www.refworld.org/cases,ECJ,4b8e6ea22.html> (*Abdulla*). Article 2(e) of the 2004 Qualification Directive is now Article 2(f) of the Recast 2011 Directive. Note that the wording of both provisions is the same.

36 *Abdulla*, [79]. It further explains: 'Within the system of the Directive, the possible cessation of refugee status occurs without prejudice to the right of the person concerned to request the granting of subsidiary protection status in the case where all the factors, referred to in Article 4 of the Directive, which are necessary to establish that he qualifies for such protection under Article 15 of the Directive are present' (at [80]).

37 UNHCR Cessation Statement 2008, above n 4, 17.

treatment or of death penalty demonstrate the absence of effective protection. Irrespective of the other criteria for protection under this Article, a situation of indiscriminate violence in the context of an armed conflict as referred to in Article 15(c) of the Qualification Directive would indicate that the security situation is not stable.[38]

Cessation – socio-economic rights and humanitarian standards

Another question which has arisen for determination in case law on cessation is whether Article 1C(5) requires consideration of the living conditions in the country of origin and, more generally, consideration of humanitarian principles. There is, of course, a 'compelling reasons' exception to cessation, but this is based on past persecution. As a result, there is a broader question about the extent to which compassionate or humanitarian considerations (including medical or socio-economic factors) should be considered in cessation decisions.

Here there has been some dispute about the standards used by UNHCR in its general declarations on cessation. The recent invocation of the cessation clause in relation to Rwanda has been particularly controversial. In 2010, UNHCR signed a joint communiqué with the governments of Uganda and Rwanda announcing that Uganda would invoke the cessation clause in relation to Rwandan refugees on 31 December 2011.[39] Subsequently, the parties agreed to postpone invocation of cessation to 30 June 2012.[40] This has been criticised by some, because although it noted that 'Rwanda enjoys a relatively stable political environment',[41] it applied cessation despite finding that 'returnees face extreme poverty, as well as land and shelter issues, lack of medical coverage, a dearth of job opportunities and the need to walk long distances in search of water'.[42] Thus, the decision to invoke cessation in relation to Rwanda has been heavily criticised by some NGOs and academic commentators.[43] For instance, Kelly McMillan argues that Rwanda has not become a democracy and there are serious problems with its

38 Ibid.

39 Statement of the Joint Committee of the 8th Tripartite Commission Meeting, 13 May 2010. The statement included the clause that 'The parties agreed to work towards ensuring all Rwandan refugees voluntarily repatriate by 31 December 2011, the date of the invocation of the Cessation Clause', as cited in *Fahamu Refugee Legal Aid Newsletter*, Issue 5, June 2010, 5, <www.pambazuka.org/images/articles/489/JuneRefugeeLegalAidNews.pdf>.

40 UNHCR, 'Tripartite Meeting: Parties Agree to Reinforce Voluntary Repatriation of Rwandan Refugees', *Refugee Bulletin*, October 2011, <www.unhcr.org/4ec3d2b19.pdf> (hereinafter UNCHR, Tripartite Meeting).

41 Ibid.

42 Ibid.

43 See e.g. K. McMillan, 'Uganda's Invocation of Cessation Regarding Its Rwandan Refugee Caseload: Lessons for International Protection' (2012) 24(2) *International Journal of Refugee Law*, 231; The Fahamu Refugee Programme, 'Rwanda: Cessation of Refugee Status Is Unwarranted', *Memorandum of Fact and Law*, 21 September 2011, <www.refugeelegalaid-information.org/sites/srlan/files/fileuploads/Memo%20of%20Fact%20and%20Law.pdf>.

recent human rights record which demonstrate there has not been a fundamental and enduring change of circumstances sufficient to satisfy the application of Article 1C(5).[44] This is of interest, as UNHCR's Guidelines on Cessation emphasise the importance of socio-economic conditions such as the right to a livelihood.

How, then, have state parties approached this issue? And to what extent do courts consider the UNHCR Guidelines on Cessation? Some of these issues were considered in two important judgements on cessation: the CJEU in *Abdulla* (2010) and more recently the decision of the UK Court of Appeal in *MA (Somalia)* (2018).[45] I discuss these in turn.

Case study: the CJEU in *Abdulla*

One of the questions referred to the CJEU by the German Federal Administrative Court in *Abdulla* was whether cessation of refugee status under Article 11(1)(e) requires that the security situation in the refugee's country of nationality be stable and the general living conditions ensure a minimum standard of living.[46] Unfortunately, the CJEU failed to address this (on the basis that there was no need to answer that question).[47] Roger Errera has criticised the CJEU for failing to answer the right to livelihood question, noting that this is 'regrettable'. He notes that their reasons for failing to do so are not justifiable, stating that '[t]he answer to questions 1 and 2(a) did not command such silence' and that '[t]he cryptic dictum of the Court is not convincing'.[48]

Although the court did not specifically answer the question of livelihood, its general position is that protection for the purpose of cessation under the Qualification Directive means protection against persecution only, and not a broader notion of 'effective protection'. Thus, one can assume that it does not endorse the view that protection encompasses such elements as a right to livelihood. Indeed, the CJEU did not formally adopt the wider interpretation of 'effective protection' advocated by UNHCR, which includes elements such as a minimum standard of subsistence.[49] This is important in terms of how the CJEU considers UNHCR guidance on

44 Ibid, 236.

45 *Secretary of State for the Home Department v MA (Somalia)* [2018] EWCA Civ 994 (*MA (Somalia)*).

46 *Abdulla*, question 2(c), set out at [43].

47 *Abdulla*, [77].

48 R. Errera, 'Cessation and Assessment of New Circumstances: A Comment on *Abdulla*, CJEU, 2 March 2010' (2011) 23(3) *International Journal of Refugee Law* 521, 535.

49 *Abdulla*, [75]. UNHCR has stated that 'the effective protection required for applying the "ceased circumstances" clause encompasses not only protection against persecution but also respect for human rights, including the right to a basic livelihood, which implies access to a subsistence minimum': UNHCR Statement on the Ceased Circumstances Clauses, p. 14. They continue: 'In UNHCR's view, in the absence of a stable security situation and of a minimum standard of living, the criteria for cessation would not be met': UNHCR Cessation Statement 2008, above n 4, 17.

refugee law because the court's failure to endorse a wider view of protection which encompasses respect for human rights (including issues of livelihood) runs counter to UNHCR guidance on cessation. UNHCR, in a statement on cessation drafted in response to the CJEU litigation in *Abdulla*, emphasised that:

> The context and the object and purpose of international protection demonstrate that the effective protection required for applying the 'ceased circumstances' clause encompasses not only protection against persecution but also respect for human rights, including the right to a basic livelihood, which implies access to a subsistence minimum.[50]

The central question, however, is whether such an interpretation is warranted by the terms of Article 1C(5) of the Refugee Convention, as informed by the objects and purposes of that instrument. As discussed in Chapter 3, I argue that the test for cessation is different to that for recognition of refugee status under Article 1A(2) and does in fact encompass wider considerations of 'effective protection'. However, it is arguable that incorporating subsistence or livelihood considerations into this 'effective protection' test would represent an overly expansive interpretation of Article 1C(5). As stated in the Introduction to this book, my approach to cessation is to establish a principled but also workable interpretation of Article 1C(5). I acknowledge that the debate about the importance of socio-economic human rights and their relevance to the Refugee Convention is a complex one which has been analysed in some depth by other commentators.[51] It is not possible, within the confines of this particular book to revisit those broader debates in detail. However, I would point out that socio-economic considerations may be best captured by the humanitarian avenues for protection established in most asylum host states and by humanitarian assistance delivered by international organisations. Further, whilst human rights principles should inform the interpretation of the Refugee Convention, refugee status is not simply a status given in response to broad humanitarian needs. As noted elsewhere in this book, refugeehood denotes a very particular type of status that results from persecution and the absence of state protection (a point discussed further in Chapter 5). Indeed, Dr Harald Dörig, a judge of the German Federal Administrative Court, speaking extra-judicially, has taken a similar position, noting that '[t]he right to a basic livelihood is . . . not necessary for the cessation of refugee status'.[52]

50 UNHCR Cessation Statement 2008, above n 4, 14.

51 See e.g. M. Foster, *International Refugee Law and Socio-Economic Rights: Refuge from Deprivation* (Cambridge University Press, 2007).

52 H. Dörig, 'A Comment on the Abdullah Decision of the CJEU from the Perspective of the Referring Court', IARLJ Conference, Lisbon, September 2010, <www.iarlj.org/general/images/stories/lisbon_sep_2010/doerig.pdf/>.

Case study: UK – *MA (Somalia)* 2018

The applicability of humanitarian standards to cessation was considered recently in the UK Court of Appeal case of *Secretary of State for Home Affairs v. MA (Somalia)*. In this case, the question at issue was whether a decision maker carrying out a cessation decision was also required to consider whether the refugee's rights under Article 3 of the European Convention on Human Rights would be violated if they were returned to their country of origin.[53] Article 3 of the ECHR provides that '[n]o one shall be subjected to torture or to inhuman or degrading treatment or punishment'. Thus, the case involved an analysis of whether humanitarian considerations formed part of the cessation criteria.

At first instance, the tribunal judge accepted that the applicant was from a minority clan. He also noted that the applicant did not know where his parents were, that he had little education, and his family in the UK would not be able to support him because they were on Social Security benefits.[54] Therefore, if the applicant was to be returned to Somalia, 'it was likely that he would have to live in conditions that fell below acceptable humanitarian standards'.[55] Therefore the tribunal held that the cessation standards set out in the UK immigration rules were not satisfied.

The UK Secretary of State then appealed to the Upper Tribunal, where Judge Lane dismissed that appeal. The Upper Tribunal found that the First-Tier Tribunal judge had clearly put weight on the lengthy period in which the respondent had been absent from Somalia while living in the UK, and had reached a conclusion which was available to it on the evidence.[56] Interestingly, the Upper Tribunal also found that the requirements set out in UNHCR Guidelines on International Protection No 3 (Cessation and Refugee status) were 'clearly not established in the case of Somalia',[57] finding that it:

> continues to have no proper functioning unitary government or system of law and justice. It remains difficult to see how the cessation of the appellant's refugee status can have been made in accordance with those guidelines and also the decision in *Abdulla*.[58]

There appeared to be some confusion in this case about the interpretation to be given to UK Tribunal country guidance on Somalia and how it should

53 Convention for the Protection of Human Rights and Fundamental Freedoms 1950, ETS No. 005 (ECHR).
54 First Tier Tribunal decision (Judge Hinson), summarised in *MA (Somalia)* [14].
55 Ibid.
56 Upper Tribunal decision (Judge Lane), summarised in *MA (Somalia)* [15].
57 Upper Tribunal decision (Judge Lane), cited in *MA (Somalia)* [16].
58 Ibid.

be applied to cessation decisions.[59] This confusion appeared to stem from the fact that humanitarian standards were referred to in UK Tribunal country guidance decision on Mogadishu[60] which showed there were changed circumstances. However, the application of this country guidance decision to the cessation proceedings was disputed. In arguments to the Court of Appeal, counsel for the applicant submitted that 'a court or tribunal which has to assess whether there has been a significant and non-temporary change would have to take into account as a relevant factor any breach of Article 3'.[61] The applicant's counsel argued that this included information in the country guidance decision about whether the applicant was likely to be exposed to living conditions falling below acceptable humanitarian standards if returned to Somalia in breach of Article 3.[62] Counsel also argued that 'there would not have been a significant and non-temporary change of circumstances if a risk of a breach of Article 3 remained so far as the [applicant] was concerned'.[63]

In response, the UK Secretary of State argued before the Court of Appeal that the first-instance decision maker (the First-Tier Tribunal) had wrongly focused on humanitarian conditions in the country of origin in applying the cessation principles.[64] The Secretary of State argued that 'the lawfulness of a cessation decision does not depend on any comprehensive verification of the country of origin's systems for protecting human rights, nor on any question relating to Article 3 [of the ECHR]'.[65] That is, Article 3 of the ECHR is a separate matter to a cessation decision. As part of its arguments, the Secretary of State also submitted that there was a distinction between cases were a person is subjected to a risk of *violence* on return and cases of *deprivation*.[66]

Ultimately, the UK Court of Appeal held, *inter alia*, that:

> The question whether Article 3 [of the ECHR] would be violated by the refugee's return to his country of origin is not part of the cessation decision but separate from it, and there is no violation by reason only of the absence of humanitarian living standards on return.

59 In the UK, the Immigration and Asylum Chamber of the United Kingdom Upper Tribunal (UKUT) produces 'country guidance' decisions on contemporary conditions in countries for the purposes of determining refugee status. These decisions bind the UKUT and government decision-makers' findings as to which groups are and are not at risk in particular countries. See an excellent discussion of these decisions in D. McDonald-Norman, 'Country Guidance Decisions in the UK and Australia', *AUSPUBLAW Blog*, 7 July 2016, <https://auspublaw.org/2016/07/country-guidance-decisions/>.

60 *MOJ and Others (Return to Mogadishu)* (CG) [2014] UKUT 442, [408].

61 *MA (Somalia)* [35].

62 Ibid.

63 Ibid [38].

64 Ibid [22].

65 Ibid [27].

66 Ibid [33].

> Article 3 is not normally violated by sending a refugee back to his country of origin where there is a risk that his living conditions will fall below humanitarian standards.[67]

Interestingly, in adjudicating upon these submissions, the UK Court of Appeal relied heavily on the findings of the CJEU in *Abdulla*.[68] The court ultimately held that 'humanitarian standards are not the test for a cessation decision'[69] and that in its findings the First-Tier Tribunal went much further than the Qualification Directive or the Refugee Convention.[70]

As discussed in Chapter 3, the test for cessation is different to that for recognition of refugee status under Article 1A(2) and does in fact encompass wider considerations of 'effective protection'. However, as I concede earlier in response to the Case Study on *Abdulla*, I agree that incorporating subsistence or livelihood considerations into this 'effective protection' test may be too expansive an interpretation of Article 1C(5) which is not warranted by the terms of that provision.

Of additional relevance to this book is the type of legal sources relied upon by the UK Court of Appeal in *MA (Somalia)*. The court acknowledged that the UNHCR Guidelines on Cessation 'appear to go further' than the interpretation given to cessation by the court.[71] The court acknowledged that the Guidelines constituted an 'important text' for the purposes of interpreting the provisions of the Qualification Directive.[72] However, the court interpreted the Guidelines as 'saying no more than that the system of protection for human rights generally would indicate whether the individual refugee would be sufficiently protected in his country of origin'.[73] Further the court noted that the Guidelines were issued before the decision of the CJEU in *Abdulla* and therefore in the event of any conflict, 'the decision of the CJEU must prevail on this point'.[74] This reflects a trend towards relegating UNHCR guidelines and the UNHCR Handbook to very much a secondary source of treaty interpretation by domestic courts (as was also seen in the Australian case of *QAAH*, discussed in Chapter 3).

Is partial cessation in a country sufficient?

The final issue that arises in relation to the 'fundamental and durable' test is whether the establishment of only 'partial cessation' is sufficient for cessation

67 Ibid [2].
68 Ibid [50]–[54], referring to *Abdulla*.
69 Ibid [56].
70 Ibid.
71 Ibid [57].
72 Ibid.
73 Ibid.
74 Ibid.

purposes. In this context, we must consider the interaction between cessation and the internal relocation test for refugee status. The use of Article 1C(5) in 'partial cessation' situations is of particular concern because cessation does not carry with it the safeguards that have been developed in relation to internal relocation, such as consideration of the 'reasonableness' of return and the requirement that the applicant not be subject to serious harm in the area of safety.

Thus, UNHCR has, on a number of occasions, cautioned against the use of Article 1C(5) in relation to part of a territory.[75] In its 2003 Guidelines on Cessation it states that cessation should not apply to regional safety:

> changes in the refugee's country of origin affecting only part of the territory should not, in principle, lead to cessation of refugee status. Refugee status can only come to an end if the basis for persecution is removed without the precondition that the refugee has to return to specific safe parts of the country in order to be free from persecution. Also, not being able to move or to establish oneself freely in the country of origin would indicate that the changes have not been fundamental.[76]

There appears to be significant differences in the acceptance of partial cessation across jurisdictions, which is itself a rather unsatisfactory situation.

Significantly, a recent decision of the UK Upper Tribunal held that the UK authorities were *not* entitled to cease the applicant's refugee status on the basis only of a change in *part* of the country.[77] In doing so, the Tribunal member confirmed the correctness of the UNHCR Cessation Guidelines on that point (although emphasising that it was not affording the UNHCR Cessation Guidelines 'a status of being determinative of the issue in question').[78]

The fact that the Tribunal placed great weight on the UNHCR Guidelines here is important.[79] The UK Secretary of State had sought to argue that cessation could be satisfied if conditions had changed in only part of the country, but no 'reasonableness' criterion would be applied to such a case. The Tribunal member, quite rightly, pointed out that such a differentiated test would raise significant fairness issues:

> if the person whose claim for asylum depends on an assessment of an internal flight option, that individual would have that issue assessed on the basis of undue harshness and the reasonableness of internal relocation. However, in the case of a person whose refugee status is to be taken away, once it is decided that there is a part of the country in which the change of circumstances is of

75 UNHCR Cessation Guidelines 2003, above n 4, [17].

76 Ibid [17].

77 *MS (Art 1C(5)-Mogadishu) Somalia* [2018] UKUT 196 (IAC), 21 March 2018, [55]–[57] (Upper Tribunal Judge Kopieczek) (*MS (Art 1C(5)-Mogadishu*).

78 *MS (Art 1C(5)-Mogadishu)*, [55]–[57] (Upper Tribunal Judge Kopieczek).

79 Ibid [52]–[53] (Upper Tribunal Judge Kopieczek).

> such a significant and non-temporary nature that the person's fear is no longer regarded as well-founded (in that area), that individual may be returned without the sort of examination of the issues of undue harshness and reasonableness of return to that particular area which would occur in considering a grant of refugee status. . . . Put another way, it would make it easier to cease a person's refugee status than to make a grant of refugee status; a position which is contrary both to logic and principle.

In contrast, a 2017 decision of the Grand Board of the Immigration Appeals Board in Norway found that cessation was satisfied in relation to two applicants from Somalia, on the basis of changes in *part* of that country. The majority of the Grand Board found that 'significant' changes had taken place in Mogadishu in relation to the situation at the time the applicant was granted refugee status and temporary residence permits. Specifically:

> the Somali authorities regained control of the city in 2012, which has led to a gradual improvement in the security situation in Mogadishu, and that al-Shabaab is no longer deemed to constitute a real risk to the appellants.[80]

Conclusions

Article 1C(5) states that the Refugee Convention will cease to apply to a refugee where '[h]e can no longer, because *the circumstances in connection with which he has been recognised as a refugee have ceased to exist*, continue to refuse to avail himself of the protection of the country of his nationality'.[81] If one reads those italicised words literally, it does mean that if the refugee was recognised as a refugee because (for instance) he could not return to his home town of Kabul, but now he can because of sufficient improvements (pursuant to relocation principles), then the circumstances 'in connection with' his recognition may have in fact ceased to exist.

However, many states have accepted that the test is 'fundamental and durable change'. Therefore, the question becomes: can there be 'fundamental' change where the change is only in one area of the country? These concerns raise the difficulties and dangers of the concept of 'localised persecution' and 'territorial protection'. Compartmentalising persecution and protection to one area of a country is problematic, particularly given the nature of contemporary armed conflict and in light of the trend towards extending the concept of 'protection'

80 See e.g. decisions of the Grand Board of the Immigration Appeals Board of Norway, above n 2. I note that a majority of the board disagreed with the majority, finding that a significant and permanent change had *not* taken place in the security situation in Mogadishu. However, the minority also seemed to be accepting and applying a 'partial' cessation test.

81 1951 Convention relating to the Status of Refugees, 189 *UNTS* 150, supplemented by the 1967 Protocol relating to the Status of Refugees, 606 *UNTS* 267 (hereinafter Refugee Convention), Article 1C(5).

to include non-state actors. There is a particular problem raised by the extension of 'protection' capabilities to non-state actors in relation to the 'changed circumstances' cessation clause. That is, return of a refugee on the basis that circumstances in their country of origin have 'changed' when a non-state actor is providing protection, and perhaps in only *part* of a country, is by definition only 'change' going to availability of protection in *part* of the country – that is, there is only *partial cessation*. This has the risk of exposing the returning refugee (or 'former refugee' once cessation is applied to him or her) to a risk of *refoulement* to the unprotected area of the country if the required safeguards are not in place.

5 Cessation and non-state actors of protection*

Introduction

An important legal issue which has arisen in relation to cessation in recent years has been whether non-state actors should be viewed as sufficient actors of protection under international refugee law. This question is significant because states have traditionally been seen as the fundamental actors in international law. States are parties to international treaties, including the 1951 Refugee Convention.[1] They are also defined as having special attributes and responsibilities, including the responsibility to protect their citizens.[2] In particular, the existence of state protection is a key element of the definition of refugee status under Article 1A(2) of the Refugee Convention.[3] Article 1C(5) also centres on the state as a protector, providing that cessation can only occur where the refugee can no longer 'continue to refuse to avail himself of the protection of the country of his nationality'.[4]

However, since the Convention was drafted in 1951, the central role of states under international law has been questioned. Whilst states continue to be the predominant actors in the international sphere, some scholars note the growing importance of non-state actors such as the United Nations, international organisations, transnational corporations, non-governmental organisations and other groups.[5]

* A version of this chapter was originally published in M. O'Sullivan, 'Acting the Part: Can Non-State Entities Provide Protection under International Refugee Law?' (2012) 24(1) *International Journal of Refugee Law* 85–110.

1 Importantly, they are the parties recognised by the UN Charter: *Charter of the United Nations*, 24 October 1945, 1 UNTS XVI, Article 4.

2 See e.g. the UK House of Lords in *Horvath* [2001] 1 AC 489, 499–500 (Hope LJ) (*Horvath*); M. Gibney, 'Liberal Democratic States and Responsibilities to Refugees' (1999) 93 *American Political Science Review* 169, 175; A. Shacknove, 'Who Is a Refugee?' (1985) 95 *Ethics* 274, 275.

3 1951 Convention relating to the Status of Refugees, 189 *UNTS* 150, supplemented by the 1967 Protocol relating to the Status of Refugees, 606 *UNTS* 267 (hereinafter Refugee Convention). Article 1A(2) of the Refugee Convention refers to an applicant's ability to seek the protection of the 'country of his nationality'.

4 Refugee Convention, above n 3.

5 Non-state actors can now, in certain circumstances, bring claims in various international fora such as the International Labour Organization and the UN Compensation Commission: see R. McCorquodale, 'An Inclusive International Legal System' (2004) 17 *Leiden Journal of International Law* 477, 489–92. See also P. Alston (ed.), *Non-State Actors and Human Rights* (Oxford University Press, 2005); A. Bianchi (ed.), *Non-State Actors and International Law* (Ashgate, 2009).

On a practical level, non-state actors are increasingly playing a role in providing assistance in refugee source countries. This ranges from the delivery of humanitarian assistance and peacekeeping functions by the United Nations and other international organisations in countries such as Rwanda[6] and Kosovo[7] to military intervention by multinational forces in Iraq and Afghanistan.[8] Despite this, the notion that international organisations and other non-state bodies can be parties to international treaties has been rejected in many areas of law.[9]

There has been a particular push to recognise non-state bodies as actors of refugee protection in so-called failed states, such as Somalia and Chad, where no functioning state apparatus exists and various clans and militias control certain territories within the state.[10] International refugee law has, to some extent, recognised the increased role of non-state actors by holding that such bodies can be agents of *persecution* under the 1951 Convention.[11] However, there now remains

6 See the United Nations Assistance Mission for Rwanda (UNAMIR), which operated between 1993 and 1996 under the authority of various UN Security Council Resolutions. It is widely considered to have been a failure on the basis that it was not able to prevent the genocide in Rwanda: see discussion of this in Thomas Demmel, 'United Nations Assistance Missions in Afghanistan and Rwanda: A Comparative Study', Suffolk University, 13 April 2008, <www.suffolk.edu/images/content/Thomas.Demmel.UN.Assistance.Missions.pdf>.

7 The literature on humanitarian intervention in Kosovo is significant, but see by way of example, J. Charney, 'Anticipatory Humanitarian Intervention in Kosovo' (1999) 32(5) *Vanderbilt Journal of Transnational Law* 1231; and P. Hilpold, 'Humanitarian Intervention: Is There a Need for a Legal Reappraisal?' (2001) 12(3) *European Journal of International Law* 437.

8 In the latter context, the activities of private security bodies have raised concerns: see J.K. Elsea, US Congressional Research Service, 'Private Security Contractors in Iraq and Afghanistan: Legal Issues', R40991, 7 January 2010, <www.fas.org/sgp/crs/natsec/R40991.pdf>.

9 For instance, the International Committee of the Red Cross (ICRC) has stated that non-state actors are incapable of becoming parties to the Geneva Conventions on the Laws of War: '[o]nly States May Become Party to International Treaties, and Thus to the Geneva Conventions and Their Additional Protocols': ICRC, *International Humanitarian Law: Answers to Your Questions*, October 2002, 12, <www.icrc.org/eng/assets/files/other/icrc_002_0703.pdf>, see discussion in Gregory Fox, *Humanitarian Occupation* (Cambridge Studies in International and Comparative Law) (Cambridge University Press, 2008), 223.

10 For instance, some courts have held that 'protection' for the purpose of refugee law can be provided by clans and militias – see e.g. *DM (Majority Clan Entities Can Protect) Somalia v. Secretary of State for the Home Department*, [2005] UKAIT 00150, UK: Asylum and Immigration Tribunal, 27 July 2005, <www.unhcr.org/refworld/docid/43fc2d6722.html> (hereinafter *DM Somalia*).

11 See UNHCR, *Handbook on Procedures and Criteria for Determining Refugee Status under the 1951 Convention and the 1967 Protocol Relating to the Status of Refugees*, HCR/IP/4/Rev.1, 1979, Re-edited, Geneva, January 1992, [65] (hereinafter UNHCR *Handbook*); *R v Secretary of State for the Home Department, Ex p Adan* [1999] 3 WLR 1274, 1289 (UK House of Lords) (*Adan* 1999); *Horvath*, 499; Walter Kälin, 'Non-State Agents of Persecution' (2000–01) 15 *Georgetown Immigration Law Journal* 415. See also Article 6 of the 2011 EU Qualification Directive, which provides that actors of persecution or serious harm include '(a) the State; (b) parties or organizations controlling the State or a substantial part of the territory of the territory of the State; (c) non-State actors, if it can be demonstrated that the actors mentioned in (a) and (b), including international organizations, are unable or unwilling to provide protection against persecution or serious harm as defined in Article 7': *Directive 2011/95/EU of the European Parliament and of the Council of 13 December 2011 on*

a deeper question as to how non-state actors fit within the broader international refugee law framework. That is, whether non-state entities can be said to be actors of ***protection*** for the purposes of cessation, and for international refugee law more broadly. Does the concept of 'protection' involve particular functions and attributes which only states can provide? And, following on from a question that I raised in earlier chapters: what is the relationship between persecution and protection under international refugee law?

The issue of non-state actors of protection has been discussed to some extent in refugee law jurisprudence in the UK, France and Canada over the last decade or so.[12] However, it has become more prominent in international refugee law discourse through the introduction of a provision on non-state actors of protection in Article 7 of the EU Qualification Directive.[13] Article 7 of this Directive, controversially, provides that protection can be provided not only by a 'state' but also 'international organizations' or 'parties'. This provision therefore presents a fundamental challenge to the traditional conception of the state as the provider of 'protection' under international refugee law. This EU development is significant on a practical level given asylum host states have for some time been attempting to return asylum seekers to fragile states, such as Iraq and Afghanistan, on the basis that protection from persecution will be provided by statal or quasi-statal authorities with the assistance of multinational troops.[14] This question therefore has significant implications for the operation of cessation under Article 1C(5) of the 1951 Refugee Convention (and its EU Qualification Directive equivalent, Article 11(1)(e), which was considered by the Court of Justice of the European Union (CJEU) in the 2010 decision in *Abdulla*).[15] This analysis also has important ramifications for other jurisdictions, as similar provisions have been set out in Australian legislation.[16]

Standards for the Qualification of Third-Country Nationals or Stateless Persons as Beneficiaries of International Protection, for a Uniform Status for Refugees or for Persons Eligible for Subsidiary Protection, and for the Content of the Protection Granted (Recast), [2011] OJ L 337/9 (hereinafter 2011 EU Qualification Directive).

12 For instance, in the Canadian case of *Ajieh, John Kenneth Andzayie v. M.C.I.*(F.C.T.D., no. IMM-4985–01), MacKay, March 3, 2003; 2003 FCT 266, the Court, *in obiter*, notes that 'potential assistance from a non-governmental agency is unlikely to be accepted as a satisfactory substitute for state protection'.

13 2011 EU Qualification Directive, above n 11.

14 See e.g. German practice, discussed below.

15 *Salahadin Abdulla, Hasan, Adem and Rashi, Jama v Bundesrepublik Deutschland, Joined Cases C-175/08. C-176/08. C-178/08 and C-179/08*, Court of Justice of the European Union, 2 March 2010, <www.unhcr.org/refworld/docid/4b8e6ea22.html> (*Abdulla*).

16 Migration Act (Cth) 1958, s 5LA(1) provides that effective protection measures are available to a person in a receiving country if '(a) protection against persecution could be provided to the person by: (i) the relevant State; or (ii) a party or organisation, including an international organisation, that controls the relevant State or a substantial part of the territory of the relevant State; and (b) the relevant State, party or organisation mentioned in paragraph (a) is willing and able to offer such protection'. Departmental Guidelines also state that the relevant protection could be provided by the party or organisation working alone or in conjunction with the State: Department of Home Affairs, 'Policy: Refugee and humanitarian – Refugee

These issues are important, as, although the role of non-state actors in international law has been discussed at some length,[17] the role of non-state bodies as actors of *protection* for the purpose of refugee law has not been the subject of detailed analysis. This is significant, as it raises questions about whether recognition of non-state actors as responsible actors of protection may need to be more constrained under refugee law than in other areas of international law.[18] These questions include:

- First, is a provision which recognises non-state actors as protectors (such as Article 7 of the EU Qualification Directive) consistent with the 1951 Refugee Convention? Has modern state practice evolved such that non-state actors should now be recognised as providers of protection under international refugee law?
- What are the particular problems posed for cessation by the inclusion of non-state actors as actors of protection?
- Should the identity of the entity affording protection to the applicant be a consideration in assessing the existence of a well-founded fear of persecution and provision of protection? (e.g. clans or militias as compared to international organisations).

The rationale given by proponents of a broad application of protection to non-state entities has been largely a pragmatic one – it is argued that it is the *fact* of protection which is important, rather than the entity concerned.[19] Whilst it is widely recognised that the Refugee Convention should be interpreted as a 'living instrument',[20] and that it should therefore be adapted to meet modern-day contingencies, there are dangers in expanding the concept of 'protection' to non-state actors on the basis of what is occurring on 'the ground' without also balancing pragmatism with principle. The aim of this chapter is to develop both a pragmatic *and* principled interpretation of the issue.

It does so by, first, outlining the theoretical construct which I use to analyse the non-state actor question. Here, I examine the meaning of 'protection' under

---

Law Guidelines', section 9.3, re-issued 1 July 2017 (Refugee Law Guidelines), cited in AAT Legal Guide, September 2018, 8.22.

17 See e.g. McCorquodale, above n 5; and A. Clapham, *Human Rights Obligations of Non-State Actors* (Oxford University Press, 2006).

18 In this context, I am referring to situations where non-state actors take over governmental powers or the administration of an area of territory within a state, rather than where non-state actors undertake humanitarian relief work in a state. For an interesting discussion of the human rights obligations of UN bodies in various contexts, including international territorial administration, refugee camps and the provision of humanitarian aid, see G. Verdirame, *The UN and Human Rights: Who Guards the Guardians?* (Cambridge University Press, 2011).

19 See e.g. UK House of Lords Select Committee on the European Union, Summary of Conclusions, *Defining Refugee Status and Those in Need of International Protection*, H.L. Paper 156, Session 2001–02, 28th Report, [116].

20 See e.g. *R v Immigration Appeal Tribunal, ex parte Shah* [1999] 2 AC 629, 657 (Hope LJ); E. Feller, 'International Refugee Protection 50 Years on: The Protection Challenges of the Past, Present and Future' (2001) 83(843) *International Review of the Red Cross* 581, 594.

international refugee law and the theoretical underpinnings of refugeehood. Next, I discuss how non-state actors have been considered in refugee decision-making and whether non-state actors can be actors of protection for the purposes of cessation. Here, I utilise the EU example as a case study, focusing on the application of Article 7 and Article 11(1)(e) of the EU Qualification Directive and the decision of the CJEU in *Abdulla*. Although some reference is made to other jurisdictions by way of comparison, the focus of this chapter is on how the EU has interpreted the issue as a case study which illustrates the broader issues that arise in relation to this question (and which also apply to other jurisdictions considering this issue). In the final section, I consider whether the concept of protection under international refugee law should be interpreted widely so as to include non-state actors. This includes discussion of the meaning to be given to 'country of nationality' and 'protection' in Article 1A(2) of the Refugee Convention, jurisprudence on non-state actors of protection and arguments for and against expansion of 'protection' to non-state entities. Significantly, it seeks to reframe the non-state actor debate by highlighting the importance of the state-citizen relationship underlying refugeehood and its link to the notion of 'protection'.

The meaning of 'protection' and the theoretical underpinnings of refugeehood

The approach to non-state bodies in international refugee law

Before examining the theoretical construct of refugeehood and the meaning of protection, there are two things to note about the refugee definition as it relates to non-state actors of protection. Firstly, the criteria for refugee status set out in Article 1A(2) and for cessation of that status in Article 1C(5) of the Refugee Convention are clearly based on a framework of the state and nationality. The centrality of the state is reflected in the requirement that a refugee must have crossed a state border and be outside their country of nationality and be unable or unwilling to avail him or herself of the protection of that country.

Secondly, the refugee definition is centred on the two concepts of 'persecution' and 'protection'. For the purpose of placing the issue of non-state actors into the broader context of refugee status determination, it should be noted that a finding that there is sufficient protection offered in a particular country can lead to a decision that a person does not face a 'well-founded' fear in that country and is therefore not a refugee. Similarly, an assessment of non-state protection in Article 1C(5) decisions goes to the ability of the refugee to 'continue to refuse to avail himself of the protection of the country of his nationality'.[21] The expansion of the concept of 'protection' to non-state actors under EU and international refugee law therefore directly affects the entitlement of an individual to refugee status and decisions about revocation of that status.

21 Refugee Convention, above n 3, Article 1C(5).

Non-state actors as persecutors

As noted earlier, international refugee law now recognises that non-state actors can constitute agents of persecution where the state is unwilling or unable to provide protection against such persecution. However, for many years, there was a difference of opinion between state parties to the Convention as to the approach to persecution by non-state bodies and the role of state culpability in persecution. On the one hand, common law countries such as the UK, Australia and Canada adopted a 'protection' approach, which says that there is no requirement to show state complicity in the persecution but only that there is a lack of state protection.[22] France and Germany, in contrast, adopted the 'accountability' theory of protection which holds that where acts of persecution are by a non-state agent, this cannot lead to recognition of refugee status unless a state can be held accountable for the persecution by showing that it perpetrates, condones or tolerates the harm.[23] Under this approach, a state is not accountable when it is shown to simply be unable to prevent the harm perpetrated by non-state actors.[24] The accountability approach has been criticised by UNHCR and commentators.[25] For instance, Zimmermann and Mahler note that:

22 This was explained by Laws LJ in *R v Secretary of State for the Home Department, Ex p Adan* [1999] 3 WLR 1274 (Court of Appeal):

> This accords with other jurisprudence in the English jurisdiction. Our courts recognise persecution by non-state agents for the purposes of the Convention in any case where the *state* is unwilling or unable to provide protection against it, and indeed *whether or not there exist competent or effective governmental or state authorities in the country in question*. This is what has been called the 'protection' theory. It is, as we have said, shared by a majority of the states signatory to the Convention and the UNHCR (at 1289, emphasis added).
>
> Andreas Zimmermann and Claudia Mahler note that this approach 'guarantees refugee protection on a broader basis and focuses on the fact that the individual might be without proper protection from his or her home State in case of severe violations of human rights by non-State actors. This approach is also more in line with the object and purpose of the 1951 Convention and should thus be favoured': A. Zimmerman and C. Mahler, 'Article 1A, Para 2, 1951 Convention', in A. Zimmerman (ed.), *The 1951 Convention Relating to the Status of Refugees and its 1967 Protocol: A Commentary* (Oxford University Press, 2011), 364–5.

23 See Kälin, above n 11, 415; Zimmermann and Mahler, above n 21, 364; S. Kneebone, 'Moving beyond the State: Refugees, Accountability and Protection', in S. Kneebone (ed.), *The Refugees Convention 50 Years On: Globalisation and International Law* (Ashgate, 2003), 282 (hereinafter Kneebone, 'Moving Beyond the State').

24 Zimmerman and Mahler, above n 21, 364.

25 See e.g. UNHCR: the 'spirit and purposes of the Convention would be contravened and the system for the international protection of refugees would be rendered ineffective if it were to be held that an asylum seeker should be denied needed protection unless a State could be held accountable for the violation of his or her fundamental human rights by a non-governmental actor': UNHCR, *Agents of Persecution: UNHCR Position*, 14 March 1995, [3], <www.refworld.org/docid/3ae6b31da3.html>. Susan Kneebone notes that 'a state centred accountability model embodies an inappropriate concept of the state in the context of the

> in refugee law, the decisive question is not whether a State may be held responsible for human rights violations or not . . . but rather whether a certain individual needs protection by a third State.[26]

Goodwin-Gill and McAdam also state:

> The Convention definition begins with the refugee as someone with a well-founded fear of persecution, and only secondly, as someone who is unable or unwilling, by reason of such fear, to use or take advantage of the protection of their government. In our view, the Convention's first point of reference is the individual, particularly as a rights-holder, rather than the system of government and its efficacy or intent in relation to protection, relevant as these elements are to the well-founded dimension.[27]

The differences in state practice, which were evident in the EU some years ago, have been ameliorated with the passing of Article 6 of the Qualification Directive, which specifically recognises that non-state actors can be actors of persecution for the purpose of refugee law without proof of any complicity on the part of state or state-like bodies in that persecution (thereby adopting the broader 'protection' view).[28] Thus, as Volker Türk has noted:

> There is now . . . broad agreement that persecution within the meaning of the 1951 Convention may emanate not only from the state but also from *de facto* authorities or from groups, even individuals, in situations where the authorities are either unwilling or unable in practice to provide the persons concerned with protection that would enable them safely to remain within, or to return to, their country.[29]

However, the other side of this issue is now at the forefront of the development of international refugee law: that is, can non-state bodies also be actors of *protection*?[30]

Refugee Convention': Kneebone, 'Moving Beyond the State', above n 22, 281. See also Zimmermann and Mahler, above n 21, 364.

26 Zimmermann and Mahler, above n 21, 364.

27 G. Goodwin-Gill and J. McAdam, *The Refugee in International Law* (Oxford University Press, 3rd ed., 2007), 10.

28 2011 EU Qualification Directive, above n 1, Article 6. This provides that actors of persecution or serious harm include '(a) the State; (b) parties or organizations controlling the State or a substantial part of the territory of the territory of the State; (c) non-State actors, if it can be demonstrated that the actors mentioned in (a) and (b), including international organizations, are unable or unwilling to provide protection against persecution or serious harm as defined in Article 7'.

29 V. Türk, 'Protection Gaps in Europe? Persons Fleeing the Indiscriminate Effects of Generalized Violence', 18 January 2011, 6, <www.unhcr.org/refworld/docid/4d37d8402.html>.

30 See e.g. 2011 Qualification Directive, above n 11, Article 7(1): 'Protection against persecution or serious harm can only be provided by: (a) the State; or (b) parties or organizations,

The position taken in this book is that the fact that international refugee law now recognises that non-state actors can carry out acts of *persecution* does not mean that the converse should be accepted, that is, that non-state actors can *provide protection*. Persecution and protection, whilst linked in the refugee definition, are two very different concepts under international refugee law. Acts of persecution, such as discrimination, physical harm and similar acts, can clearly be carried out by both state and non-state actors. However, the concept of 'protection' involves positive attributes such as, *inter alia*, the provision of physical security and safety, the existence of a functioning government and basic administrative structures, including a functioning legal and judicial system, and an adequate infrastructure to enable residents to exercise their rights.[31] It is therefore necessary to adopt a stricter approach to interpreting 'protection' as it relates to non-state actors.[32] It is also necessary to reconcile the Convention's emphasis on the state and nationality with this central element of 'protection' and to maintain the focus of the Convention on the individual's well-founded fear of persecution. In order to do this, I argue that the theoretical underpinning of 'refugeehood' offers a suitable framework for examining the issue of non-state actors of protection. In particular it offers a way of considering the protection needs of an individual refugee claimant in a social and political context, thereby focusing on the individual at risk rather than simply the capacity of the state to provide protection.[33]

Theory of refugeehood

A number of eminent refugee law commentators have written on the theory of refugeehood, including Atle Grahl-Madsen and Andrew Shacknove. Grahl-Madsen notes that a refugee is distinguished from ordinary aliens[34] by the existence

---

including international organizations, controlling the State or a substantial part of the territory of the State provided they are willing and able to offer protection in accordance with paragraph 2'.

31 See also UNHCR, *UNHCR Statement on the 'Ceased Circumstances' Clause of the EU Qualification Directive*, August 2008, 14, <www.unhcr.org/48a2f2a42.pdf> (hereinafter UNHCR Cessation Statement 2008).

32 James Hathaway and Michelle Foster have also highlighted the risks of recognising non-state actors as agents of protection, arguing that this 'confuses the object and purpose of the Refugee Convention': J.C. Hathaway and M. Foster, *The Law of Refugee Status* (Cambridge University Press, 2nd ed., 2014), 291.

33 Guy Goodwin-Gill and Jane McAdam criticise the focus in some jurisprudence on state protection on the basis that it shifts the focus of protection from the individual at risk to the state of origin and its capacity to provide protection: Goodwin-Gill and McAdam, above n 26, 10.

34 Although earlier writers have pointed to the fact that aliens are human beings and therefore in need of protection also. See, for instance, Hermann Cohen, 19th century philosopher, quoted in H. Freedman (ed.), *Jeremiah, Hebrew Text and English Translation with an Introduction and Commentary 1949*, 52: 'The alien was to be protected, not because he was a member of one's family, clan, or religious community, but because he was a human being. In the alien, therefore, man discovered the idea of humanity' (cited at the commencement of the Introduction to this book).

of a controversy between the refugee and the 'authorities' of his or her home country and that this controversy:

> is of a political nature – i.e. relating to how the country shall be governed and who shall govern it – and that is so serious as to impair the basic relationship between the individual and the government of the said country.[35]

Grahl-Madsen continues:

> it is characteristic of the situation of political refugees that the normal mutual bond of trust, loyalty, protection, and assistance between an individual and the government of his home country has been broken (or simply does not exist) in their case, and that they are afraid of returning to that country lest they shall become victims of political persecution, or at least shall have to make a complete political submission to a government which they consider repugnant and maybe also 'illegal'.[36]

Andrew Shacknove echoes the approach of Grahl-Madsen. He notes that the definition of refugee in various jurisdictions is predicated on an implicit argument (or conception) that:

> a a bond of trust, loyalty, protection and assistance between the citizen and the state constitutes the normal basis of society;
> b in the case of the refugee, this bond has been severed;
> c persecution and alienage are always the physical manifestations of this severed bond; and
> d these manifestations are the necessary and sufficient conditions for determining refugeehood.[37]

He states that this conception supplies the theoretical basis for the definition of a refugee[38] and describes refugeehood as 'exclusively a political relation between the citizen and the state, not a territorial relation between a countryman and his homeland'.[39] Significantly, he places persecution within the broader issue of state protection, stating that:

> Persecution is but one manifestation of the broader phenomenon: the absence of state protection of the citizen's basic needs. It is this absence of state

35 A. Grahl-Madsen, *The Status of Refugees in International Law* (A.W. Sijthoff-Leyden, Vol. 1, 1966), 78.

36 Ibid 79.

37 Shacknove, above n 2, 275. As Shacknove notes in his paper, Grahl Madsen also uses the language of a bond of trust and loyalty between citizen and state (see Shacknove at 275, footnote 4).

38 Ibid 275.

39 Ibid 283.

> protection of the citizen's basic needs which constitutes the full and complete negation of society and the basis of refugeehood.[40]

Alexander Aleinikoff also notes that as 'involuntary migrants' refugees 'evidence a breach of the relationship between the citizen and the state-of-origin'.[41]

This ties in with writings about nationality as a relationship between individual and state, which has been discussed in detail in international jurisprudence.[42] For instance, in the *Nottebohm* case, the International Court of Justice stated that nationality is 'a legal bond having as its basis a social fact of attachment, a genuine connection of existence, interests and sentiments'.[43] It is also linked to the views of Matthew Price (discussed earlier in Chapter 1) on temporary protection. Price distinguishes temporary protection from asylum by noting that '[a]sylum confers a *political* good – *membership*', whereas recipients of temporary protection are simply given permission to remain in the country for a period of time.[44] He further notes that 'asylum should be reserved for those exposed to serious harm because they *lack political membership*'.[45]

Given the preceding analytical framework, I now turn to examine the cessation and non-state actor provisions of the EU Directive as a case study to establish whether this is a justifiable extension of protection under international refugee law.

Case study: cessation and actors of protection under the EU Qualification Directive

The starting point of my analysis is Article 11(1)(e) of the Qualification Directive, which was the focus of consideration in the CJEU decision on non-state actors in *Abdulla.* Article 11(1)(e) provides, similarly to Article 1C(5) of the Refugee Convention, that a person shall cease to be a refugee, if he or she:

> can no longer, because the circumstances in connection with which he or she has been recognised as a refugee have ceased to exist, continue

40 Ibid 277. This view was referred to by the Federal Court of Canada in *Zalzali v Minister of Employment and Immigration* [1991] 3 F.C. 605, [18].

41 T.A. Aleinikoff, 'State Centred Refugee Law: From Resettlement to Containment' (1992–1993) 14(1) *Michigan Journal of International Law* 120, 121.

42 See e.g. *Administrative Decision No 1* of the Mixed Claims Commission between the US and Germany, 18 A.J. (1924); and *Messih v Minister of the Interior*, Egyptian Conseil d'Etat, Int. Law Reports, 291, 292, discussed in P. Weis, *Nationality and Statelessness in International Law* (Sijthoff and Noordhoff, 2nd ed., 1979), 30–1.

43 *Nottebohm (Liechtenstein v Guatemala) Second Phase*, ICJ reports (1955), 4, as discussed in Weis, ibid 31. Leading refugee law scholars, Paul Weis and Antonio Fortin, have written extensively about nationality and its link to the rights and duties of states, see Weis, above n 41, 239; and A. Fortin, 'The Meaning of "Protection" in the Refugee Definition' (2001) 12(4) *International Journal of Refugee Law* 548, 551.

44 M.E. Price, 'Persecution Complex: Justifying Asylum Law's Preference for Persecuted People' (2006) 47 *Harvard International Law Journal* 413, 431.

45 Ibid 431 (emphasis in original).

> to refuse to avail himself or herself of the protection of the country of nationality.[46]

Article 11(2) then provides that in considering this question, EU Member States shall 'have regard to whether the change of circumstances is of such a significant and non-temporary nature that the refugee's fear of persecution can no longer be regarded as well-founded'.[47] This must be read in light of other articles in the EU Qualification Directive, including Article 7.

An important aspect to note here is that both Article 7 and Article 11 of the EU Directive were amended in the Recast 2011 version of the Directive. I therefore summarise both the 2004 and 2011 Directives here. This is necessary as the CJEU decision in *Abdulla*, handed down in 2010, considered the 2004 version of Article 7.

Article 7 of the EU Qualification Directive

Article 7(1) of the 2004 Qualification Directive stated that protection can be provided by:

> (1) (a) the State; or
> (b) parties or organizations, including international organizations, controlling the State or a substantial part of the territory of the State.

Article 7(2) of the 2004 Qualification Directive then set out guidance as to when protection will be 'generally provided' and the factors that Member States must consider in its assessment:

> (2) Protection is generally provided when the actors mentioned in paragraph 1 take reasonable steps to prevent the persecution or suffering of serious harm, inter alia, by operating an effective legal system for the detection, prosecution and punishment of acts constituting persecution or serious harm, and the applicant has access to such protection.[48]

46 2011 EU Qualification Directive, above n 11, Article 11(1)(e).

47 2011 EU Qualification Directive, above n 11, Article 11(2).

48 Recital (19) to the EU Qualification Directive, above n 11 repeats this: 'Protection can be provided not only by the State but also by parties and organizations, including international organizations, meeting the conditions of this Directive, which control a region or a larger area within the territory of the State'. Article 7(3) of both the 2004 and 2011 Qualification Directives also provide that 'When assessing whether an international organization controls a State or a substantial part of its territory and provides protection as described in paragraph 2, Member States shall take into account any guidance which may be provided in relevant Council acts'.

The Recast 2011 Qualification Directive amends Article 7 by emphasising the willingness and ability of the non-state actor to provide protection (amendments in italics):

1 Protection against persecution or serious harm can only be provided by:

(a) the State; or (b) parties or organizations, including international organizations, controlling the State or a substantial part of the territory of the State *provided they are willing and able to offer protection in accordance with paragraph 2.*

2 *Protection against persecution or serious harm must be effective and of a non-temporary nature. Such* protection is generally provided when the actors mentioned *under points (a) and (b) of* paragraph 1 take reasonable steps to prevent the persecution or suffering of serious harm inter alia by operating an effective legal system for the detection, prosecution and punishment of acts constituting persecution or serious harm, and the applicant has access to such protection.[49]

Before analysing Article 7 in greater depth, it is important to note a number of things about its drafting history. The original version of this article in the proposal for the 2004 Qualification Directive[50] was worded differently to that of the finalised Article 7. Whilst the original version recognised protection could be provided by 'international organisations', it restricted the scope of other non-state actors to 'stable quasi-state authorities', rather than the broader term 'parties' contained in the final 2004 version. Also, it applied only to those international organisations and quasi-state authorities which 'control a clearly defined territory of significant size and stability' and 'who are able and willing to give effect to rights and to protect an individual from harm *in a manner similar to an internationally recognised State*'.[51] It therefore required a level of *effectiveness* of protection and attributes similar to a state. In contrast, the *final* version of the 2004 Directive did not contain any such criteria.

Further, Article 7(2) in the 2011 version of the Directive seeks to set out a general test for sufficiency of state protection which refers to whether the state has taken 'reasonable steps' to provide protection against persecution. However, Article 7(2) is a rather weak qualification on Article 7(1). It only requires that the non-state actors take 'reasonable steps' to prevent persecution and other harm, rather than requiring that the state and/or non-state authority *actually* provide protection.

49 2011 EU Qualification Directive, above n 11, Article 7 (emphasis added).

50 European Commission, 'Proposal for a Council Directive on minimum standards for the qualification and status of third country nationals and stateless persons as refugees or as persons who otherwise need international protection' [2002] OJ C 51 E/325, Article 9(3).

51 Ibid (emphasis added).

Existing commentary on Article 7

Permitting non-state actors to provide 'protection' is a controversial notion under international refugee law, as traditionally states have been seen as the only bodies which can provide such protection. As a result, UNHCR, academic commentators and non-governmental organisations have been heavily critical of Article 7, particularly on the basis that non-state entities are not accountable under international law.[52] UNHCR has also argued that non-state actors normally only exercise authority in a state on a temporary or transitional basis and have a limited ability to enforce the rule of law.[53] These concerns have been echoed by a number of non-governmental organisations such as the European Council of Refugees and Exiles,[54] the UK Immigration Law Practitioners' Association,[55] Justice[56] and the UK Refugee Council.[57] In particular, Justice and ECRE have questioned the ability of non-state bodies to provide sufficiently stable and durable protection.[58]

In this context, it is significant to note that the European Economic and Social Committee has disagreed with the extension of actors of protection to non-state actors. It stated it was 'inappropriate' to extend the definition of actors of protection to non-state bodies such as NGOs and international organisations.[59] The committee noted that while such actors may be willing

52 UNHCR, *Annotated Comments on the EC Council Directive 2004/83/EC of 29 April 2004 on Minimum Standards for the Qualification and Status of Third Country Nationals or Stateless Persons as Refugees or as Persons Who Otherwise Need International Protection and the Content of the Protection Granted (OJ L 304/12 of 30.9.2004)*, 28 January 2005, 18; European Council on Refugees and Exiles (ECRE), 'Information Note on the Council Directive 2004/83/EC of 29 April 2004 on Minimum Standards for the Qualification of Third Country Nationals and Others in Need of International Protection', IN/10/2004/ext/CN, 1 October 2004, 7, <www.ecre.org/resources/ECRE_actions/292>; 'Memorandum by Guy Goodwin-Gill, Professor of International Refugee Law, University of Oxford, and Agnes Hurwitz, Refugee Studies Centre, University of Oxford', House of Lords Select Committee, above n 19, [12].

53 UNHCR, Annotated Comments, above 50, 18. See also UNHCR comments on the European Commission's proposal to recast the Directive in 'UNHCR comments on the European Commission's proposal for a Directive of the European Parliament and of the Council on minimum standards for the qualification and status of third country nationals or stateless persons as beneficiaries of international protection and the content of the protection granted, COM(2009)551, 21 October 2009, 5, <www.unhcr.org/4c5037f99.pdf>.

54 ECRE, Information Note, above n 50, 7.

55 'Memorandum by the Immigration Law Practitioners' Association', House of Lords Select Committee, above n 19, [22].

56 'Memorandum by JUSTICE', House of Lords Select Committee, above n 19, [9–11].

57 'Memorandum by the Refugee Council', House of Lords Select Committee, above n 19, [4].

58 'Memorandum by the European Council on Refugees and Exiles', House of Lords Select Committee, above n 19, 42; 'Memorandum by JUSTICE', House of Lords Select Committee, above n 19, [4].

59 'Opinion of the European Economic and Social Committee on the "Proposal for a Directive of the European Parliament and of the Council on minimum standards for the qualification

and able to protect people from a given country, 'ultimate responsibility for this does not lie with them. International organisations are answerable to Member States, while NGOs are answerable to their members and financial backers'.[60] The committee therefore stated that:

> Only the State can provide valid and effective protection in the medium and long term, as it is answerable to its own people, who obviously have the greatest interest in its viability and stability. While actors of protection may provide useful or even vital services in the short term, especially in resolving humanitarian issues, responsibility for the protection of persons in a given country cannot be entrusted to them, not even partially. The presence of such actors cannot be cited as grounds for refusing international protection.[61]

I will be presenting my own analysis of this issue later in this chapter. However, before doing so, we must first examine how the CJEU interpreted this provision in the context of cessation.

The CJEU in Abdulla

The Court of Justice of the European Union handed down an important judgement in 2010 in the case of *Abdulla*, in which it made findings (albeit in very brief terms) about the proper interpretation of Article 7 of the Qualification Directive in relation to cessation. The court was asked to interpret Article 7(1) of the Directive as part of a reference to it by the German Federal Administrative Court (*Bundesverwaltungsgericht*). The referral involved five separate cases which were referred to the CJEU together.[62] The cases involved applicants from Iraq whose refugee status had been revoked by German authorities on the basis that they no longer feared persecution due to the overthrow of Saddam Hussein's regime.

In the original German case on cessation which led to the referral, *BVerwG 10 C 33.07*,[63] the German Federal Administrative Court made a number of statements as to its understanding of the role of non-state actors

---

and status of third country nationals or stateless persons as beneficiaries of international protection and the content of the protection granted (recast)"', COM(2009) 551 final/2–2009/0164 (COD) 2011/C 18/14, [4.2].

60 *Abdulla* [4.2].

61 Ibid.

62 For further details, see [2008] OJ C 197, 3–6.

63 *Bundesverwaltungsgericht* (Federal Administrative Court, Germany), *10 C 33.07*, 7 February 2008, (*BVerwG 33.07*). The German Federal Administrative Court is the final court of appeal in relation to administrative matters.

in refugee law. It noted that, in accordance with previous case law of the court, a non-state actor could be said to provide 'protection' if it exercises de facto territorial authority in an area and has established an order with a certain degree of stability and 'having the power in principle to protect and persecute'.[64] The court stated that the factors that are *not* decisive in relation to this question are the legitimacy of the exercise of power, its acceptance by all or a majority of those subject to it, the rulers' freedom from arbitrariness, observance of a minimum standard of human rights and the capacity to be held liable under international law.[65] In the context of Iraq, the court noted that previous case law (*BVerwG 10 C 34.06*) had held that the Iraqi government, at least with the assistance of multinational forces, had 'an effective statal or quasi-statal authority in portions of its territory'.[66] In relation to cessation, the German Federal Administrative Court held in *BVerwG 33.07* that the characteristic of 'protection of country' suggests that fundamentally there must be a state,[67] reflecting that the era in which the 1951 Refugee Convention was created 'was one of nation states'.[68] It held, however, that since that time, it has been recognised that quasi-statal and international protection may be of 'equivalent worth' to state protection, as reflected in Article 7(1) of the Directive.[69] It therefore stayed the proceedings in this and four other related cases and sought a preliminary ruling from the CJEU seeking clarification as to the correct approach to this issue.[70]

Prior to the handing down of the decision of the CJEU, Advocate General Mazák of the court was asked to provide an advisory opinion in the case. On the issue of multinational troops, Advocate General Mazák stated:

> In my view, where the assistance of multinational troops is employed by a State such employment could be viewed as a reasonable step to prevent persecution in the country of nationality of a refugee. I consider however that in order to comply with the terms of Article 7 of Directive 2004/83, a State may only rely on the assistance of multinational troops provided such troops operate under the mandate of

64 *BVerwG 33.07* [27].
65 Ibid.
66 Bundesverwaltungsgericht (Federal Administrative Court, Germany), *10 C 34.06*, 20 March 2007, cited in *BVerwG 33.07* [27].
67 *BVerwG 33.07* [28].
68 Ibid.
69 Ibid.
70 It posed the following question in relation to non-state actors: 'Does the cessation of refugee status pursuant to Article 11(1)(e) of the Directive . . . presuppose that in the country of which the refugee is a citizen, a) an actor of protection within the meaning of Article 7(1) of the Directive is present, and in this case is it sufficient if protection can be provided only with the assistance of multi-national troops' (*10 C 33.07*, [2]).

the international community, for example under the auspices of the United Nations.[71]

The CJEU, which handed down its judgement in *Abdulla* in March 2010, took a slightly different approach to that of Advocate General Mazák in relation to the question of non-state actors. The court simply stated that the actors of protection referred to in Article 7(1) 'may comprise international organizations controlling the State or a substantial part of the territory of the State, *including by means of the presence of a multinational force in that territory*'.[72] It did not give any further guidance as to the nature of such a force (for instance, whether it should be present in the country for a defined period) or what its role should be (for example, whether forces undertaking peacekeeping or humanitarian functions would suffice or whether it had to be carrying out state-like functions relating to rule of law institutions within the country in question). It also did not specify whether it should be supported by a UN or other international mandate.[73] Further, although it reiterated that cessation requires a 'significant and non-temporary' change in circumstances, pursuant to Article 11(2) of the Qualification Directive, it did not link this requirement with Article 7. That is, it did not specifically address the issue of the transitional nature of the occupation of Iraq by multinational forces as that relates to the need to establish durability of change under the test for cessation. It also failed to include Advocate General Mazák's important rider about the need for multinational forces to be supported by a mandate of the international community. The requirement of a mandate is an important qualification on the broad nature of Article 7(1), as it provides (depending on the nature of the mandate) a means of introducing a level of accountability to the actions of an international organisation and some certainty as to powers, functions and durability of stay in a country.[74] This is of concern, as it is arguable that multinational troops without backing of a UN mandate and without a set period of presence are only temporary in nature and should not be considered as constituting effective protection for both the purposes of granting *and* ceasing refugee status.

71 Opinion of Advocate General Mazák in Joined Cases C-175/08, C-176/08, C-178/08 and C-179/08, *Salahadin Abdulla and Others*, 15 September 2009, [54].

72 *Abdulla*, [101] (emphasis added). The court also discussed this issue at [75].

73 See Lord Plant of Highfield, 'Minutes of Evidence', House of Lords Select Committee, above n 19, 11.

74 See e.g. UN Security Council Resolution 1212 on Haiti which stressed the commitment of the international community to a long-term programme of support for Haiti (SC Res. 1212, 25 November 1998, [8]). See also UN Security Council Resolution 1244 on Kosovo which provided for an interim administration whose functions included '[m]aintaining civil law and order, including establishing local police forces', '[p]rotecting and promoting human rights' and '[a]ssuring the safe and unimpeded return of all refugees and displaced persons to their homes in Kosovo': SC Res. 1244, 10 June 1999, [10(i-k)].

Moreover, neither Article 7 nor the CJEU decision in *Abdulla* reflects the particular nuances which come into play when one considers the 'protection' capabilities of non-state actors such as the United Nations. This is significant as decisions of the French *Commission de Recours* have, for instance, held that there is a difference in protection provided by UN forces established under Chapter VI and Chapter VII of the UN Security Council. It has held that UN forces established under Chapter VI are *not* actors of protection, but that those established under Chapter VII *are*.[75] The rationale is that under Chapter VII of the UN Charter, UN missions have administrative and coercive powers.[76] There are also broader concerns about the resource limitations of the UN and its past history of providing humanitarian and other protection in countries. Indeed, Madeline Garlick, EU Officer for UNHCR, has stated similar concerns with Article 7:

> UNHCR's concern is that while international organizations continue to provide the best level of support and protection that they can, limited resources and legal authority may systematically handicap their efforts. This renders unrealistic the suggestion that international organizations can 'control' territory and 'protect' people in the same way that a State can.[77]

In the light of the preceding, I next turn to consider whether a provision such as Article 7(1) is compatible with the 1951 Refugee Convention.

Non-state actors of protection under international refugee law

The text and context of the 1951 Refugee Convention

Unfortunately, the 1951 Refugee Convention is silent on the issue of non-state actors. As the *travaux préparatoires* reflect, the drafters of the Convention did not refer to the notion of non-state actors as agents of either persecution or protection. Rather, both Article 1A(2) and Article 1C(5) refer to protection of the 'country of nationality'. Does it indicate that only states can provide protection?

75 See ECRE, 'The Impact of the EU Qualification Directive on International Protection', October 2008, 95 (hereinafter ECRE Impact).

76 See *Charter of the United Nations*, 24 October 1945, 1 UNTS XVI, Chapter VII.

77 M. Garlick, 'UNHCR and the Implementation of Council Directive 2004/83/EC on Minimum Standards for the Qualification and Status of Third Country Nations or Stateless Persons as Refugees or as Persons Who Otherwise Need International Protection and the Content of the Protection Granted' (The EC 'Qualification Directive'), in K. Zwaan (ed.), *The Qualification Directive: Central Themes, Problem Issues, and Implementation in Selected Member States* (Nijmegen: Wolf Legal Publishers, 2007), 65.

There are strong arguments in favour of interpreting 'protection' as used in the Refugee Convention as requiring protection by a *state* entity only. Both Article 1A(2) and Article 1C(5) of the Convention quite clearly refer to the refugee's *country of nationality*, or in the case of stateless persons, the *country of former habitual residence*. I submit that 'country' in this context should be interpreted as meaning the 'state' – the government and associated state apparatus such as a functioning legal system, police force, security forces and so on, rather than simply the physical *territory* of a country. Given that 'nationality' connotes a relationship involving citizenship; of a bond between state and citizen, this supports a finding that it is the *state entity* which must provide protection. This is particularly so when one considers the linking of 'protection' and 'country of nationality' in the Convention, as it indicates it is talking about the protection offered by the *state* to its *citizens*, not simply the protection offered in the *territory* of a country.

This view is supported by taking a holistic approach to the Convention and examining other articles in the Convention.[78] In this context, the other cessation clauses set out in Article 1C(1) to 1C(4), which deal with actions such as re-establishment in the country of origin and reacquisition of nationality, are relevant.[79] Fitzpatrick and Bonoan emphasise that these clauses require careful analysis of a number of criteria, including 'capacities of State authorities'.[80] In particular, Article 1C(1), which applies to refugees who voluntarily re-avail themselves of the protection of the country of nationality, is said to involve consideration of the bond between citizen and state. For instance, Grahl-Madsen argues that in light of jurisprudence on Article 1C(1):

> and considering the system of Article 1C, it seems justified to conclude that physical presence in the territory of the home country does not *per se* constitute re-availment of protection in the sense of Article 1C(1) . . . ; it is the conscious subjection under the government of that country – or, in other words the normalization of the relationship between State and individual which matters.[81]

78 The need to take a holistic interpretation of the whole Convention, rather than simply its constituent parts, has been emphasised by UNHCR, courts and academic commentators: see UNHCR, 'The International Protection of Refugees: Interpreting Article 1 of the 1951 Convention Relating to the Status of Refugees' (2001) 20(3) *Refugee Survey Quarterly* 77, 78; V. Türk and F. Nicholson, 'Refugee Protection in International Law: An Overall Perspective', in E. Feller et al. (eds.), *Refugee Protection in International Law: UNHCR's Global Consultations on International Protection* (Cambridge University Press, 2003), 42–3; UK House of Lords in *Januzi (FC) (Appellant) v Secretary of State for the Home Department and Others* [2006] 2 WLR 397, [4] (Lord Bingham).

79 Refugee Convention, above n 3, Articles 1C(1)–(4). See S. Kneebone and M. O'Sullivan, 'Article 1C', in A. Zimmermann (ed.), *The 1951 Convention Relating to the Status of Refugees and Its 1967 Protocol: A Commentary* (Oxford University Press, 2011).

80 J. Fitzpatrick and R. Bonoan, in E. Feller et al., *Refugee Protection in International Law: UNHCR's Global Consultations on International Protection* (Cambridge University Press, 2003), 491, 523.

81 Grahl-Madsen, above n 34. See also Kneebone and O'Sullivan, above n 76, 496–7; J.C. Hathaway, *The Law of Refugee Status* (Butterworths, 1991), 196–7 (hereinafter Hathaway, *Law of Refugee Status*).

He makes similar comments in relation to the other clauses of Article 1C. For instance, Grahl-Madsen notes that Article 1C(2), which deals with reacquisition of nationality, is also designed (like Article 1C(1)) to cover 'normalization of relations between individuals and their country of origin'.[82] This point has also been echoed by other writers.[83] In particular, Goodwin-Gill and McAdam argued that evidence of having obtained protection for these purposes:

> comprises all such actions by the refugee as indicate the establishment of normal relations with the authorities of the country of origin, such as registration at consulates or application for and renewal of passports or certificates of nationality.[84]

In addition to Article 1C, Article 1E of the Refugee Convention also deals with rights pertaining to nationality. Article 1E provides that the Convention will not apply to a person who is recognised by the authorities of the country of residence 'as having the rights and obligations *which are attached to the possession of the nationality of that country*'.[85] Thus, the emphasis in this clause of the Convention is not merely on protection from persecution, but on rights and obligations which attach to possession of *citizenship* and *nationality*.[86]

There have, however, been suggestions in some jurisprudence that 'country' for the purpose of the 1951 Convention is merely a territorial construct. For instance, in the United Kingdom, the term 'country' has been interpreted by courts as a geographical rather than political construct. In the case of *Dyli*, the UK Asylum and Immigration Tribunal held that 'country' in Article 1A(2) is used only in the geographical sense.[87] In making this finding, the court pointed to the fact that Article 1A(2) does not include the word 'authorities' and thus the phrase 'outside the country' refers to it in a geographical sense. However, I submit that this approach is, with respect, flawed. Simply because Article 1A(2) does not contain the word 'authorities' or 'state authorities' does not lead to the conclusion that country is used in a geographical sense. Indeed, had the founders wished to simply refer to the *territory* of a country, they could have utilised the

82 Grahl-Madsen, above n 34, 393. In the context of 1C(4), Grahl-Madsen also notes re-establishment requires more than mere 'physical presence' in the country of origin (at 372).

83 See Hathaway, *Law of Refugee Status*, above n 78, 196–7, where he discusses this as 'normalization of relations between the refugee and her state of origin'; and Kneebone and O'Sullivan, above n 76, 498.

84 Goodwin-Gill and McAdam, above n 26, 136.

85 Refugee Convention, above n 3, Article 1E (emphasis added).

86 See related discussion of citizenship and nationality in the context of Article 1E of the Refugee Convention in S. Kneebone, 'Strangers the Gate: Refugees, Citizenship and Nationality' (2004) 10 *Australian Journal of Human Rights* 33.

87 E.g. in *Fadil Dyli v. Secretary of State for the Home Department*, HX5171700(00TH02186), United Kingdom Asylum and Immigration Tribunal/Immigration Appellate Authority, 30 August 2000, [12]–[13], <www.unhcr.org/refworld/docid/3dec84942.html> (*Dyli*). Note that starred determinations are significant in that they are considered binding on later decisions of the UK Asylum and Immigration Tribunal.

term 'territories', as they did in both Articles 31 and 33 of the Refugee Convention.[88] This view is supported by the scholar Hemme Battjes, who notes that 'the Refugee Convention employs the term "territory" where a geographical designation in contrast to the institutional entity "country" is meant'.[89] He argues that if 'country' was used merely to refer to the geographical territory of a state then the term 'protection within the territory of that country' would arguably have been used in the 1951 Convention. He therefore concludes that the word 'country' in Article 1A(2) of the Refugee Convention refers to a 'state'.[90]

In addition to the text of the 1951 Convention, it is necessary to examine the Convention as a 'living instrument' and whether subsequent state practice establishes a new norm of non-state protection.[91] However, state practice on the issue of non-state actors of protection is somewhat contradictory. Although the signing of the EU Qualification Directive by the 26 EU Member States is evidence of agreement of those states to the content of Article 7, the national legislation of those states, which purports to transpose Article 7 into national law is inconsistent.[92] Also, the way in which Article 7 is interpreted in jurisprudence is not consistent amongst EU Member States.[93]

Looking more broadly at the practice of other contracting states to the 1951 Refugee Convention, there are also marked differences in approach to the issue of non-state actors. Although a number of courts, including those in the UK, Canada, France, Germany and Australia, have recognised that 'protection' under the 1951 Refugee Convention may be provided other than by a state, there is strong disagreement in the jurisprudence as to the required attributes of such an organisation. In the UK, a starred determination of the Asylum Immigration Tribunal has held that the nature of the body providing the protection under the Convention is 'irrelevant'.[94] Others, such as the French Commission de Recours,

88 Article 31 of the Refugee Convention prohibits contracting states from imposing certain penalties on refugees who come directly from a 'territory' where their life or freedom was threatened. Article 33 of the Refugee Convention provides that states must not *refoule* a refugee to the frontiers of 'territories' where they may face a well-founded fear of persecution.

89 H. Battjes, ***European Asylum Law and International Law*** (Martinus Nijhoff, 2006), 248 (citations omitted).

90 Ibid.

91 Article 31(3)(b) of the Vienna Convention on the Law of Treaties (23 May 1969, 155 UNTS 331) provides that, in interpreting international treaties, account is to be taken of any subsequent practice in the application of the treaty which establishes the agreement of the parties regarding its interpretation. This is discussed in Chapter 2 of this book.

92 ECRE Impact, above n 72, 93–5.

93 See European Commission, 'Report from the Commission to the European Parliament and the Council on the Application of Directive 2004/83/EC', COM(2010) 314 Final, 16 June 2010, 6.

94 *Dyli*, [13]. In *obiter* dicta comments in the case of *Gardi*, the UK Court of Appeal, questioned the wide interpretation of protection set out in *Dyli* stating that protection should be by an entity which is accountable under international law: *Gardi v Secretary of State for Home Department* [2002] EWCA Civ 750 (Ward, Keene and Nourse JJ), [37] (*Gardi*). However, the wide approach in *Dyli* has been endorsed in later decisions of the Asylum and Immigration Tribunal and appears to be the accepted approach in the UK: see e.g. *DM Somalia* [32]; *SF (Sufficiency of Protection-KAA-Michigan Guidelines) Iraq CG* [2002] UKIAT 07376, [13] (*SF Iraq*).

have limited the concept to entities created under certain UN powers,[95] whilst the Canadian courts have required that there be a type of 'agency' relationship established whereby the non-state entity undertakes the powers and responsibilities of a state.[96] Notably, some decisions have simply not accepted that non-state actors can provide protection under the Refugee Convention at all.[97]

What conclusions can be drawn from state practice in this area? It seems that although a number of countries, particularly some EU Member States, appear to embrace the broad notion of non-state actors as including 'parties' and 'international organizations', as set out in the EU Qualification Directive, others have qualified this approach by either requiring the entity to act 'like a state' or to be supported by a particular UN mandate. It is therefore my submission that there is no coherent line of authority which supports a broader interpretation of 'protection' to encompass non-state actors.

What then is the answer to this question – how should we approach this issue in a way which respects the text of the Refugee Convention, whilst also interpreting it within a modern-day context? My answer is to look more deeply at what occurs when a person flees their country in terms of both a political and a legal act – the essence of refugeehood. This involves shifting the focus of the debate from the sufficiency of protection provided by a non-state entity and towards a more principled approach to the issue. A simple textual analysis, particularly where the text of the Convention is ambiguous as to meaning, is not sufficient to deal with the complex legal and political issues posed by the question of non-state actors of protection. A deeper analysis is required of this, which necessitates examining questions about the theoretical underpinnings of refugeehood.

A more appropriate conceptual framework – the theoretical underpinnings of refugee status

The complexities of the legal issues raised by the question of non-state actors in refugee law suggest it is necessary to not merely examine this issue from the point of view of international legal accountability or whether non-state bodies are capable of providing protection as a question of fact. The fact that non-state bodies lack international accountability supports the main argument in this

95 See decisions of the French Commission de Recours discussed in ECRE Impact, above n 72.

96 The Canadian Federal Court in *Elmi* (1999) upheld the view of the Immigration and Refugee Board that a clan is capable of providing protection if it is acting as the 'de facto government agent of protection': *Elmi v. Minister of Citizenship and Immigration*, IMM-580–598, Canada: Federal Court, 12 March 1999, [17]. Note that this 'agency' relationship is discussed in P. Mathew et al., 'The Role of State Protection in Refugee Analysis, Discussion Paper No. 2, Advanced Refugee Law Workshop, International Association of Refugee Law Judges (IARLJ), New Zealand, October 2002' (2003) 15(3) *International Journal of Refugee Law* 444, 457. They say that without a clear and accountable agency relationship, protection offered by the UN ordinarily will not constitute the 'protection of that country' for the purposes of Article 1A(2) of the Convention.

97 See e.g. UK Court of Appeal in *Gardi*.

chapter – that it is highly problematic to accept such bodies as sufficient providers of refugee protection. However, the accountability issue is only part of the legal problem. The debate about this matter also needs to be moved on to question in a deeper fashion what it means to be a refugee and how that relates to the political relationship between individual and the state. Thus, we must reconceptualise the debate to encompass more fundamental issues about the nature of the relationship between citizen and state and the essence of refugeehood. This is the more appropriate conceptual approach to the issue of non-state actors of protection, which allows us to reconcile the pragmatic need to reflect the modern-day reality of refugee protection, whilst also furthering the protection of refugee rights. In particular, I submit that the theoretical underpinnings of refugeehood provide the means of understanding the relationship between individual and state and whether this is *political* or merely *geographical* in nature. The essence of refugeehood is the breaking of the bond between citizen and state. It therefore involves the severance of a *political* relationship with the country of nationality, and, as Shacknove points out, not simply a 'territorial relation between a countryman and his homeland'.[98]

When applied to the issue of non-state actors of protection, this means that the presence of non-state actors in a country of origin cannot be equated with state protection, because on a fundamental level, it cannot repair the severed bond between citizen and state which was ruptured when persecution took place, when the protection of the state failed and refugeehood was established. Rather, the relationship between citizen and state can only be repaired by the presence of a functioning government, able and willing to provide protection to its people, which operates with the consent of the governed.

In recognition of the reality of contemporary international practice, I argue that in some, very limited circumstances, certain international organisations such as the United Nations, *may* provide 'protection' if they are acting as a *stable, state-like authority* and they are acting in an agency relationship, that is, in place of a 'failed state' or with the consent of the government in question.[99] That is, they must not simply be in the territory of the country in question, but must administer the apparatus of the state and have the attributes of a state in terms of control of the legal system, police force and so on. Such UN forces would also need to be present in the country for a durable and stable period of time and be supported by an international mandate. In this context, I note that the capacity of the United Nations to provide protection is also recognised in Article 1D of the

98 Shacknove, above n 2, 283.

99 Similar arguments have been made by a member of the UK House of Lords Select Committee on the EU, Minutes of Evidence, Lord Plant of Highfield, above n 19, 11. For an example of such an arrangement, see the remit of the UN Interim Mission in Kosovo (UNMIK). UNMIK was established under a United Nations resolution and the Federal Republic of Yugoslavia had in effect ceded control to it: see UN Security Resolution 1244, above n 71, [5], [10]. Note that under UNMIK Regulation 1999/1, UNMIK was vested with '[a]ll legislative and executive authority with respect to Kosovo, including the administration of the judiciary': UNMIK Regulation 1999/1, 25 July 1999.

1951 Convention.[100] This concession is justified by the fact that a stable, state-like authority acting in an agency capacity which meets the preceding criteria may be seen as having, to some extent at least, repaired the bond between citizen and state. It also allows consideration of the practical realities and pragmatic concerns arising in this area by recognising the protective responsibilities of such bodies.

However, a broader notion of non-state actors which encompasses 'international organisations' and 'parties', without any criteria of stability or legitimacy, such as set out in Article 7 of the Qualification Directive, will not normally fit these requirements. This is particularly so in relation to groups such as militias and clans which may have control over part of a country. This type of protection, based on exercise of territorial power, is by its nature fluid and changeable and open to challenge by rival groups and militias within that state. Such local territorial control is not of the same nature as the widespread political, economic and legal power exercised by a functioning state, particularly where that state governs democratically and with the legitimacy of the consent of the governed.

In particular, the issue of the bond between citizen and state has great significance to the question of *multinational forces* as actors of protection. Multinational forces have been endorsed as acceptable actors of protection in the recent decision of the CJEU in *Abdulla*.[101] However, viewed in the context of the basis of refugeehood, I submit that this finding is incorrect. Grahl-Madsen stated that refugeehood may exist where an individual must submit to a government the citizen finds 'repugnant' or 'illegal'.[102] Moreover, Shacknove specifically addresses the issue of foreign troops and protection, stating that '[t]he *sine qua non* of the political commonwealth is to defend the citizen "from the invasion of foreigners and the injuries of one another"'.[103] As the legitimacy of a government is drawn from the consent of the governed, the political relationship between citizen and state cannot be re-established if multinational forces are present in a country, particularly if they are so present without the consent of the governed.[104]

The writing of political scientists also provides valuable guidance in this area, particularly in relation to the legitimacy of states. Michael Walzer has, for instance, noted that '[t]he state is constituted by the union of people and government'[105]

100 Refugee Convention, above n 3. Article 1D provides: 'This Convention shall not apply to persons who are at present receiving from organs or agencies of the United Nations other than the United Nations High Commissioner for Refugees protection or assistance. When such protection or assistance has ceased for any reason, without the position of such persons being definitively settled in accordance with the relevant resolutions adopted by the General Assembly of the United Nations, these persons shall *ipso facto* be entitled to the benefits of this Convention'.

101 *Abdulla*, [75–76].

102 Grahl-Madsen, above n 34.

103 Shacknove, above n 2, 278, citing Hobbes, *Leviathan* (1958), 142.

104 This is significant given that the German Federal Administrative Court stated in *BVerwG 33.07* that the factors that are *not* decisive in relation to this question are the legitimacy of the exercise of power and its acceptance by all or a majority of those subject to it.

105 M. Walzer, 'The Moral Standing of States: A Response to Four Critics' (1980) 9(3) *Philosophy and Public Affairs*, 209, 212. Walzer was discussing the issue of military intervention.

and that 'a state is legitimate or not depending upon the "fit" of government and community, that is, the degree to which the government actually represents the political life of its people'.[106] In particular, he raises an important issue about the problems of legitimacy caused by the presence of foreign troops in a country, noting the strength of foreign troops depends:

> upon the character of their own government and community, their historical traditions, loyalties, and so on, and bears no relation at all to the history and culture of the people, whose fate they are determining.[107]

The preceding discussion is very significant to the issue of 'protection', because if an international organisation or multinational forces are in a country by force or otherwise present without the consent of the government or people, then it also may affect the ability of nationals to seek the protection of the state or state-like body. For instance, an Iraqi national may not be reasonably expected to seek protection from US forces.

This is one of the strengths of utilising the Grahl-Madsen/Shacknove 'refugeehood' framework in this context. To date, the focus of jurisprudence has been centred on the sufficiency of protection in the state, which has pushed the focus away from the individual refugee. As Goodwin-Gill and McAdam have noted, there is a need for refugee law to focus more squarely on the individual refugee and his or her well-founded fear of persecution.[108] The 'refugeehood' framework better reflects this aspect of refugee law and protection.

Particular problems which arise in cessation cases

The preceding analysis has dealt with the ramifications for non-state actors of protection for international refugee law, with brief reference to cessation. However, it is also necessary to analyse the ramifications for cessation in more detail.

The question of the protection provided (or not provided) by non-state actors is of particular concern in cessation cases because in that context persecution of the individual has *already* been proven to have occurred, and refugee status granted on that basis. In addition, as noted in Chapter 4, it is generally agreed by UNHCR and academic commentators that changes in the country concerned need to be fundamental, stable and durable in order for cessation to apply.[109]

106 Ibid 214.

107 Ibid 222. There is also a problem of effectiveness. For instance, Erin D. Mooney, writing about the presence of UN troops in the former Yugoslavia, notes that despite the presence of 14,000 troops from the UN Protection Force, ethnic cleansing from UN Protected Areas 'continued virtually unchecked' during 1992: see E.D. Mooney, 'Presence, Ergo Protection? UNPROFOR, UNHCR and the ICRC in Croatia and Bosnia and Herzegovina' (1995) 7(3) *International Journal of Refugee Law* 407, 414.

108 Goodwin-Gill and McAdam, above n 26, 10.

109 UNHCR, Executive Committee Conclusion No. 65, *General Conclusion on International* Protection, UN GAOR, 46th Sess., (q) (1991); UNHCR *Handbook*, above n 11, [135];

Indeed, the need for durability of change in the country of origin is explicitly recognised in Article 11(2) of the Qualification Directive, which provides that states must consider whether the changes in the country are 'significant and non-temporary' before applying cessation.[110] It is questionable whether this can be demonstrated where the protector is a non-state entity. This is particularly so where the stability of the country conditions are being supported by multinational troops.

In this context, the concept of refugeehood is particularly important once refugee status has been recognised by an asylum state. In this case, the act of recognition leads to a status in international law which gives a refugee certain rights akin to that of nationals of the asylum host state, including employment, education and work rights.[111] Recognition of refugee status therefore leads to a break in the political relationship between refugee and his or her home state. This ties in with my discussion of the acquired rights of asylum seekers and refugees pursuant to Articles 3–34 of the Convention in Chapter 2 of this book where I note that cessation has the effect of withdrawing the acquired rights of a refugee. This supports the central argument of this book that a cessation decision is not merely the opposite or mirror to a recognition decision (that is, absence of persecution) but involves wider considerations relating to effectiveness of protection, such as positive evidence of the provision of human rights and the rule of law in the country of nationality and the absence of armed conflict.

Recognition of non-state bodies as actors of protection also raise concerns where protection is being provided in only a *part* of a country of origin. This raises an interesting issue of comparison with the Internal Flight Alternative (IFA), which in effect allows states to exclude a person from refugee status in situations where that person has a well-founded fear of persecution in relation to a region within their country of origin but can relocate to another area within their country of origin.[112] The use of Article 1C(5) in 'partial protection' situations is of particular concern because cessation does not carry with it the safeguards or humanitarian aspects that have been developed in relation to IFA, such as consideration of the 'reasonableness' of return and the requirement that the applicant not be subject to serious harm in the area of safety.[113] In particular, UNHCR has noted that in a

---

Goodwin-Gill and McAdam, above n 26, 143; M. O'Sullivan, 'Withdrawing Protection under Article 1 C (5) of the 1951 Convention: Lessons from Australia' (2008) 20(4) *International Journal of Refugee Law* 586, 593.

110 EU Qualification Directive, above n 11, Article 11(2).

111 Refugee Convention, above n 3, Articles 3–34.

112 The differences between the criteria for cessation and internal relocation are discussed in further detail in M. O'Sullivan, 'Territorial Protection: Cessation of Refugee Status and Internal Flight Alternative Compared', in S. Juss, *The Ashgate Research Companion to Migration Law, Theory and Policy* (Ashgate, 2013), 209–31.

113 Most jurisdictions recognise that in order for IFA to be found in relation to a particular applicant, it must be 'reasonable' for that applicant to relocate: see e.g. US Asylum Regulation 208.13(b)(1)(i); US Regulations 8 CFR § 208.13(b)(2)(ii).; *Randhawa*, 124 ALR 265, 270 (Black C.J); 280 (Whitlam J). See also UNHCR, *Guidelines on International*

situation of internal armed conflict, which by its nature is volatile, internal relocation should not be applied.[114] In its 2003 Guidelines on IFA, it states:

> In most cases, countries in the grip of armed conflict would not be safe for relocation, especially in the light of shifting armed fronts which could suddenly bring insecurity to an area hitherto considered safe.[115]

In examining comparative law, it is interesting that similarly, US regulations also require decision makers dealing with relocation to consider 'serious harm' and 'ongoing civil strife':

> whether the applicant would face other serious harm in the place of suggested relocation; any ongoing civil strife within the country; administrative, economic, or judicial infrastructure; geographical limitations; and social and cultural constraints such as age, gender, health and social and familial ties.[116]

The reference here to serious harm is of interest, as states have thus far not accepted that risk of serious harm is a separate criterion for consideration as part of the cessation clauses. This is reflected in the decision of the CJEU in *Abdulla*, which held that the criteria for refugee status and complementary protection were completely separate and thus serious harm was not part of the criterion for cessation.[117]

In addition to these specific questions, the link between cessation and IFA raises a broader issue of whether a more consistent approach and holistic interpretation should be taken of 'safety' and 'protection' across international refugee law (including the EU Qualification Directive).[118]

Counterarguments

Although the views of Grahl-Madsen and Shacknove have been endorsed by a number of commentators,[119] these views were expressed some time ago –

Protection: "Internal Flight or Relocation Alternative" Within the Context of Article 1A(2) of the 1951 Convention and/or 1967 Protocol Relating to the Status of Refugees, HCR/GIP/03/03 (2003), [20] (hereinafter UNHCR, IFA Guidelines 2003).

114 UNHCR, 'Note on the Cessation Clauses', UN Doc. EC/47/SC/CRP.30, 30 May 1997, [27].

115 UNHCR, IFA Guidelines 2003, above n 111, [27].

116 US Regulations 8 CFR, § 208.13(b)(3).

117 *Abdulla*, [78]–[79]. See discussion of this aspect of the judgement in Chapter 4 of this book.

118 It is widely recognised that it is necessary to take a holistic interpretation of the whole of the Convention when analysing its constituent articles. See UNHCR, 'The International Protection of Refugees: Interpreting Article 1 of the 1951 Convention Relating to the Status of Refugees' (2001) 20(3) *Refugee Survey Quarterly* 78; and V. Türk and F. Nicholson, 'Refugee Protection in International Law: An Overall Perspective', in Feller et al., above n 75, 42–3.

119 See e.g. Hathaway, *Law of Refugee Status*, above n 78, 125; C. Phuong, *The International Protection of Internally-Displaced Persons* (Cambridge University Press, 2005), 20–2; M.

Grahl-Madsen in 1960 and Shacknove in 1985. Are the arguments still relevant today given the reduction in the power of nation states and the increasing role of non-state actors in some countries?

The theory of refugeehood put forward by Andrew Shacknove, and endorsed by Hathaway, has been questioned by some authors.[120] Aleinikoff, for instance, states that it is odd that the concept of refugee status, which is directly linked to humanitarian concerns, is explained by these authors in membership terms and criticises the state-centred nature of such an analysis.[121] He also argues that the notion of a 'severed social bond' is not an appropriate term given the complexity of societies and social relations[122] and that recognition as a refugee does not demand the showing of such a severed bond.[123] In response, I note that although the Refugee Convention does not explicitly speak of the severance of a social bond, such a framework provides a useful way of explaining the political context of refugeehood – one which can exist alongside the humanitarian considerations to which Aleinikoff refers. Further, although non-state actors are increasingly playing an important role in international relations and international law, it remains the case that *states* are still the main repositories of power over individuals and that the 1951 Refugee Convention is an agreement between *states* and which obliges only *states* to grant protection to those who come within the definition of a 'refugee'. Similarly, I would argue that citizenship remains an important repository of rights.[124] Thus the Grahl-Madsen/Shacknove refugeehood framework remains relevant in analysing the non-state actor of protection debate.

Some may also question the refugeehood approach on the basis that the repugnancy or illegality of a governing body has no relevance to the finding that a

---

Bradley, 'The Conditions of Just Return: State Responsibility and Restitution for Refugees', *University of Oxford Refugee Studies Centre Working Paper Series, RSC Working Paper No. 21*, March 2005, 4, 7–8, 17, <www.rsc.ox.ac.uk/publications/working-papers/RSC-workingpaper21.pdf>; E. Haddad, *The Refugee in International Society: Between Sovereigns* (Cambridge University Press, 2008), 33–4.

120 Haddad, above n 116, 34. Although Haddad endorses Shacknove's approach, she highlights its flaws. Niraj Nathwani criticises Grahl-Madsen's bond theory on the basis that it can lead to questionable results in practice, namely in relation to obtaining the benefits of nationality under cessation: see N. Nathwani, *Rethinking Refugee Law* (Martinus Nijhoff, 2003), 14.

121 T.A. Aleinikoff, 'State Centred Refugee Law: From Resettlement to Containment' (1992–1993) 14 *Michigan Journal of International Law*, 120, 123, footnote 14.

122 Ibid 123, footnote 14.

123 Aleinikoff acknowledges that '[a]lthough refugee status is grounded in the idea of loss of membership, refugee law does not guarantee attainment of membership elsewhere': 124. He later says: 'If refugee status constitutes dissolution of "social bonds," then unmaking refugees demands the creation or reestablishment of "social bonds" – either in the country of origin or elsewhere. In short, a durable solution repairs the tear in the state system fabric by ensuring that no individual lacks membership in some state' (Ibid 125).

124 Indeed, lack of citizenship is reflected in the significant numbers of stateless persons worldwide. UNHCR estimates that approximately 10 million people were stateless around the world in 2016 (although exact numbers are not known): UNHCR, *Global Trends in Forced Displacement 2016*, June 2017, <www.unhcr.org/globaltrends2016/>.

person has a well-founded fear of persecution under the Refugee Convention. As noted earlier, Grahl-Madsen makes a valid point in underlining the political nature of refugeehood and the importance of the re-establishment of the bond between citizen and state. However, it is true that some caution must be exercised in stating that refugeehood may arise where a person is required to make a political submission to a government the citizen finds 'repugnant' or 'illegal'. A person's view as to the 'repugnancy' or otherwise of a government does not lead to a finding that the individual has a well-founded fear of persecution on Convention grounds. However, it may be of relevance to the stability of the protection provided by non-state actors. Indeed, a number of leading political scientists have recognised that the legitimacy of governing bodies has an important bearing on political stability in post-conflict societies.[125] Thus, arguably the political legitimacy of a non-state actor is a relevant factor in relation to protection, as it is likely to greatly influence the stability of conditions in a refugee's country of nationality. This will be particularly relevant to decisions involving cessation of refugee status under Article 1C(5) of the Refugee Convention, which is widely recognised as requiring stability and durability of country conditions. It also supports the classification of protection as involving a political element, rather than merely territorial in nature.

Further, some may point to the developments in the broader school of international law to expand the legal accountability of non-state actors[126] as reason for also taking a broad interpretation of protection under international refugee law. However, the debate over non-state actors under international law has been focused primarily on the lack of international legal accountability. Whilst accountability is an important factor, and one which provides further argument against reliance on non-state actors for refugee protection purposes, the non-state actor debate under international *refugee* law raises different considerations. This is particularly so given that the act of returning a refugee to a country protected by non-state actors may breach the prohibition against *refoulement*.[127] The issue at stake is not simply one of the international legal personality of the relevant non-state body but whether it can be said that, due to the 'protection' offered by that

125 On the issue of the link between legitimacy of governments and failed/weak states, see R. Rotberg, 'The New Nature of Nation-State Failure' (2002) 25(3) *The Washington Quarterly* 85, 85; and L. Diamond, 'Promoting Democracy in Post-Conflict and Failed States: Lessons and Challenges', *National Policy Forum on Terrorism, Security and America's Purpose*, 6–7 September 2005, Washington DC, 19, 24–25. See also M. Saul, 'Local Ownership of Post-Conflict Reconstruction in International Law: The Initiation of International Involvement' (2011) 16(1) *Journal of Conflict and Security Law* 165.

126 See e.g. J.E. Nihman, 'Non-State Actors and the International Rule of Law: Revisiting the "Realist Theory" of International Legal Personality', in C. Ryngaert, *Non-State Actor Dynamics in International Law: From Law-Takers to Law-Makers* (Routledge, 2010). Nihman argues, amongst other things, that the international rule of law would benefit from the reconstitution of non-state actors as legal persons.

127 Under Article 33 of the Refugee Convention (above n 4), states parties are prohibited from returning a refugee to territories where his or her life or freedom would be threatened for a Convention reason.

body, a person who fears persecution in their home country does not face a 'well-founded' fear and is not a refugee. That is, expansion of the concept of 'protection' in this way affects the entitlement of an individual to refugee status. In the context of international refugee law, then, extreme caution must be exercised in expanding 'protection' to encompass non-state actors. There are a number of reasons why non-state actors may not be able to protect citizens in the same way as states: clans and militias are typically more vulnerable to overthrow by opposing clans and militias, and non-state bodies usually operate as 'protectors' when the state has failed or there is ongoing civil war within a country. In such situations, a non-state actor may have only a tenuous hold of power.

Another criticism which may be raised against my approach is that it is necessary to take a pragmatic approach to the issue of non-state actors of protection.[128] My answer to this is that I agree that the 1951 Convention must continue to provide a suitable legal framework for addressing contemporary refugee problems. Thus, as stated previously, I recognise that in light of the modern practice of humanitarian intervention by the UN, it is arguable that certain international organisations, such as the United Nations, *may* provide such protection, if they are acting as a *stable, state-like authority*, are supported by an international mandate and are acting in an agency relationship, that is, in place of a 'failed state' or with the consent of the government in question.[129] However, these are strict requirements which will not normally be met by non-state actors such as multinational forces, clans and militias.

Finally, leading UK judge and academic commentator Hugo Storey has argued that we should not base definition of a state for refugee law purposes on a narrow liberal democratic model of political community.[130] In particular, he contends that:

> Attempts by certain commentators to reject the potential viability of protection being afforded by international organizations or (in certain limited circumstances) majority clans remain unconvincing, featuring as they do contradictory reliance on notions of State accountability rejected in other contexts, and equivocal and unjustified deviation from the principle of refugee protection as surrogate protection, which in essence is based on a factual or functional approach.[131]

128 See the UK Asylum and Immigration Tribunal in *SF Iraq* [13]: 'there are cogent reasons for taking a pragmatic or functional approach according to which the issue of whether a de facto entity could afford Refugee Convention protection is essentially a question of fact'.

129 Similar arguments have been made by a member of the UK House of Lords, Lord Plant of Highfield, Minutes of Evidence, House of Lords Select Committee, above n 19, 11.

130 H. Storey, 'The Meaning of "Protection" Within the Refugee Definition' (2016) 35(3) *Refugee Survey Quarterly* 1, 32–34. See also H. Storey in J.C. Hathaway and H. Storey, 'What Is the Meaning of State Protection in Refugee Law? A Debate' (2016) 28(3) *International Journal of Refugee Law* 480, 484; H. Storey, 'The Law of Refugee Status, 2nd edition: Paradigm Lost?' (2015) 27(2) *International Journal of Refugee Law* 348, 360.

131 J.C. Hathaway and H. Storey, 'What Is the Meaning of State Protection in Refugee Law? A Debate' (2016) 28(3) *International Journal of Refugee Law* 480, 482.

Storey argues that the 'frequent tendency' of commentators to take a very narrow approach to state protection agencies (such as police, army and security forces) must be rejected. He notes that actors of the state can also include 'acts of the legislature and judiciary; and can extend further in certain circumstances to include acts done by private individuals or groups acting under the control or direction of organs or entities empowered to exercise governmental authority'.[132]

I agree with Hugo Storey that there is nothing in Article 1A(2) which prescribes how the overall assessment of the level of protection is to be determined. I also agree that the interpretation of state protection should encompass not only the machinery of government but also a system of legal norms and a political community. Thus, obviously the acts of the judiciary and legislature are relevant in considerations as to the adequacy of state protection. However, Storey also argues that protection is a 'composite notion' and, as such, can encompass:

- Situations where organs or entities of the State machinery other than the police, army and security personnel (for example, the social services of a State) carry out protective functions, directly or indirectly;
- Situations where private individuals or groups act under the control or direction of organs or entities empowered to exercise governmental authority;
- Situations where the government is supported by international organisations or personnel from a friendly State or States.[133]

Storey argues that 'if civil society bodies like families, community associations, tribes, clans, or women's shelters and so forth serve to reduce the need for State actors to actively take protective steps' then effective and durable protection will be provided and the state has shown that it is both able and willing to achieve that.[134] In response to these statements, James Hathaway has acknowledged that state protection does not have to be *directly* provided by traditional state agencies (such as police, army and so forth). As such, Hathaway notes that 'an assessment of protection may reasonably include *contracted-out mechanisms of protection*, which are genuinely accessible and for which the State remains fully accountable'.[135] Therefore, he agrees that these mechanisms

> might include, for example, sub-national authorities, tribal or ethnic governments, civil society contractees, and so forth. The relevant question is always, however, whether the national government – acting directly and/or indirectly – is, or is not able, to afford protection.[136]

My perspective on these debates is that much depends on whether one takes a conceptual or merely functional approach to protection. I believe that a practical,

132 Ibid 483.
133 Ibid.
134 Ibid 489.
135 Ibid 486 [emphasis in original].
136 Ibid 486.

contextual approach should be taken to the meaning of protection to ensure that refugee law is fit for purpose. That is does, in fact, work in practice. I also concede that taking a very 'statist' approach to protection reflects western liberal democratic values of the centrality of state institutions that may not be relevant in other political contexts. This point is illustrated by reports on civil society in Afghanistan, which note the importance of civil society in the governing of that country:

> In the case of Afghanistan, the absence of formal state institutions beyond district headquarters, both historically and in the contemporary context, has often led to a *dual role for civil society actors* in local settings, as they have taken a governing role in terms of decision-making and resource distribution, and a civil society role in terms of bridging the voices of their local constituents to the state and other institutions outside their communities. Consequently, the defining lines between the *civil society and government appear to be blurred.*[137]

Thus, I agree that regard must be had to local cultural norms around the reliance on civil society and other groups (such as clans). To fail to accept the protection of clans may be seen as being too narrowly focused on a 'western' paradigm and failing to take account of other notions of community. However, I would point out that going beyond functionality, one must also consider conceptual issues. That is, whilst acts done by non-governmental organisations may provide a protective function, they do not have the durability or legitimacy of the state.

At the heart of this debate is the very complex question of what is the purpose of a state? An in-depth examination of this question is well beyond the scope of this chapter. However, if we say that the role of a state is merely a *functional* one – to provide services to its inhabitants – then perhaps the functional approach is sufficient. But if we accept that states do *more than this* (and should do more than this), then perhaps one also has to look at the concept of a state and what it offers to *democratic cohesion* in a country.

Civil society[138] is a typically fractured protective agent. If we focus specifically on NGOs as part of civil society, I would point out that the influence of such bodies is very limited: they do not have control over the whole of a state, or

137 Afghanistan Research and Evaluation Unit (AREU), *The Role of Civil Society in Promoting Good Governance in Afghanistan*, July 2016, 5, <www.refworld.org/docid/57d93f264.html> (emphasis added).

138 Defined for these purposes to include local civil society organisations (not international bodies such as the UN); media, local organisations (such as voluntary associations). As Alice Nah has pointed out, 'local civil society actors are also different operationally and structurally from UNHCR and INGOs. Often formed and run by very committed, independent-minded, strong-willed leaders, they tend to be smaller and have fewer resources than their international and regional counterparts. They often struggle to meet overwhelming needs and to keep programmes viable in the face of scarce financial resources': A.M. Nah, 'Networks and Norm Entrepreneurship Amongst Local Civil Society Actors: Advancing Refugee Protection in the Asia Pacific Region' (2016) 20(2) *The International Journal of Human Rights* 223, 231.

perhaps even part of a state. This leads into the problem that the protection will be partial. Partial protection may be acceptable under Article 1A(2) under which internal relocation is permitted. However, for the reasons outlined in the previous chapter, I argue that relocation should not be a factor in relation to cessation. That is, that partial cessation of circumstances in the country of origin is not sufficient to satisfy Article 1C(5). Following on from this, I would also underline the need to consider the very particular exigencies and fragilities which exist in *post-conflict situations*. Here, the legitimacy of the non-state actor is relevant in terms of the acceptability of that actor to the people it is said to protect and also the likelihood that any change of circumstances will be stable and durable. As Karavias notes:

> the operation of an actor within the territory of the State without that State's consent, as is the case in the civil war context, may translate into a situation of tension, or – even worse – of hostilities between the two parties.[139]

Further, if there is a finding that a particular state is supported by civil society in the provision of fundamental services to inhabitants then it indicates there is a *structural problem* within that state. That fundamental structural problem must be considered as a conceptual matter in any assessment of the durability of that protection.

Civil society is also limited in its influence of the state which it may be seen as 'supporting'. It is rare that a civil society organisation will have central control of what happens in an entire country. Further, they are often viewed as a counterbalance or check on the state. Importantly, civil society is bound to comply with the laws of the state as are individual citizens and cannot directly change the laws. Their authority is therefore more likely to come under threat. Civil society organisations are often the target of state repression and attacks.[140] These factors should be considered in the legal and functional interpretation to be given to them for the purposes of refugee protection.

In addressing the question of whether a purely functional interpretation of protection is acceptable, the work of Robert Rotberg on failed states is instructive. Rotberg emphasises that citizens of states 'inform the local political culture, and together give content to the social contract between ruler and ruled that is at the core of regime/government and citizenry interactions'.[141] The danger

139 M. Karavias, 'Non-State Actors in Control of Territory as "Actors of Protection" in International Refugee Law' (2014) 2 *Revue Belge De Droit International* 487, 507.

140 See, for instance, in Afghanistan: 'Civil society activists [. . .] risk violence from Anti-Government Elements and Afghan national security forces due to the nature of their work and sometimes their influential role in society'. UNAMA, Afghanistan: Annual Report on the Protection of Civilians in Armed Conflict 2016, February 2017, 32, <www.refworld.org/docid/58bd20104.html>; Amnesty International, 'Human Rights Defenders under Threat: A Shrinking Space for Civil Society', 16 May 2017, 36, <www.refworld.org/docid/5a7db6494.html>.

141 R. Rotberg, 'Failed States, Collapsed States, Weak States: Causes and Indicators', in R. Rotberg, *State Failure and State Weakness in a Time of Terror* (World Peace Foundation; Brookings Institution Press, 2003), 3, <www.wilsoncenter.org/sites/default/files/statefailureandstateweaknessinatimeofterror.pdf>.

in giving a purely functional interpretation to protection is that obfuscates this important political relationship.

Moreover, whilst protection by clans might form a functional protection role, there is a danger that this will lead to disparate groups providing differentiated levels of protection and the related danger that bodies such as clans and militias will conflict with each other in the absence of strong centralisation. This can lead citizens to turn more to sectional and community loyalties,[142] which may lead to political instability and further conflict between groups.

Ultimately, the core dispute is whether protection is merely a functional good or a political good. For the reasons discussed throughout this chapter, it is my contention that it is both, and thus, assessment of protection must not therefore merely be based on functionality.

Conclusions

Recognition of non-state actors of protection, such as provided in Article 7 of the Qualification Directive, reflects a pragmatic approach to international refugee law, under which the primary focus is whether protection can be provided as a question of fact, whether that be by a state or non-state entity.

Although international refugee law must be interpreted in a dynamic fashion, taking account of the changing nature of humanitarian intervention by the UN and other bodies, along with international legal developments relating to non-state actors, any such interpretation must advance the protection provided by the 1951 Refugee Convention. In my opinion, the extension of protection to include non-state actors does not achieve this purpose and, in fact, may result in return of refugees to situations of precarious security and the real chance of persecution. This is particularly so in cessation cases where persecution of an individual (via recognition of refugee status) has already shown to have occurred and the asylum host state is attempting to return the refugee to that country of origin based on an alleged change in circumstances. The presence of non-state actors, such as multinational troops, which have a finite existence in asylum states, is not likely to lead to the stability and durability of change in country conditions which is required for cessation.

The implications of an overly wide interpretation of actors of protection such as that set out in Article 7 of the Qualification Directive is that if protection is provided by a temporary, transitional non-state entity, there is a risk that refugees will be returned to a country where they will be at risk of persecution contrary to the principle of *non-refoulement*.[143] This is particularly so in relation to clans and militias who have obtained political control of a certain part of a state – such political control and the provision of security to individuals should not be equated with the high level of 'protection' required for the purposes of international refugee law. Likewise, the presence of multinational troops should not be viewed as providing such protection, particularly where there is an ongoing

142 Ibid 9.
143 Refugee Convention, above n 3, Article 33.

armed conflict occurring within the state in question (such as Iraq and Afghanistan). Thus, a broad interpretation of non-state actors which includes 'parties' and 'international organizations', such as set out in Article 7(1) of the EU Qualification Directive, is not justifiable on a principled level, nor advisable in practice.

As a result, I argue that Article 7 of the Qualification Directive is inconsistent with the 1951 Refugee Convention and should be amended to limit the remit of non-state actors to international organisations with established mandates and who have state-like functions. It should not be utilised to recognise non-state actors of protection in cessation decisions. Although the 2011 Recast Qualification Directive made certain improvements to the provisions of Article 7 in relation to ability and willingness to protect, it is the submission of this book that these changes are not adequate to remedy the risks inherent in recognising non-state actors as actors of protection for the purposes of international refugee law.

To date, the jurisprudence on this issue has focused on the ability of the non-state actor to provide protection, its level of control over territory or the existence of international legal accountability. However, the debate about non-state actors (both for the purpose of recognition and cessation of refugee status) must be re-conceptualised and a new approach taken to the issue which builds on the framework set out by Grahl-Madsen and Shacknove on the theoretical underpinnings of refugeehood. Due to the nature of refugeehood as involving the relationship between the individual and state, the mere fact that a body or group may be *able* to provide protection in a region or country is not sufficient to constitute 'protection' under the Refugee Convention. We must also consider notions of legitimacy and durability of presence. Moreover, the political imperative to return refugees to countries such as Iraq and Afghanistan cannot override the words of the Convention (as interpreted purposively). That means only states and state-like bodies can provide 'protection' under refugee law. Thus, the fact of protection is not the only consideration under the Convention; the *nature* of the body, its attributes, power and link to the country in question must also be considered. As I have discussed in this chapter, refugeehood is a political relationship, not simply a geographical one.

The push towards a broad interpretation of non-state actors, as seen in Article 7 of the EU Qualification Directive, is also indicative of a wider trend in international law to recognise the international legal rights and obligations of non-state actors. The debate in international refugee law is different in that this does not simply raise the question of attributing legal personality to a non-state actor. Rather, it raises the far more complex question as to whether non-state actors are capable in principle of protecting individuals against persecution in the same way that a state can. This involves broader questions of nationality, allegiance and the role of the state.

Any change to international refugee law must be both sustainable in theory and reflect contemporary practice. I have provided a theoretical model for extending the concept of protection to non-state actors, which I submit reflects both a principled and pragmatic approach to the area, and one which advances the core purpose of the Convention – the protection of refugees.

6 Onus of proof, past persecution and the compelling reasons exception to cessation

Introduction

One question which has arisen in jurisprudence on cessation is what onus of proof should apply to decisions under Article 1C(5) of the 1951 Refugee Convention.[1] This procedural question is important, given the seriousness of revoking an individual's refugee status and exposing them to return to their country of origin. As noted in Chapter 4, many states agree that the burden of proof in cessation cases should be on the state and that the standard of proof is one of 'fundamental, stable and durable' change,[2] or variants on those criteria.[3] However, some jurisdictions, notably Australia, have not endorsed these procedural requirements.[4] This chapter examines this in greater depth by examining the relevance of past persecution to cessation and, in particular, the so-called compelling reasons exception to Article 1C(5).

Debates about the applicable burden of proof in cessation cases are obviously linked closely with the question of whether cessation is the mirror of the recognition decision in Article 1A(2). Indeed, the relationship between these two clauses in the Convention is a theme that threads through many of the other key interpretative questions about cessation.

1 Convention Relating to the Status of Refugees, 28 July 1951, 189 U.N.T.S. 150 (hereinafter Refugee Convention).

2 UNHCR ExCom, Conclusion No. 69, *Cessation of Status*, U.N. GAOR, 47th Sess. (1992), [b]; UNHCR, *Handbook on Procedures and Criteria for Determining Refugee Status under the 1951 Convention and the 1967 Protocol Relating to the Status of Refugees*, HCR/IP/4/Rev.1, 1979, Reedited, Geneva, January 1992, [135] (hereinafter UNHCR *Handbook*); G. Goodwin-Gill and J. McAdam, *The Refugee in International Law* (Oxford University Press, 3rd ed., 2007), 142–3; J.C. Hathaway, *The Rights of Refugees under International Law* (Cambridge University Press, 2005), 922–35.

3 The EU Qualification Directive sets out slightly different wording: *Directive 2011/95/EU of the European Parliament and of the Council of 13 December 2011 on Standards for the Qualification of Third-Country Nationals or Stateless Persons as Beneficiaries of International Protection, for a Uniform Status for Refugees or for Persons Eligible for Subsidiary Protection, and for the Content of the Protection Granted (Recast)*, [2011] OJ L 337/9, Article 11(2) and Article 14 (hereinafter 2011 Qualification Directive).

4 *Minister for Immigration and Multicultural Affairs v QAAH of 2004*, [2006] HCA 53 (*QAAH*).

Here the link between past persecution and cessation raises complex legal issues. It is generally accepted that the refugee definition under Article 1A(2) involves an assessment of ***prospective*** risk of persecution.[5] Thus, it is not necessary for applicants to demonstrate that they have already been persecuted in their home country in order to be granted refugee status. However, evidence of past persecution may be considered as indicative of any future risk of harm. Indeed, some jurisdictions establish a type of a 'presumption' of a current well-founded fear of persecution where there has been past persecution.[6] The question raised by this is as follows: if a particular jurisdiction sets out a 'presumption' of a well-founded fear where there has been past persecution for ***recognition*** cases, can refugees also avail themselves of this in ***cessation*** cases?

In the European Union (EU), this issue is dealt with by the presence of what is known as a 'facilitated standard of proof'[7] for past persecution set out in Article 4(4) of the EU Qualification Directive.[8] Article 4(4) provides that where past persecution is shown to have been experienced by a refugee, this is a 'serious indication' of the applicant's well-founded fear of persecution.[9] The presence of Article 4(4) in the Qualification Directive raises a number of legal questions. For instance, how should Article 4(4) apply to cessation decisions where an applicant claims that they fear persecution for reasons which are ***different from***, or only ***partially linked to***, the reasons that gave rise to the original decision to grant him or her refugee status?

To date, this question has not been addressed in the academic literature on refugee law. For instance, Article 4(4) of the EU Qualification Directive has not yet been analysed in any great depth in refugee law literature, with only a very small number of papers having been written on the issue to date.[10] Article 4(4)

5 See e.g. House of Lords in *Adan v Secretary of State for the Home Department*, [1999] 1 AC 293, 306 (Lloyd LJ); J.C. Hathaway and M. Foster, *The Law of Refugee Status* (Cambridge University Press, 2nd ed., 2014), 162.

6 The term 'presumption' has been used by the German Federal Administrative Court to describe Article 4(4) of the EU Qualification Directive: see e.g. *BVerwG 10 C 21.08*, VGH 3 UE 460/06.A, 5 May 2009, [8]. The term 'presumption' is also commonly used to refer to the use of past persecution under US law: see T. McIlmail, 'Toward a More Reasonably Rebutted Presumption: A Proposal to Amend the Past Persecution Asylum Regulation – 8 C.F.R. 208.13(B)(1)' (1997–1998) 12 *Georgetown Immigration Law Journal* 265.

7 The term 'facilitated' standard of proof is used by the German Federal Administrative Court: see e.g. *BVerwG 10 C 4.09*, VGH 8 A 611/08.A, 27 April 2010, [9], [21]; and *BVerwG 10 C 21.08*, VGH 3 UE 460/06.A, 5 May 2009, [1], [19], [24]–[25].

8 2011 EU Qualification Directive, above n 3, Article 4(4).

9 Ibid: 'The fact that an applicant has already been subject to persecution or serious harm or to direct threats of such persecution or such harm, is a serious indication of the applicant's well-founded fear of persecution or real risk of suffering serious harm, unless there are good reasons to consider that such persecution or serious harm will not be repeated'.

10 There are only a handful of academic papers which discuss Article 4(4) in any detail. These include G. Noll, 'Evidentiary Assessment and the EU Qualification Directive', *UNHCR New Issues in Refugee Research, Working Paper No. 117*, 2005, 11–12. Although there are a number of US journal articles which analyse the past persecution presumption under US law, the only journal article to have addressed the issue of past persecution and cessation in the

and the way in which it interacts with *cessation*, therefore, requires analysis. This chapter attempts to analyse some of these emerging legal questions. It will do so by focusing on case studies from Germany and the Court of Justice of the European Union (CJEU).

Further, this chapter addresses the humanitarian aspect of past persecution via applicability of the 'compelling reasons' proviso to cessation under Article 1C(5). This sets out an exception to cessation where there are compelling reasons arising out of past persecution. According to the wording of Article 1C(5), this proviso only applies to *statutory* refugees defined in Article 1A(1), rather than *1951 Convention* refugees defined under Article 1A(2). In this section I examine an issue which is contested amongst refugee law scholars: whether that 'exception' to Article 1C(5) should be extended beyond its literal words to *all* Convention refugees.

The onus of proof for Article 1C(5) cessation

There is broad agreement amongst states, UNHCR and academics that the onus of proof in cessation decisions is on the state seeking to apply those provisions. That is, the state authorities bear the onus of demonstrating that circumstances in the refugee's country of origin have changed.[11] Article 14(2) of the EU Qualification Directive also provides that it is the EU Member State which must demonstrate that cessation has occurred:

> Without prejudice to the duty of the refugee in accordance with Article 4(1) to disclose all relevant facts and provide all relevant documentation at his or her disposal, the Member State which has granted refugee status shall, on an individual basis, demonstrate that the person concerned has ceased to be or has never been a refugee in accordance with paragraph 1 of this Article.[12]

This is echoed in the national laws of some EU Member States. For instance, jurisprudence and policy statements from the UK appear to support the placement of the burden on the relevant decision maker in relation to Article 1C(5) decisions.[13]

EU is R. Errera, 'Cessation and Assessment of New Circumstances: A Comment on *Abdulla*, CJEU, 2 March 2010' (2011) 23(3) *International Journal of Refugee Law* 521.

11 US Immigration and Nationality Act 1952 (as amended), 8 USC 1158, § 208 (c)(2)(A) § 208(c)(2)(d); Immigration and Refugee Protection Act 2001, Canada, s 108(1); UNHCR, 'The International Protection of Refugees: Interpreting Article 1 of the 1951 Convention Relating to the Status of Refugees', April 2001, [10]; UNHCR Lisbon Roundtable Meeting of Experts, Summary Conclusions, May 2001, published in E. Feller et al. (eds.), *Refugee Protection in International Law: UNHCR's Global Consultations on International Protection* (Cambridge University Press, 2003), 550; Goodwin-Gill and McAdam, above n 2, 143; J. Fitzpatrick and R. Bonoan, 'Cessation of Refugee Protection', Chapter 8 in E. Feller et al. (eds.), *Refugee Protection in International Law: UNHCR's Global Consultations on International Protection* (Cambridge University Press, 2003), 544.

12 2011 Qualification Directive, above n 3, Article 14(2).

13 UK Home Office, *Asylum Policy Instruction: Revocation of Refugee Status (Version 4.0 19)*, January 2016, 15; *Arif v Secretary of State for the Home Department*, [1999] INLR 327,

However, the Australian High Court has departed from this international position. In the leading case of *QAAH*, the High Court of Australia held that it was incorrect to say that there is an 'onus' upon the relevant decision maker to establish the existence of an effective, substantial and durable change. That is, the reasoning of the majority of the High Court was that the placing of such an onus and standard of proof was inconsistent with the nature of the Refugee Review Tribunal (RRT) as an inquisitorial body.[14] Thus, to some extent, the Australian jurisprudence may be explainable due to the nature of the relevant tribunal under examination in that case.

The relevance of past persecution to cessation

As noted earlier, it is generally accepted that the test for well-founded fear of persecution involves a forward-looking assessment. However, it is not yet clear how this relates to new claims of persecution made as part of a cessation decision-making procedure. In particular:

- Does the fact that past persecution occurred have evidentiary value in assessing any new claims of persecution, even if the link to the past persecution is only partial?
- If the 'new' claims of persecution are linked, even partially, to the reasons for which the refugee was first recognised as a refugee, is the proper test one of cessation under Article 1C(5) under which the state in question must demonstrate that the refugee does not have a well-founded fear of persecution?
- Moreover, where a refugee relies on entirely new, different circumstances of persecution, should the person be treated as making a new application for refugee status and be assessed under Article 1A(2) of the Refugee Convention?

In this part of the chapter, I focus on two case studies: US state practice and EU jurisprudence, particularly on the interpretation of Article 4(4) of the EU Qualification Directive. These examples illustrate the legal complexities arising from the interaction between past persecution and cessation. In order to answer these questions, it is necessary to examine one of the first major international cases which established this presumption: the decision of the US Board of Immigration Appeals (BIA) in the 1989 case of *Chen*, and subsequent legislation and case

---

331; *Fadilt Dyli v The Secretary of State for the Home Department*, [2000] UKIAT 00001 (UK Immigration Appeal Tribunal); *In re B (FC) (Appellant) (2002) Regina v Special Adjudicator Ex parte Hoxha (FC)* [2005] 1 W.L.R. 1063, [66] (*Hoxha*, House of Lords); *The Secretary of State for the Home Department v MM (Zimbabwe)*, 22 June 2017 [2017] EWCA Civ 797, [36]; Upper Tribunal (Immigration and Asylum Chamber), UK, *Appeal RP/00068/2017*, [13], <https://tribunalsdecisions.service.gov.uk/utiac/rp-00068-2017>; Upper Tribunal (Immigration and Asylum Chamber), UK, *Appeal RP/00077/2016*, [17], <https://tribunalsdecisions.service.gov.uk/utiac/rp-00077-2016>.

14 *QAAH* [40].

law in the United States.[15] Although there are differences between the past persecution provisions in EU and US law, discussion of the US past presumption is instructive, as there is very little indication of the underlying rationale for Article 4(4) in EU jurisprudence, commentary or other material. A discussion of the US approach also illustrates some of the problems arising from adjudicating upon the connection to be proven between past and future persecution.

The development of past persecution presumption – the United States

The notion that past persecution can give rise to an evidentiary presumption of a well-founded fear of persecution was established in the US Board of Immigration Appeals (BIA) decision in *Chen*. In that case, the BIA held that a 'rebuttable presumption arises that an alien who has been persecuted in the past by his country's government has reason to fear *similar* persecution in the future'.[16] The use of the word 'similar' by the BIA here is important, as one of the questions about the element of past persecution in cessation cases is whether the past persecution must be *connected* to the new claims of persecution. In particular, is the *fact* that persecution has taken place sufficient to raise the presumption? Alternatively, must the *reason* for the claimed future persecution be the same or at least similar to that of the past persecution suffered?

The facts of *Chen* are important in understanding the possible answers to these questions: The applicant claimed that both he and his family were persecuted in China during the so-called Cultural Revolution, from approximately 1966 through the mid-1970s. The applicant claimed to have been sent for 're-education' on a number of occasions in the 1970s and to have suffered other ill-treatment during this period. The board found that it was 'beyond dispute that the respondent has in fact suffered persecution in China'.[17] However, it held that, since the time of the Cultural Revolution, conditions in China have changed significantly and therefore it was 'not persuaded by the evidence presented that a reasonable person in the respondent's circumstances would have a well-founded fear of persecution on account of his religion, if returned to the China of 1989'.[18] It therefore held that the applicant had not met his burden of establishing a well-founded fear of persecution. The board then held that the applicant was eligible for asylum under Ministerial discretion because the chance of persecution based on the applicant's religion had not been totally eliminated:

> While conditions in China have changed since the time the respondent was persecuted, the basic form of government there has not changed, human

15 *Matter of Chen*, United States Board of Immigration Appeals, 25 April 1989, 20 I. & N. Dec, 16.

16 *Chen*, 18 (emphasis added).

17 Ibid 20

18 Ibid 21.

> rights are still sometimes abused, and there is little religious freedom. The respondent is closely identified with a religious family. While he may not have a 'well-founded fear' of future persecution in China, we do not think that all chance of persecution on account of his religion has been eliminated by the change in regime since the Cultural Revolution. Moreover, it is evident that the respondent still genuinely fears returning to China.[19]

The approach in *Chen* was codified in US Code 8 CFR § 208.13(b)(1), which provides for two bases for asylum: either where the applicant has a well-founded fear of future persecution, or where the applicant has suffered actual past persecution.[20] Specifically, US Code 8 CFR § 208.13(b)(1) provides that an applicant shall be found to be a refugee on the basis of past persecution if:

> the applicant can establish that he or she has suffered persecution in the past in the applicant's country of nationality . . . on account of race, religion, nationality, membership in a particular social group, or political opinion, and is unable or unwilling to return to, or avail himself or herself of the protection of, that country owing to *such persecution*. An applicant who has been found to have established such past persecution shall also be presumed to have a well-founded fear of persecution on the basis of the original claim. That presumption may be rebutted if an asylum officer or immigration judge makes one of the findings described in paragraph (b)(1)(i) of this section.

US Code 8 CFR § 208.13(b)(1) also specifically provides that '[i]f the applicant's fear of future persecution is *unrelated* to the past persecution, the applicant bears the burden of establishing that the fear is well-founded'.[21]

There are two bases upon which the past persecution presumption can be rebutted under US legislation: first, where there has been a fundamental change of circumstances,[22] and, second, where the applicant could avoid persecution by relocating to another part of their country of nationality.[23] However, if a refugee falls within these two grounds, they may nevertheless be able to obtain asylum as a result of the exercise of the decision maker's discretion under US Code § 208.13(b)(1)(iii). This can be where: the applicant demonstrates 'compelling

19 Ibid.

20 8 CFR, § 208.13(b)(1).

21 8 CFR, § 208.13(b)(1) (emphasis added).

22 8 CFR, § 208.13(b)(1)(ii), which states that where an applicant can demonstrate past persecution, the decision maker bears the evidential burden of establishing by a 'preponderance of the evidence' that there has been a relevant change in circumstances.

23 8 CFR, § 208.13(b)(1)(i) provides that a decision-maker may exercise a discretion to deny asylum granted on the basis of past persecution where 'it is found, by a preponderance of evidence that there has been a fundamental change in circumstances such that the applicant no longer has a well-founded fear of persecution in the applicant's country of nationality for a Convention reason; or if the applicant could avoid future persecution by relocating to another part of the applicant's country of nationality'.

reasons for being unwilling or unable to return to the country arising out of the severity of the past persecution'; or the applicant 'has established that there is a reasonable possibility that he or she may suffer other serious harm upon removal to that country'.[24]

A number of decisions of the BIA have taken a strict view of the requisite link between past and present persecution. In the BIA case of *In re N-M-A*, decided in 1998, the board held that the evidentiary presumption in § 208.13 is extinguished by changed conditions in the country of origin which show that the particular threat which led to the past harm no longer exists.[25] In doing so, it focused on establishing that the claim of future persecution is from the *same source* as that of the past persecution. Thus, it found that:

> once an applicant has demonstrated that he has suffered past persecution on account of a statutorily protected ground, and the record reflects that country conditions have changed to such an extent that the applicant no longer has a well-founded fear of persecution from his *original persecutors*, the applicant bears the burden of demonstrating that he has a well-founded fear of persecution from any new source.[26]

The board indicated that the presumption would not apply to persecution which arose from circumstances 'substantially different' from those claimed in any current proceedings.[27] Thus after *In re N-M-A*, it was understood that US authorities could rebut a presumption of well-foundedness arising from past persecution by demonstrating that the applicant's previous persecutor no longer posed a continuing threat.

After *In re N-M-A*, there was a series of asylum cases involving applicants who had been subjected to Forced Genital Mutilation (FGM), which gave rise to divergent opinions in the US courts. In these cases, the evidentiary link between past and future persecution was contested. In a controversial decision of the BIA in 2007, *In re A-T*, the Board held that there had to be a risk of *identical* persecution in order for an applicant to obtain the benefit of the past persecution presumption in §208.13.[28] Controversially, it held that because female genital mutilation is a type of harm that generally is inflicted only once, the procedure itself will normally constitute a 'fundamental change in circumstances' such that an asylum applicant no longer has a well-founded fear of persecution based on the fear that she will again be subjected to FGM.[29] However, the next year, the US Court of Appeals Second Circuit in *Bah v. Mukasey*, disagreed with this

24 8 CFR, § 208.13(b)(1)(iii).
25 *In re N-M-A*, US Board of Immigration Appeals, Interim Decision No. 3368, 21 October, 1998, 313.
26 Ibid (emphasis added).
27 Ibid 320.
28 *In re A-T*, 24 I. & N. Dec. 296 (BIA 2007) (*In re A-T, BIA*).
29 Ibid 299.

approach, finding that there was nothing in § 208.13 which suggests that 'the future threats to life or freedom must come in the same *form* or be the same *act* as the past persecution'.[30] It noted that: '[w]e have never held that a petitioner must fear the repetition of the exact harm that she has suffered in the past. Our definition of persecution is not that narrow'.[31]

UNHCR has endorsed this approach, stating in its Guidelines on FGM that:

> there is no requirement that the future persecution feared should take an identical form to the one previously endured, as long as it can be linked to a Convention ground.[32]

Subsequently, the BIA's finding on past persecution in *In re A-T* was vacated by the US Attorney General in September 2008, so that case no longer controls future BIA deliberations.[33] The Attorney General took a similar approach to that of the Second Circuit of the US Court of Appeals in *Bah*, finding that the BIA was wrong in focusing on whether the applicant would suffer 'identical' future harm.[34] The Attorney General noted that the appropriate focus of the inquiry is whether future harm would be carried out 'on account of the *same statutory ground*', that is, whether harm would be inflicted on account of the applicant's particular social group.[35] This is of interest, as the UNHCR Guidelines on FGM require only a link to *a* Convention ground, not the *same* Convention ground upon which past persecution took place.[36] That is, UNHCR does not appear to require that the new claim of persecution be linked to the *same Convention ground* as that which applied to the past persecution. This is significant, as this link is the approach suggested in the US Attorney General's decision in *In re A-T*.[37] Thus, although the Attorney General's decision in *In re A-T* is wider than that of the original BIA's decision, it is strongly arguable that it is still too narrow and should be widened to include any future persecution linked to the past persecution, whether referable to the same Convention ground or not.

The approach taken in the US to past persecution has been criticised by some academics. For instance, Susannah Vance notes that the landmark case of *Chen*

30 *Bah v. Mukasey*, 529 F.3d 99, 114 (2d Cir. 2008).

31 Ibid 115.

32 UNHCR, *Guidance Note on Refugee Claims Relating to Female Genital Mutilation*, May 2009, 9.

33 *In re A-T*, 24 I. & N. Dec. 617, at 617 (A.G. 2008) (*In re A-T (AG)*).

34 Ibid 622: 'the Board was wrong to focus on whether the future harm to life or freedom that respondent feared would take the "identical" form – namely, female genital mutilation – as the harm she had suffered in the past'.

35 Ibid.

36 UNHCR, Guidance Note Female Genital Mutilation, above n 32, 9.

37 *In re A-T (AG)*, above n 32.

'does not indicate that past persecution triggers a presumption only of similar or identical persecution in the future'.[38] She states:

> Moreover, the Convention and the *Handbook* . . . support the view that the presumption is limited only by the *basis* of the applicant's fear, an internal standard – not the identity of the persecutor, an external one.[39]

According to Vance, the correct reading of *Chen* and the UNHCR Handbook is that government authorities must demonstrate:

> that the applicant no longer has any present fear of persecution based on the same protected ground that formed the basis of the past persecution, without respect to the form or source of the threat.[40]

I agree that such a reading of the legal situation is correct, and accords with a good faith interpretation of the Refugee Convention in line with accepted principles of treaty interpretation (discussed in Chapter 2).

In light of this background, I now turn to analyse cessation decisions and the role of past persecution.

Past persecution under Article 4(4) of the Qualification Directive

Article 4(4) of the Qualification Directive provides that where past persecution is shown to have been experienced by a refugee, this is a 'serious indication' of the applicant's well-founded fear of persecution.[41] Specifically, it provides that:

> The *fact* that an applicant has already been subject to persecution or serious harm or to direct threats of such persecution or such harm, is a serious indication of the applicant's well-founded fear of persecution or real risk of suffering serious harm, unless there are good reasons to consider that *such* persecution or serious harm will not be repeated.[42]

38 S. Vance, 'An Enduring Fear: Recent Limitations on the Past Persecution Ground for Asylum' (2002–03) 91 *Kentucky Law Journal* 957, 978.

39 Ibid 978 (emphasis in original).

40 Ibid 979.

41 2011 EU Qualification Directive, above n 3, Article 4(4).

42 Ibid (emphasis added). It is significant to note that a proposal for amendment to the Qualification Directive currently being considered by the EU Parliament will remove the last sentence of Article 4(4) ('unless there are good reasons to consider that such persecution or serious harm will not be repeated'): Proposal for a Regulation of The European Parliament and of the Council on standards for the qualification of third-country nationals or stateless persons as beneficiaries of international protection, for a uniform status for refugees or for persons eligible for subsidiary protection and for the content of the protection granted and amending Council Directive 2003/109/EC of 25 November 2003 concerning the status of

Importantly, Article 4(4) states that past persecution will not serve as a serious indication of well-founded fear if there are good reasons to consider that *such* persecution will not be repeated. The provision is somewhat contradictory in that the first sentence refers to the 'fact' of persecution. This indicates that the facilitated standard of proof applies due to the *fact* that persecution has occurred, rather than requiring a linkage between the *reason* or *source* for the past and future claims of persecution.

However, the second part of the provision then sets out a type of proviso which states that the facilitated standard of proof will not apply where there are good reasons to consider that *such* persecution (that is, the original persecution) will not be repeated. However, a reference to 'such persecution' does not necessarily require the repetition of exactly the *same* persecution. If the object of the facilitated standard of proof in Article 4(4) is to recognise the evidentiary link between past and future persecution, such a link may be shown even if the *source* or *reason* for the persecution is different. For instance, certain groups may be the subject of persecution by a regime no matter who is in power, due to systemic historical, political and social factors. For instance, women in Afghanistan continue to be recognised as a persecuted group within Afghan society despite the regime change which has taken place in that country. It is of interest here to note that this 'good reasons' proviso may be deleted from Article 4(4) in the future, as this is currently the subject of an amendment by the European Parliament.[43] Such an amendment would make it far easier for applicants to use evidence of past persecution in both recognition and cessation cases.

I now turn to how the CJEU and German courts have interpreted past persecution in the context of cessation of refugee status.

The CJEU and the German Federal Administrative Court jurisprudence

There are two important European cases on cessation and standard of proof which have been handed down in recent years: the Court of Justice ruling in *Abdulla*[44] and the decision of the German Federal Administrative Court in *A and R v. Federal Republic of Germany, BVerwG 10 C 3.10*.[45] As discussed in earlier chapters, the CJEU found that there is symmetry between recognition and cessation. This raises the question: if cessation is merely the mirror image of the recognition decision, should a ceased refugee not be able to avail themselves of

---

third-country nationals who are long-term residents', 13.7.2016, COM/2016/0466 final – 2016/0223 (COD) (Proposal for EU Qualification Regulation).

43 Ibid.

44 *Salahadin Abdulla and Others v. Bundesrepublik Deutschland*, C-175/08; C-176/08; C-178/08 & C-179/08 Court of Justice of the European Union, 2 March 2010 (*Abdulla*).

45 *A and R v Federal Republic of Germany, BVerwG 10 C 3.10, Bundesverwaltungsgericht* (German Federal Administrative Court), 24 February 2011 (*BVerwG 10 C 3.10*).

the protection of Article 4(4) in the same way that an asylum seeker lodging a refugee claim can? Does the change of circumstances for the purposes of cessation necessarily extinguish the existence of the past persecution for the purpose of any fresh claims for persecution?

Onus and standard of proof for new claims of persecution

In relation to the standard of proof which should apply in cessation decisions, the CJEU was asked to answer two questions. Firstly, which standard of proof should apply where an applicant makes new claims of persecution not related to the recognition decision? Secondly, should cessation decisions and applications containing new claims of persecution be considered in light of the more relaxed standard of proof in Article 4(4) of the Qualification Directive?[46]

In response to the first question, the CJEU held that where the competent authorities of the Member State find that circumstances which resulted in the granting of refugee status have ceased to exist, consideration of whether there are any *other* circumstances which could justify a fear of persecution[47] attracts the same standard of probability as that applied when refugee status was granted.[48] This approach therefore reflects its central finding in the case that cessation should be treated as the 'mirror image' of recognition.

In relation to the meaning of Article 11(2) of the Qualification Directive, which sets out the 'significant and non-temporary' standard for change, the court held that this provision applies only to the reasons for persecution on which recognition of refugee status was originally based. In contrast, if the ceased refugee makes new claims for persecution, then this is not assessed under Article 11(2) but using the well-founded fear test as applied to recognition of refugee status.[49] The CJEU also held that under Article 11(2), the change of circumstances will be of a 'significant and non-temporary' nature 'when the factors which formed the basis of the refugee's fear of persecution may be regarded as having been permanently eradicated'.[50] As was discussed in Chapter 4 of this book, whilst the use of the term 'permanently eradicated' is a high threshold for states to meet in relation

46 *Abdulla*, [43].

47 Either for the same reason as that initially at issue or for one of the other reasons establishing refugee status set out in Article 2(c) of the Directive.

48 *Abdulla*, [91].

49 Ibid [83] and [88], cited with approval in *BVerwG 10 C 3.10*, [19]. In *BVerwG 10 C 3.10*, the German Federal Administrative Court also noted: 'Therefore the extinction of refugee status does not depend on whether comprehensive protection against any form of persecution is afforded in the country of origin': [19].

50 *Abdulla* [73]: 'The change of circumstances will be of a "significant and non-temporary" nature, within the terms of Article 11(2) of the Directive, when the factors which formed the basis of the refugee's fear of persecution may be regarded as having been permanently eradicated. The assessment of the significant and non-temporary nature of the change of circumstances thus implies that there are no well-founded fears of being exposed to acts of persecution amounting to severe violations of basic human rights within the meaning of Article 9(1) of the Directive'.

to change of circumstances, the reference to the cessation of the refugee's fear of persecution is not in fact the same criteria as set out in Article 1C(5). Whilst cessation is clearly linked to the factors which led to the original decision as to the existence of a well-founded fear of persecution, the words of Article 1C(5) clearly state that cessation will only apply where the '*circumstances in connection with which* he has been recognized as a refugee have ceased to exist'.[51] Further, Article 1C(5) does not simply refer to the absence or otherwise of persecution. Thus the 'circumstances in connection with which' a person has been recognised as a refugee may encompass much broader considerations than merely the factors which formed the basis of the refugee's fear of persecution. These may include the continuation of armed conflict or other security issues, problems with corruption or serious political structural problems which may impact upon the provision by the state of protection.

In relation to past persecution, the CJEU did recognise that the more relaxed standard of proof under Article 4(4) may apply where new claims of persecution, unrelated to the original basis of recognition of refugee status, are made:

> in so far as it provides indications as to the scope of the evidential value to be attached to previous acts or threats of persecution, Article 4(4) of the Directive may apply when the competent authorities plan to withdraw refugee status under Article 11(1)(e) of the Directive and the person concerned, in order to demonstrate that there is still a well-founded fear of persecution, relies on circumstances other than those as a result of which he was recognised as being a refugee.[52]

However, the court placed a proviso on this statement, indicating that this may usually only be the case 'when there are earlier acts or threats of persecution which are *connected* with the *reason* for persecution being examined at that stage'.[53]

There are a number of things to note about the approach of the CJEU to this question. First, the ruling means that where a ceased refugee relies on the *same* reason for persecution as that accepted when refugee status was granted, the assessment to be carried out will normally be dealt with as a cessation decision under Article 11(2), rather than as a recognition decision under Article 2(c) and Article 4(4) of the Directive.[54] This is because where the *reason* for persecution is the *same*, but circumstances have changed, this falls to be decided as a *cessation* case, rather than a fresh claim. So for instance, if an Afghan applicant was originally recognised as a refugee on the basis of persecution by the Taliban and in cessation proceedings they claim they continue to face such persecution, despite the changes in Afghanistan, this is treated as a cessation decision. The burden is then

51 Refugee Convention, above n 1, Article 1C(5) (emphasis added).
52 *Abdulla* [100].
53 Ibid.
54 Ibid [98].

on the state to demonstrate that, indeed, circumstances have sufficiently changed under Article 11(1)(e) such that the applicant no longer has a well-founded fear of persecution on this basis. There is therefore no need for the applicant to argue for the procedural benefit provided by Article 4(4) of the Directive. Indeed, this is echoed by UNHCR which states that:

> Article 4(4) of the Directive would only be relevant if the new circumstances were to be examined in the context of the assessment of a new asylum application, lodged after the application of the "ceased circumstances" clause.[55]

The second implication of the CJEU's finding is that if there are fresh claims which are *different* to those originally made in the first recognition decision, the new acts of persecution must be *connected* to that past persecution and that connection is to the *reason* for the persecution. This indicates that the *fact* that persecution has taken place in the past is not sufficient. It must be demonstrated that the *reason* is connected. However, does 'reason' for persecution require that the persecution be from the same *source* of persecution, or upon the same Convention *ground* of persecution? The court did not give further detail as to what would be a sufficient 'connection' between the reason for past and future persecution in cessation cases. It is therefore helpful to examine the opinion of CJEU Advocate General Mazák in *Abdulla* for further guidance.[56]

AG Mazák took a slightly different approach to the use of past persecution in cessation decisions in that he defined the term 'new, different circumstances founding persecution' (as that term was used in the referral questions to the CJEU) as relating to 'entirely novel circumstances which have no link, even partial, to the previous circumstances, on the basis of which the person concerned was granted refugee status'.[57] Upon this basis, he took the position that where factors relating to the original persecution still exist in the country of origin that are linked 'even partially' to that original persecution, than the relevant test is that of cessation under Article 11(2) of the Qualification Directive.[58] In contrast, where a refugee argues that there are entirely new, different circumstances of persecution, Advocate General Mazák views that as 'making a new application for refugee status and that those circumstances must be assessed in order to establish whether that person has a well-founded fear of being persecuted in accordance with Article 2(c) of Directive 2004/83'.[59] Significantly, Advocate General Mazák

55 UNHCR, 'UNHCR Statement on the "Ceased Circumstances" Clause of the EC Qualification Directive' (2008), 18, <www.unhcr.org/refworld/docid/48a2f0782.html> (citations omitted) (hereinafter UNHCR Cessation Statement 2008).

56 Opinion of Advocate General Mazák in Joined Cases C-175/08, C-176/08, C-178/08 and C-179/08 *Salahadin Abdulla and Others*, 15 September 2009, [54], <http://curia.europa.eu/> (hereinafter AG Mazák Opinion).

57 Ibid [70].

58 Ibid [71].

59 Ibid [73]. AG Mazák noted that '[t]he standard of probability to be applied is thus the standard applicable to the grant of refugee status pursuant to Article 13 of Directive 2004/83'.

states that new claims for persecution based on 'entirely different circumstances' should not be considered in line with the relaxed standard of proof in Article 4(4) of the EU Qualification Directive:

> The fact that a person was granted in the past refugee status owing to a well-founded fear of persecution based on entirely different circumstances does not in my view amount to a serious indication in accordance with Article 4(4) of Directive 2004/83 of the applicant's current well-founded fear of persecution.[60]

Mazák noted that there must be a link between the past persecution or threats of persecution and the new claims of persecution. However, that link need only be 'partial':

> the relaxation of the rules of assessment contained in Article 4(4) . . . requires in my view a link, if only partial, between past persecution or direct threats of such persecution and, new, different circumstances founding persecution.[61]

As to the basis on which such a connection should be decided, AG Mazák leaves this point open for national courts to decide.[62]

The issue of the standard of proof for *new* claims of persecution in cessation cases was the subject of further consideration by the German Federal Administrative Court in 2011 in *A and R v. Federal Republic of Germany*.[63] This case concerned husband and wife applicants from Iraq. The applicants were recognised as refugees by the German Federal Office in February 2002 on the basis that the Iraqi authorities viewed a mere application for asylum in another country as political opposition.[64] In 2005, the German Office revoked the applicants' refugee status following a finding that their fear of persecution had permanently ceased to exist due to the changed political conditions in Iraq. The applicants made new claims that the husband had been involved in the Democratic People's Party in Iraq prior to leaving the country. The German Federal Administrative Court held that there was a link between the new claims and the previous basis for recognition and thus the case could be assessed as a cessation decision (that is, whether there has been a non-temporary change in country conditions under Article 11(2)). The party in which the applicant had been involved was at that time in opposition to Saddam Hussein's regime and thus the court viewed this as sufficiently linked to the previous claim for refugee status upon which the applicant had been granted refugee status:

60 Ibid [74].
61 Ibid [75].
62 Ibid [76]: 'It is for the national court to assess, inter alia, whether the circumstances in question are novel or linked to the circumstances, on the basis of which the person concerned was granted refugee status'.
63 *BVerwG 10 C 3.10.*
64 Ibid [2].

> Although the recognition of his refugee status was not *founded* on this argument, it was nevertheless *connected* with opposition to the regime at the time – which was presumed by the Iraqi authorities because he had filed an application for asylum – and was therefore *connected* with political opinion as a reason for persecution.[65]

Thus, despite the CJEU requiring a 'connection' between the reason for persecution between the past and future, the German Federal Administrative Court appears to have interpreted this quite widely here, in that the past persecution had not been based on the applicant's involvement in the Democratic People's Party. However, it does appear that this case law requires a connection to exist between the same Convention *grounds* (e.g. in *A and R v. Germany*, political opinion), which may be overly narrow given that many persecution claims straddle more than one Convention ground.

In applying this to the facts of the case, the German Federal Administrative Court held that:

> If the Complainant is threatened with persecution in relation to his involvement with the 'Democratic People's Party', this would indeed need to be taken into account in the examination under Article 11(2) of Directive 2004/83/EC, with regard to the question of whether the established change in circumstances – specifically, the cessation of persecution by the Saddam Hussein regime and the establishment of a new government . . . is sufficiently significant that the Complainant's fear of persecution should no longer be considered well founded.[66]

Problems with the CJEU and German Federal Administrative Court approach

A number of interpretative issues and difficulties arise from the jurisprudence of the CJEU and German Federal Administrative Court. In order to illustrate these, I first compare the EU approach to that taken to past persecution in US cases and then go on to illustrate some of the problems which may arise from the EU jurisprudence when applied in practice.

In coming to a principled and reasoned interpretation of Article 4(4) and its interaction with cessation, it is important to foresee the types of cases to which it may apply. In relation to cessation and past persecution, certain difficulties arise because of the heavy reliance on country information about changes which have taken place in a certain country. Care must therefore be taken in this context not to simplify what may in fact be a very complex situation.

It is useful to point to an example using Afghanistan to illustrate this issue. A cursory examination of the situation in Afghanistan may lead to the conclusion that

65 Ibid [24].
66 Ibid (emphasis added).

the Taliban are no longer in power and therefore a refugee who was in the past persecuted by the Taliban based on his or her political opinion, can be subject to cessation on the basis that the Taliban has been overthrown and no longer holds power as a governing political entity. If that refugee then claims that they now face persecution from another source, for example because they are Shi'a Muslims fearing persecution by Shi'ites, this may well be said to be *unconnected* with the refugee's past persecution by the Taliban, as it from a different source and involves a different ground of persecution.[67] Does this mean that a ceased refugee in such a situation should be denied the benefit of the facilitated proof in Article 4(4) that they would otherwise enjoy if they were asylum seekers applying for asylum in the first instance? Does the past persecution by the Taliban provide any evidentiary proof of the person's well-founded fear of persecution? On one level it does – because the past persecution demonstrates that the state was unable or unwilling to protect the applicant from persecution. In this context, it is noted that the well-founded fear concept is in fact comprised of two limbs – the existence of a well-founded fear of persecution and lack of state protection from that persecution.[68] Thus, arguably, even if the *type* of persecution set out in a new claim by a ceased refugee is different from the *type* of persecution which founded the original refugee status determination, remnants of the previous persecutors may still remain in the country (for instance, in the context of Afghanistan, country information suggests that the Taliban continues to be influential in significant parts of the state).[69]

Another illustration can be made using the example of Iraq where many asylum seekers were recognised as refugees on the basis of persecution by Saddam Hussein's regime (for reasons of religion or political opinion). Upon regime change in Iraq, many applicants claimed persecution for reasons such as fear of persecution from the Ba'ath party[70] due to political opinion and fear of persecution due to being a returnee from a Western country or having worked with/for the Allied forces. Further, although 'regime change' took place in Iraq, experts noted that many of the networks from Saddam Hussein's regime remained.[71] Thus, despite

67 See Minority Rights International, 'State of the World's Minorities Asia and Oceania and Indigenous Peoples 2010', 114: 'Many Shia in Afghanistan, including Hazara, endured grave human rights abuses under the religious strictures of the Taliban'.

68 Refugee Convention, above n 1, Article 1A(2) provides that refugee status arises 'owing to a well-founded fear of being persecuted for reasons of race, religion, nationality, membership of a particular social group or political opinion, is outside the country of his nationality and is unable or, owing to such fear, is unwilling to avail himself of the protection of that country'.

69 See e.g. UK Home Office, *Country Policy and Information Note Afghanistan: Security and Humanitarian Situation*, Version 5.0, April 2018, 10, 17–21; S. Sharifi and L. Adamou, 'Taliban Threaten 70% of Afghanistan, BBC Finds', *BBC World News Service: Kabul*, 31 January 2018, <www.bbc.com/news/world-asia-42863116>.

70 The previous ruling party of Iraq, led by Saddam Hussein.

71 For instance, during the period in which cessation was applied to refugees from Iraq by Australian authorities, Charles Tripp advised the Australian Refugee Review Tribunal by way of expert evidence that 'From all the evidence, most of those networks are still intact. They haven't dissolved. What did dissolve was the public state, the looted ministries, the collapsed education system, the dissolved army. What didn't dissolve, as far as one can tell, are the networks of the shadow state': Charles Tripp, Expert Evidence to the Refugee Review

a regime change in a country, problems with lack of state protection may persist and be similar in nature to the problems with state protection experienced by refugees in the past. As a result, the *state authorities* may be different but the *underlying political, economic and social problems in the governmental structure and society in general, may be the same.* For instance, there are continuing problems with political and social instability, religious and other conflict and other security issues in both Iraq and Afghanistan which impede the ability of the current state authorities to provide protection to its citizens. Thus, the fact that a refugee has suffered persecution in his/her home country should be a factor in any decision-making and should lead to a lowered standard of proof.

In this regard, I would emphasise that often past and future persecution cannot be easily divided from each other. This has been recognised by UNHCR, which has highlighted the complexities and linkages of persecution in Iraq. For instance, in its 2009 Eligibility Guidelines on Iraq it noted:

> political polarization along religious lines goes back in time to the policies of past regimes, and is exacerbated by the post-2003 emphasis on religious and ethnic identities. Thus, in many cases, while an individual's religious affiliation is a factor in making that person a target for persecutory measures, political opinion is also imputed into the religious affiliation and the individual targeted for that reason as well.[72]

The UK Immigration Appeals Tribunal has also underlined the problems with separating the past from the future in refugee status decision-making.[73] Thus, although a change in circumstances under cessation provisions may well 'extinguish'[74] the well-foundedness of the persecution, it does not extinguish the evidentiary value of the past persecution, because it does not extinguish or override the *past persecution itself.*

The preferable interpretation of Article 4(4) in cessation cases

Given the preceding discussion, what interpretation should be given to Article 4(4) in cessation decisions involving fresh claims? It is not disputed that some connection between past persecution and present claims must be demonstrated in order for Article 4(4) of the Qualification Directive to apply. A link is required because Article 4(4) is an evidentiary concept, not a humanitarian one. However, for a number of reasons, this connection requirement should be interpreted

---

Tribunal (RRT), cited in many RRT decisions on Iraq, including V04/17185 [2005] RRTA 39 (6 April 2005); V05/17773 [2005] RRTA 295 (17 November 2005).

72 UNHCR, 'Eligibility Guidelines for Assessing the International Protection Needs of Iraqi Asylum-Seekers', April 2009, [34], <www.unhcr.org/refworld/docid/49f569cf2.html>.

73 *Kaja (Political asylum; standard of proof) (Zaire)* [1994] UKIAT 11038 (10 June 1994), [1995] Imm AR 1, UK Immigration Appeal Tribunal, [34].

74 This borrows a phrase used in *In re N-M-A*, discussed above.

liberally in the context of cessation. First, as argued throughout this book and elsewhere,[75] cessation is not the 'mirror image' of recognition, contrary to the interpretation of the ECJ in *Abdulla*. Secondly, it must be recognised that applicants who are subject to cessation proceedings are *recognised refugees*. They are therefore in a different legal position to asylum seekers who are seeking to lodge a first-time refugee application. Recognised refugees hold a status under both international and domestic law, and have rights associated with that status as set out in Articles 3–34 of the Refugee Convention.

For the preceding reasons, a liberal interpretation of past persecution in cessation decisions is necessary. Thus, I prefer and generally agree with the approach taken by Advocate General Mazák in his opinion in *Abdulla*. That is, if the 'new' claims of persecution are linked, even partially, to the reasons for which the refugee was first recognised as a refugee, then the proper test is one of cessation under Article 11(1)(e) of the Qualification Directive (or Article 1C(5)) and the burden is on the state in question to demonstrate that the refugee does not have a well-founded fear of persecution based on those linked factors. Where a refugee relies on entirely new, different circumstances of persecution, then the person should be treated as making a new application for refugee status and be assessed under Article 1A(2) of the Refugee Convention (or Article 2(c) of the Qualification Directive). If such claims are to be treated as part of the recognition procedure, then they should be able to benefit from the facilitated standard of proof set out in Article 4(4) of the Qualification Directive. This would ensure that the connection required with the contemporary claim of persecution is not to the *same* persecution but, more broadly, to the underlying facts which gave rise to the original persecution.

I note in this regard that past behaviour and events are considered in many other contexts in law. For instance, the past behaviour of a criminal offender is considered in sentencing decisions. In another area, administrative law, the granting of licences and permits is often contingent on consideration of the applicant's past behaviour. In these situations, the past behaviour of the applicant is evidentiary in nature – it is being used to assist the decision maker in considering the likely future behaviour of the person. For instance, is the criminal offender likely to re-offend? However, the use of such predictions based on past events is far more complex and problematic in the area of refugee law. This is because rather than dealing with individual behaviour, the prediction deals with *state* behaviour. That is, a decision maker must consider the likelihood that a state (or non-state actor) will continue to persecute a particular person or group and/or that it will provide protection in the event of any persecution. This complexity and reliance on country information should result in cautious use of cessation and also a beneficial use of past persecution for ceased refugees.

I now turn to consider the final legal issue arising from past persecution and cessation: application of the compelling reasons proviso to Article 1C(5).

75 M. O'Sullivan, 'Withdrawing Protection under Article 1 C (5) of the 1951 Convention: Lessons from Australia' (2008) 20(4) *International Journal of Refugee Law* 586, 603.

The compelling reasons exception to cessation based on past persecution

Article 1C(5) sets out an exception or 'proviso' to the operation of cessation where there are 'compelling reasons' arising out of previous persecution. Specifically, Article 1C(5) provides that it:

> shall not apply to a refugee falling under section A(1) of this Article who is able to invoke compelling reasons arising out of previous persecution for refusing to avail himself of the protection of the country of nationality.[76]

Importantly, the proviso is phrased so as to be limited to *Article 1A(1)* of the Convention, that is, pre-1951 refugees. This has caused great difficulties in adopting a modern-day interpretation of the provision.

Although the drafting history of the Refugee Convention is not particularly helpful for the main test to be used for cessation (change in circumstances), some useful insights can be gleaned from the *travaux préparatoires* documents in interpretation the compelling reasons exception.

First, a brief discussion held during the drafting process suggests that the compelling reasons proviso was limited to pre-1951 refugees due to the concerns of states as to the uncertainty of obligations arising under the 1951 Convention if it were not so restricted.[77] It is notable that when the 1967 Protocol to the Refugee Convention was ratified and the temporal limitation relating to 1951 was deleted from Article 1A(2),[78] there was no decision to delete the reference to pre-1951 refugees from the compelling reasons proviso in Article 1C(5) and (6).[79]

Second, the provision initially referred to 'compelling family reasons'. However, during the Conference of Plenipotentiaries, that phrase was deleted from the draft and instead the draft was amended to refer simply to 'compelling reasons arising out of previous persecution', which is now set out in the final version

76 Refugee Convention, above n 1, Article 1C(5).

77 'In the matter of the practical difficulty arising out of the uncertainty of the obligations to be assumed by Governments, the Israeli delegation's suggestion was that refugees falling under sub-paragraph (1) of paragraph A of article 1, where to all intents and purposes the obligations were known, should alone be referred to . . .', Statement of Robinson (Israel), Conference of Plenipotentiaries, UN Doc. A/CONF.2/SR.23 (1951), 20, summarising the Swedish view.

78 The definition of a refugee under Article 1 A para. 2 of the 1951 Convention was originally limited to those who 'As a result of events occurring before 1 January 1951' held a well-founded fear of persecution on a 1951 Convention ground.

79 See *Hoxha*, House of Lords, 1063 [69] (Brown LJ): 'The failure in 1967 to amend it, as it could so easily have been amended simply by deleting the "(1)" from the reference to "section A (1)", seems to me eloquent of the continuing intention of the contracting parties to confine the benefit of the proviso to the diminishing number of statutory refugees who would otherwise have remained vulnerable to the loss of their Convention rights under the cessation clause'.

of Article 1C(5).[80] This is significant, as family reunification is often at the heart of refugee cases.

The compelling reasons exception is important because it recognises that even if the circumstances in a refugee's country of origin are viewed as having changed pursuant to Article 1C(5), the clause will not apply if there are sufficient reasons arising from the past persecution endured by that applicant. As to what will constitute such 'compelling reasons' will depend on a case-by-case analysis. However, the UNHCR Handbook suggests that the proviso applies to 'atrocious forms of persecution'.[81] Grahl-Madsen explains that what the drafters of the 1951 Convention had in mind when they drafted the compelling reasons proviso was:

> the situation of refugees from Germany and Austria, who were unwilling to return to the scene of the atrocities which they and their kin had experienced, or to avail themselves of the protection of a country which had treated them so badly. The fact was appreciated that the persons in question might have developed a certain distrust of the country itself and a disinclination to be associated with it as a national.[82]

The main problem with the compelling reasons proviso is not so much the level of compelling reasons required, but its *temporal application*. That is, it is stated to only apply to *statutory* refugees defined in Article 1A(1), rather than *1951 Convention* refugees defined under Article 1A(2). Due to the 1951 temporal limitation upon the proviso and arguments that it should be extended beyond its literal words, the compelling reasons exception has become a controversial and disputed provision. This is so for two main reasons. First, the criteria for refugee status set out in Article 1A(2) are *forward-looking* – paragraph (2) requires a present or prospective risk of persecution. In contrast, the compelling reasons proviso permits refugee status to be continued on the basis of *past* persecution. Secondly, both Article 1(2) and Article 1C(5) involve *objective* criteria, whereas

80 During the 28th Meeting of the Conference of Plenipotentiaries, Petrén (Sweden) 'suggested that the word "compelling" should be inserted before the words "reasons arising out of" in the Israeli amendments to sub-paras. B(5) and (6) (A/CONF.2/81, A/CONF.2/82/Rev.1)'. Statement of Petrén (Sweden), Conference of Plenipotentiaries, UN Doc. A/CONF.2/SR.28 (1951), at 10. Robinson (Israel) accepted the Swedish suggestion, see Statement of Robinson (Israel), Conference of Plenipotentiaries, UN Doc. A/CONF.2/SR.28 (1951), 10.

81 See UNHCR *Handbook*, above n 2, [136]: 'It is frequently recognized that a person who – or whose family – has suffered under atrocious forms of persecution should not be expected to repatriate. Even though there may have been a change of regime in his country, this may not always produce a complete change in the attitude of the population, nor, in view of his past experiences, in the mind of the refugee'.

82 A. Grahl-Madsen, *The Status of Refugees in International Law* (A.W. Sijthoff-Leyden, Vol. 1, 1966), 410.

the compelling reasons proviso reflects *subjective* criteria relating to the psychological hardship suffered and the state of mind of the refugee.[83]

This raises the question as to whether the literal words of the proviso should be extended to all refugees, both statutory and non-statutory. UNHCR has consistently argued that the exception reflects a 'more general humanitarian principle' which should be applied to all Convention refugees.[84] I would argue that, given that the Convention has been acknowledged as a 'living instrument'[85] and should therefore be interpreted in accordance with modern developments and interpretation, it is strongly arguable that the compelling reasons exception should apply to not only pre-1951 but all Convention refugees. This approach also accords with the Preamble to the 1951 Convention, which makes it clear that its object and purpose is to assure to refugees 'the widest possible exercise of . . . fundamental rights and freedoms'.[86] It is therefore strongly arguable that a good faith implementation of Article 1C(5) requires states to apply the 'compelling reasons' proviso to all 1951 Convention refugees.

It is significant, as the House of Lords in *Hoxha* noted,[87] that the states parties to the 1951 Convention did not decide to broaden the application of the compelling reasons proviso to all 1951 Convention refugees in 1967 when the 1967 Protocol was ratified. However, arguably the fact that this was not done should not carry undue weight. At that time, states parties were not utilising temporary residence permits as they are today, and states parties had not yet commenced systematic application of Article 1C(5) to refugees. Thus, of greater significance is contemporary state practice relating to the proviso.

As noted in Chapter 3 of this book, subsequent international practice in applying a treaty may indicate an agreement as to how the terms of that treaty should be interpreted pursuant to Article 31(3)(b) of the Vienna Convention on the

83 The issue of psychological harm in the context of the compelling reasons proviso is discussed by D. Milner, 'Exemption from Cessation of Refugee Status in the Second Sentence of Article 1C(5)/(6) of the 1951 Refugee Convention' (2004) 16(1) *International Journal of Refugee Law* 91, 99–102.

84 UNHCR *Handbook*, above n 2, [136]. See also *Guidelines on International Protection No. 3: Cessation of Refugee Status under Article 1C(5) and (6) of the 1951 Convention Relating to the Status of Refugees (the 'Ceased Circumstances' Clauses)*, 10 February 2003, HCR/GIP/03/03 (hereinafter UNHCR Cessation Guidelines 2003), [31]; UNHCR, *UNHCR Annotated Comments on the EC Council Directive 2004/83/EC of 29 April 2004*, 28 January 2005, 25.

85 Various national courts have highlighted the need to interpret the Refugee Convention as a 'living instrument': see e.g. *R v Secretary of State for the Home Department, Ex p Adan* [2001] 2 A.C. 477, 500 (House of Lords, Laws LJ); *Sepet v Secretary of State for the Home Department* [2003] 1 W.L.R. 856, 862 (House of Lords). The Supreme Court of Canada has held that 'International conventions must be interpreted in the light of current conditions': *Suresh v Canada* (Minister of Citizenship and Immigration) [2002] 1 SCR 3, 87.

86 Refugee Convention, above n 1, Preamble.

87 *Hoxha*, House of Lords, [69] (Brown LJ).

Law of Treaties.[88] Thus, I now turn to examine in further detail as to how states have approached the compelling reasons exception.

State practice on the compelling reasons exception

Many states explicitly recognise the compelling reasons exception in their domestic legislation and apply it broadly to all refugees. Notably, Article 11(3) of the Recast 2011 EU Qualification Directive provides that cessation under Article 11(1)(e):

> shall not apply to a refugee who is able to invoke compelling reasons arising out of previous persecution for refusing to avail himself or herself of the protection of the country of nationality or, being a stateless person, of the country of former habitual residence.[89]

Laws in France, Belgium, Norway, Canada and the US have also interpreted the exception as applying broadly to all refugees.[90] For instance, Section 73 of the German Asylum Procedure Act provides that cessation shall not apply:

> if the foreigner has compelling reasons, based on earlier persecution, for refusing to return to the country of which he is a citizen, or, if he is a stateless person, in which he had his usual residence.[91]

The Canadian Immigration and Refugee Protection Act also sets out a compelling reasons proviso to cessation in Section 108(4), which refers to 'compelling reasons arising out of previous persecution, torture, treatment or punishment'.[92]

The approach taken in the UK warrants more detailed treatment. Historically, case law in the UK has taken a literal approach to the exception, holding that it

88 Vienna Convention on the Law of Treaties, 23 May 1969, 155 UNTS 331.

89 2011 EU Qualification Directive, above n 3, Article 11(3).

90 USA: 8 CFR, § 208.13(b)(1)(iii)(A); Canada: Section 108 (4), *Immigration and Refugee Protection Act 2001*; Norway: Immigration Act s 37; Germany: *Asylum Procedure Act* s 73(1); France: Refugee Appeals Commission (France), decision of 18 October 1999, *Molina*, No 336763; For instance, s108(4) of the Canadian legislation states that cessation for changed circumstances 'does not apply to a person who establishes that there are compelling reasons arising out of previous persecution, torture, treatment or punishment for refusing to avail themselves of the protection of the country which they left, or outside of which they remained, due to such previous persecution, torture, treatment or punishment' *Canada (Minister of Employment and Immigration) v. Obstoj*, [1992] 2 FC 739, 748–52; See also the discussion in Goodwin-Gill and McAdam, above n 2, 145–9.

91 Asylum Procedure Act, Germany, Section 73(1).

92 Immigration and Refugee Protection Act 2001 Canada, Section 108(4).

is only applicable to statutory refugees.[93] For instance, the UK Court of Appeal in *Hoxha* held that:

> Where one has clear and express language imposing a restriction upon the scope of a particular provision, as is the case with the proviso to Article 1C(5), it must require very convincing evidence of a widespread and general practice of the international community to establish that that restriction is no longer to be applied as a matter of international law. . . . A number of states do adopt a more generous approach towards Article 1C(5) than is required by the terms of the Convention itself, but they represent . . . a minority of the signatories.[94]

This was considered in the House of Lords case of *Hoxha*. In this case, the applicants had attempted to argue that, despite the fact that they had not been determined to be refugees, the compelling circumstances proviso of Article 1C(5) should be applied to them in relation to their claim of persecution under Article 1A(2).[95] The House of Lords held that the appellants were unable to avail themselves of the compelling circumstances protection in Article 1C(5) because they did not come within the first part of Article 1C(5), that is, they were not regarded as having been 'recognised' as refugees within the meaning of 1C(5) (even if they may have previously fulfilled the 1A(2) criteria at some earlier point in time).[96] In this case, Lord Hope, concurring with the observations made by Lord Lloyd in *Adan*, held that 'the cessation provision in Article 1C(5) takes effect naturally when the refugee ceases to have a current well-founded fear'.[97] His Honour added that such an interpretation 'is in symmetry with the definition in Article 1A(2)'.[98]

Despite this jurisprudence, current UK policy guidance allows for the application of compelling circumstances when refugee status is revoked. However, the guidance puts the threshold for the exception at a very high level, stating that it 'applies to cases where refugees, or their family members, have suffered *truly atrocious forms of persecution* and it is *unreasonable* to expect them to return to their country of origin or former habitual residence'.[99] It sets out some examples of instances where the exception might apply:

- Ex-camp or prison detainees;
- Survivors or witnesses of particularly traumatic violence against family members, including sexual violence;

93 *Hoxha*, House of Lords, [26], affirming the findings of the Court of Appeal in *Hoxha v. Secretary of State for the Home Department* [2002] EWCA Civ 1403 (Eng. C.A.) (*Hoxha, CA*).
94 *Hoxha, CA*, [47], endorsed in *Hoxha*, House of Lords, [26].
95 Ibid 1077 (Brown LJ).
96 Ibid (Lord Nicholls of Birkenhead, Lord Steyn, Lord Hope of Craighead, Baroness Hale of Richmond and Lord Brown of Eaton-under-Heywood).
97 Ibid 1067 (Hope LJ).
98 Ibid.
99 UK Home Office, *Asylum Policy Guidance, Revocation of Refugee Status*, 19 January 2016, 26.

- Those who are severely traumatised.[100]

Similarly, the European Asylum Support Office (EASO) has indicated that

> The prime example of compelling reasons arising out of the circumstances of persecution is where refugees have escaped genocide or severe maltreatment at the hands of the local population with whom they would have to live together if they returned. The loss of close relatives through persecution may also be relevant, as may be experiences in camps or prisons. Return to the country of origin may have unacceptably severe consequences if the mental suffering of a person who received a psychotrauma during the original persecution would greatly increase upon return.[101]

However, the threshold test for trauma appears to be interpreted differently by EU Member States. For instance, the German Higher Administrative Court of Baden-Württemberg has held that a diagnosis of Post-Traumatic Stress Disorder (PTSD) is, in and of itself, neither necessary nor sufficient to engage Article 11(3).[102] This indicates that further harmonisation on this issue may be required.

The compelling reasons exception as a rule of customary international law

Due to the fact that the compelling reasons exception in Article 1C(5) does not explicitly apply to post-1951 refugees and because a number of states do not recognise an exception to Article 1C(5), it has been argued that these states should nevertheless apply it as a rule of customary international law.

Adopting a definitive legal opinion on the applicability of the compelling reasons exception has been difficult, as there is some disagreement about the extent to which state parties are obliged to apply the exception to all Convention refugees and some confusion amongst academics about the result of applying the exception more widely to contemporary refugees.

I note here that the transposition of Article 11(3) of the EU Qualification Directive by EU Member States will give great weight to the argument that the

100 Ibid. The guidance notes that 'The presumption is that such persons have suffered grave acts of persecution, including at the hands of elements of the local population, and therefore cannot reasonably be expected to return. Application of the 'compelling reasons' exception is interpreted to extend beyond the actual words of the provision to apply to Article 1A(2) refugees and reflects a general humanitarian principle. As this provision is expected to apply only in the most exceptional of cases, any decision not to proceed with revocation on this basis must be taken by a senior caseworker'.

101 EASO *Ending International Protection: Articles 11, 14, 16 and 19 Qualification Directive (2011/95/EU) A Judicial Analysis*, 39–40 (citations omitted).

102 Higher Administrative Court of Baden-Württemberg (Germany), *A 6 S 1097/05*, [26], cited in EASO, ibid 40.

exception has become a rule of customary international law. Until that time, however, there is still a level of divergence on this issue amongst other state parties to the Refugee Convention and thus some uncertainty as to its status as a rule of customary international law. Indeed, leading academic commentators have disagreed on the status of the exception as a rule of customary international law. Joan Fitzpatrick noted that 'practice and principle support the recognition of exceptions to cessation for Convention refugees'.[103] Guy Goodwin-Gill and Jane McAdam argue that Article 1C(5) should be interpreted in light of state practice, which they say is sufficiently developed to establish agreement between the state parties that the compelling reasons exception should be more broadly applied to all refugees.[104] Others, such as James Hathaway and Michelle Foster, disagree, stating that 'there is neither compelling evidence of relatively uniform state practice – especially in the less developed world where most cessation occurs – nor of the required *opinio juris*'.[105]

I argue in this book that as the Convention has been acknowledged as a 'living instrument' and should therefore be interpreted in accordance with modern developments and interpretation, the compelling reasons exception should apply to not only pre-1951 but to all Convention refugees. It is strongly arguable therefore that a good faith implementation of Article 1C(5) requires states to apply the compelling reasons exception to all Convention refugees. Although there are some states that have not yet recognised this broader application of the proviso formally, such as Australia, there are a number of countries which *have* implemented a compelling reasons exception.[106] These recent developments may mean that the argument in favour of customary international law has been strengthened. However, there still remain doubts about whether there

103 J. Fitzpatrick, 'Current Issues in Cessation of Protection under Article 1C of the 1951 Convention and Article I.4 of the 1969 OAU Convention, UNHCR Background Paper for Expert Roundtable Discussion on Cessation (2001), [70].

104 Goodwin-Gill and McAdam, above n 2, 148–9.

105 Hathaway and Foster, above n 5, 491.

106 US, Canada, Germany, Zimbabwe. Germany: Section 73(1) Asylum Act provides that cessation is applicable if the conditions on which the recognition of status was based have ceased to exist *and* the refugee 'can no longer refuse to claim the protection of the country of which he is a citizen, or if he, as a stateless person, is able to return to the country where he had his usual residence'. Accordingly, revocation of the status cannot be based only on a change of circumstances in the country of origin, but it also has to be ascertained whether the refugee can be *reasonably expected to return to the country of origin*. This is not the case if, for example, a refugee has 'compelling reasons, based on earlier persecution' to refuse to return. Case law has established that trauma or mental disorders which result from persecution constitute compelling reasons within the meaning of this provision: Federal Administrative Court, Decision *1 C 21/04* of 1 November 2015, asyl.net, M7834. See also K. Eichler, Leitfaden zum Flüchtlingsrecht (Guideline to Refugee Law), 2nd ed. (2016), 105, cited in <www.asylumineurope.org/reports/country/germany/content-international-protection/status-and-residence/cessation-and-review#footnote3_51cgspp>.

is sufficient state practice such that the proviso has become a rule of customary international law.

Conclusions

The legal questions posed in this chapter have important practical implications for the types of cases which have thus far been subjected to cessation decisions, that is, applicants from Iraq and Afghanistan. These two countries have undergone significant changes in country conditions, but remnants of the old regimes in both countries still remain and many non-governmental organisations report that persecution continues to occur. This continuance of persecution sometimes applies to the same groups that were persecuted prior to the regime change, but also to different groups.[107] In this regard, the case law on cessation from the German Federal Administrative Court, which has been applied to a substantial number of Iraqi cases, is of great importance.

As noted earlier, it is generally agreed that the onus of proof in cessation decisions is on the governmental authorities seeking to revoke a refugee's status. However, the standard of proof in relation to new claims asserted by applicants as part of cessation procedures is more complex. In this context, I generally agree with the approach taken by Advocate General Mazák in his opinion in *Abdulla*. That is, if the 'new' claims of persecution are linked, even partially, to the reasons for which the refugee was first recognised as a refugee, then the proper test is one of cessation under Article 11(1)(e) of the Qualification Directive (or Article 1C(5)) and the burden is on the state in question to demonstrate that the refugee does not have a well-founded fear of persecution based on those linked factors. Where a refugee relies on entirely new, different circumstances of persecution, then the person should be treated as making a new application for refugee status and be assessed under Article 1A(2) of the Refugee Convention (or Article 2(c) of the Qualification Directive).

However, where I depart from AG Mazák is in relation to the required connection for consideration of past persecution. AG Mazák opines that:

> The fact that a person was granted in the past refugee status owing to a well-founded fear of persecution based on entirely different circumstances does not in my view amount to a serious indication in accordance with Article 4(4) of Directive 2004/83 of the applicant's current well-founded fear of persecution.[108]

107 For instance, UNHCR has noted the continuing discrimination against Hazaras and other groups in Afghanistan: see 'Eligibility Guidelines for Assessing the International Protection Needs of Asylum-Seekers from Afghanistan', 30 August 2018, HCR/EG/AFG/18/02, 93–94.

108 AG Mazák Opinion, above n 56, [74].

I would argue that the fact that a refugee has suffered persecution in his or her home country should be a factor in any decision-making and should lead to a lowered standard of proof. Although the reasons for the persecution may be different, the lack of state protection may be the same.

Thus, it is my view that, despite any change of circumstances in the country of origin which mean that the reason for the previous persecution has been removed, the fact that past persecution occurred has evidentiary value in assessing any new claims of persecution, even if the link to the past persecution is only partial. That should be reflected in a liberal interpretation of connection, as set out earlier in this chapter. Whilst it is acknowledged that some level of connection must be established between the past and future persecution in order for this evidentiary link to apply, given the nature of persecution, state protection and the uncertainty in foreseeing future persecution, I argue that the level of connection between the past and future need only be partial and that an overly narrow view (as that taken by US courts), should not be followed.

It is also strongly arguable that a good faith implementation of Article 1C(5) requires states to apply the compelling reasons exception to all Convention refugees. I note here that the transposition of Article 11(3) of the EU Qualification Directive by EU Member States will give great weight to the argument that the exception has become a rule of customary international law.

In making conclusions on these legal issues, the nature of the act of cessation should be borne in mind. Cessation is a serious decision which takes away international protection from a recognised refugee. As UNHCR has emphasised, as a result of this, cessation provisions must be exercised with great caution.[109] The judgements of the CJEU and the German Federal Court on the standard of proof are of significance given that the interaction between cessation and past persecution has to date not been analysed in detail in jurisprudence. It is also important in terms of the wider debate as to the proper interaction between recognition of refugee status and its cessation.

I also note that although the focus of my analysis in this chapter has been on the EU Qualification Directive and European jurisprudence, this case law and legislation also has wider ramifications. The Qualification Directive is explicitly stated to be based on the 1951 Refugee Convention, and all EU Member States are signatories to that Convention. Thus, the jurisprudence of the CJEU and German courts discussed in this paper also has implications for international refugee law more broadly. In assessing the relationship between past persecution and cessation of refugee status, decision makers must take an approach which fully reflects the long-term effects of past persecution and takes a principled

109 UNHCR, 'Guidelines on International Protection: Cessation of Refugee Status under Article 1C(5) and (6) of the 1951 Convention Relating to the Status of Refugees (the "Ceased Circumstances" Clauses)', HCR/GIP/03/03, 10 February 2003, [7]; UNHCR, Executive Committee Conclusion No. 69, *Cessation of Status*, U.N. GAOR, 47th Sess. (1992), Preamble, [4].

approach which reflects the nature of persecution in practice. In the context of Article 4(4) of the Qualification Directive, it should be borne in mind that past persecution should and cannot be cleanly separated from the consideration of future persecution and the *fact* that past persecution has occurred may be of evidential value to findings on future persecution, even if the *reasons* or *grounds* for that persecution are not the same. A liberal interpretation of past persecution and its connection to new claims in the cessation area will reflect this, and also the long-term effects of past persecution – both in terms of its evidentiary value and humanitarian aspect.

7 Cessation and deportation

Duration of stay and integrative links

Introduction

In previous chapters, I discussed the legal test to be applied in cessation decisions under Article 1C(5) and the interaction between cessation and various other provisions of the Refugee Convention. Specifically, Chapter 2 examined the interaction between Article 1C(5) and Article 34 of the Refugee Convention which obliges contracting states to attempt as far as possible to assimilate and naturalise refugees.[1] I reconciled these two provisions of the Refugee Convention by adopting the position that whilst asylum host states can give only temporary protection to refugees, at some point those refugees must be provided with a path to naturalisation and citizenship. Now I wish to discuss a related issue: the considerations which should apply when a state has successfully applied Article 1C(5) to a refugee and is *seeking to return that person* to their country of origin. This is an important legal point because it is generally understood that states have sovereign competence to decide the conditions of residence of non-citizens and a wide discretion in terms of legal admission to citizenship. Such state sovereignty includes the right to deport former refugees where cessation requirements are satisfied.[2] However, there are several indicators – including the presence of Article 34 and the acquired rights framework in the Refugee Convention – to show that the power of the state to return former refugees is constrained (at least to some extent).

The fact that cessation applies to persons who have been *recognised as refugees* is important legally, as it renders the deportation considerations more complex than cases involving *first-instance asylum seekers*.[3] This is because recognised refugees

1 Convention relating to the Status of Refugees, Geneva, 28 July 1951, in force 22 April 1954, 1989 UNTS 137, supplemented by the Protocol relating to the Status of Refugees, New York, 31 January 1967, in force 4 October 1967, 19 UST 6223, 6257 (hereinafter Refugee Convention).

2 On this, see G. Goodwin-Gill and J. McAdam, *The Refugee in International Law* (Oxford University Press, 3rd ed., 2007), 554.

3 That is, those who have not been recognised as a refugee previously. Whilst I recognise that first-instance asylum seekers may have also lived in a state for a number of years whilst awaiting processing of their claim, they are in a different legal position vis-à-vis the Refugee Convention to those who have been recognised as a refugee and are subjected to return (as reflected in Article 1C). Further, as I am dealing in this book with cessation of refugee status, I focus on the test to be applied to *recognised* refugees.

are entitled to a range of rights under the 1951 Refugee Convention.[4] Further, refugees on a temporary residence or protection permit may have lived in a host state for a significant number of years. This is particularly likely given that many current refugee-producing situations are of a protracted nature.[5] Such refugees may have established what I call 'integrative links' to that state. These refer to the ways in which a refugee may become embedded in the community and economy of the host state: they may marry a citizen of the asylum host state and establish a family, they may purchase a house or they may become involved in the political affairs or other activities of the community.[6] Such long-term participation in the duties and obligations of civic life may demonstrate a level of membership in the polity and society. They can be seen as 'citizen-like' activities – those which are equivalent to public demonstrations of belonging, commitment or adherence to the community of the host state. Obviously, there are certain 'citizen-like' activities which temporary residents may *not* be able to undertake (such as the right to vote and participation in jury service).[7] However, refugees may in many other ways establish integrative links which form indicia of social/political membership in the host state.[8] This means that although refugees on a temporary residence permit may not hold *formal permanent residence status* (as defined by the domestic law of that host state), they may have what I call *social* citizenship.[9]

When one examines the practice of asylum host states, it appears that some countries have a process which permits consideration of aspects of refugee integration as part of cessation or deportation. However, these tests differ markedly

4 See discussion below in my analysis of the 'acquired rights' to which refugees are entitled under Articles 2 to 34 of the Convention.

5 UNHCR defines a protracted refugee situation as one in which 25,000 or more refugees from the same nationality have been in exile for 5 or more years in a given asylum country: UNHCR Ex Com, 'Protracted Refugee Situations', 10 June 2004, EC/54/SC/CRP.14, [5].

6 For instance, Ruvi Ziegler notes that refugees can express themselves politically – they 'can contribute to public discourse, for instance, by writing newspaper columns, by using social media and other channels of communication, by protest and lobbying, and by joining civil society organisations'. R. Zieger, *The Voting Rights of Refugees* (Cambridge University Press, 2017), 208.

7 See e.g. the Commonwealth Electoral Act 1918 (Cth), s 93 (Australia). However, Ruvi Ziegler argues that refugees should have the right to vote in the political community where they reside (assuming that this community is a democracy and that its citizens have the right to vote): see R. Ziegler, *The Voting Rights of Refugees* (Cambridge University Press, 2017). He argues that 'recognised CSR1951 refugees have stronger inclusion claims than other non-citizen residents due to their "civic limbo"' (at 203).

8 As Michelle Foster has noted: 'a focus on formal civil rights alone is a questionable barometer of commitment to or membership of the body politic and arguably represents a sterile view of membership that is far from the reality of people's lives': M. Foster, 'An "Alien" by the Barest of Threads: The Legality of the Deportation of Long-Term Residents from Australia' (2009) 33(2) *Melbourne University Law Review* 483, 497.

9 Some commentators see citizenship as more than a legal right but also encompassing political activity and collective identity and sentiment: see e.g. L. Bosniak, 'Citizenship Denationalized', 7 (2000) *Indiana Journal of Global Legal Studies* 447, 456–88, discussed below. Others, like Shachar, argued that individuals who have a 'real and effective link' to the political community should be entitled to claim citizenship: A. Shachar, *The Birthright Lottery: Citizenship and Global Inequality* (Harvard University Press, 2009), 165.

across jurisdictions. For instance, in Germany, the decision on the residence permit must take into account personal reasons which might argue for a stay in Germany, such as length of stay, degree of integration, employment situation and family ties.[10] Similarly, Belgium law provides that the level of integration of a refugee into Belgian society must be taken into account in cessation proceedings.[11] However, others set a very high threshold for permanency and link that closely to the compelling circumstances exception based on past persecution.[12] This narrower state practice is probably best summarised by the position taken by the Immigration Appeals Board of Norway, which explains that a person will not lose a residence permit 'if he or she has special cause to object to being returned due to previous persecution. In practice, it will take a lot for this to form the basis for a decision not to revoke a permit'.[13] Additionally, other countries such as Australia do not expressly compel decision makers to consider integrative factors in cessation decisions.[14]

The application of cessation to return decisions is therefore more complex than it appears from the terms of Article 1C(5). Contributing to this complexity is the fact that the social and political absorption of a refugee may exist as a *practical* matter, but may not be officially recognised by the host state in a *legal* sense. This represents a significant gap in the law given that return of a refugee after an extended period may not lead to sustainable return (i.e. it may eventually result in secondary movement). The need to ensure that a former refugee can re-establish him or herself is an important factor to consider, given the recognised imperatives and benefits of providing refugees with a durable solution.[15] Here, of course, I note that many refugees may wish to return to their country of origin when conditions are sufficiently safe. The point of this chapter is to set out standards for considering integrative links where a refugee does *not* wish to return, but the asylum host state is attempting to *compel* that return.

10 See European Council on Refugees and Exiles (ECRE), *Asylum in Europe: Country Report: Germany* (undated), <www.asylumineurope.org/reports/country/germany/content-international-protection/status-and-residence/cessation-and-review#footnote9_usduc57>. Under German law, a person whose deportation has been suspended shall be granted a residence permit 'if he or she has become integrated lastingly into the way of life in the Federal Republic of Germany' (Section 25b(2) Residence Act). This residence permit is granted for a maximum of 2 years.

11 Article 11(3)(1) *Aliens Act* (Belgium), cited in European Council on Refugees and Exiles (ECRE), *Asylum in Europe: Country Report: Belgium*, <www.asylumineurope.org/reports/country/belgium/content-international-protection/status-and-residence/cessation-and-review>.

12 Discussed in Chapter 6 of this book.

13 Immigration Appeals Board of Norway (UNE), 'Revocation Cases', <www.une.no/en/case-types-and-countries/case-type-revocation-cases/>.

14 This is primarily because Australia applies Article 1A(2) instead of Article 1C(5) in cessation proceedings (see detailed discussion of this in Chapter 3 of this book).

15 See e.g. UNHCR, *Framework for Durable Solutions for Refugees and Persons of Concern*, 2003, <www.unhcr.org/en-au/partners/partners/3f1408764/framework-durable-solutions-refugees-persons-concern.html>.

The application of the legal test for cessation therefore needs to better reflect the way in which temporary residence permits and temporary protection visas are operating in practice in the contemporary world. This situation raises some important questions which are addressed in this chapter: should the level of integration by a refugee in a host state be a relevant consideration in relation to the decision to cease refugee status and residency (and the resulting deportation decision)?[16] If so, what considerations should apply?

In answering these questions, I return to the concepts of political membership and refugeehood (which I introduced in Chapters 2 and 5), together with the acquired rights framework in the Refugee Convention and international human rights law norms (specifically, the right to family and private life). Further, I utilise some case studies from outside the refugee sphere by examining the way in which integrative links have been considered in *other migration areas*, with a focus on visa cancellation decisions and deportation processes in the EU, Australia and the United States. Although some of these case examples do not deal with refugee protection as such (but migrants as a more general class), they do provide a useful indication of the legal complexities which arise when a state seeks to deport persons who have resided (either lawfully or unlawfully) in that state for many years. I note also, that I refer throughout this chapter to a 'long-term refugee resident' or 'long-term resident'. That can be interpreted in a number of ways depending on the context. However, I use it here to refer to a refugee who has resided in a host state for more than 5 years.[17]

In terms of coverage of issues in this chapter, the focus here is on the *international law* implications for refugee protection arising from differing national approaches to residency, protection and status. As part of this analysis, I do not address the domestic *constitutional* implications of temporary stay for refugees. However, I note that there may be a legal question as to whether a person who resides in a host state for a long period may in fact become so 'absorbed' that they may cease to be 'aliens' for the purpose of domestic law.[18]

Before embarking on this analysis, it is important to recognise an important procedural point: that cessation of refugee status does not *necessarily* or

16 I note that these decisions are often separate: there will be a determination about cessation by a state authority, and then the person will be open to deportation. There will then be a decision to deport the person, which may involve human rights considerations (e.g. European Convention of Human Rights, Articles 3 and 8). Former refuges may also apply for an adjustment of status (e.g. to obtain another migration visa or humanitarian protection). Note that refugee status typically attracts a higher level of domestic protection than other statuses (e.g. social security benefits, work rights) so I argue that integrative links should be applied to the cessation decision (to ensure refugee status is not improperly revoked without good reason) and also to any resulting deportation decision.

17 As discussed further below, this is recognised by many commentators as the time at which persons may have a moral claim to be treated as 'settled' or given citizenship status by the state.

18 For instance, there may be an argument under Australian law that a refugee who resides for a number of years in Australia and establishes integrative links may cease to be an 'alien' for the purposes of the federal constitutional head of power allowing Parliament to pass laws in relation to such persons.

automatically lead to return of the former refugee to their country of nationality. In some cases, a former refugee may be able to argue that they are entitled to complementary protection under human rights law or some form of humanitarian protection. Thus, in some countries, a refugee who has his or her refugee status revoked under a cessation procedure will be able to apply for another status and may be issued with another residence permit.[19] For instance, certain applicants may be able to argue that deportation gives rise to a breach of provisions of the European Convention on Human Rights (ECHR),[20] namely Article 3 (torture and other inhuman treatment) or Article 8 (right to private and family life). However, human rights protections such as these are not necessarily available in other jurisdictions.[21] Further, alternative avenues to protect against deportation can be quite discretionary and do not therefore provide a reliable avenue for some applicants.[22] For instance, in Australia, the Minister for Home Affairs retains a residual discretion under the Migration Act to grant a visa to a rejected asylum seeker for humanitarian reasons.[23] However, there are problems associated with this discretion.[24] Further, for the purposes of refugee protection, the loss of refugee status does in fact render a former refugee liable to deportation (under both the Refugee Convention and Australian domestic law). Thus, I examine cessation and integrative links in that light – that loss of refugee status is a trigger for return.

I now turn to examine important framework issues, namely, the notion of 'social citizenship' before then examining how this applies to refugees via the 'acquired rights' regime established by the Refugee Convention and the relevant human rights principles which may inform cessation decisions for long-term residents.

Belonging, social membership, political community and citizenship

The granting of citizenship is a core aspect of state sovereignty. The granting of citizenship is an act which is squarely in the control and discretion of the state

19 See for instance, the procedures applicable in Germany discussed in ECRE 'Asylum in Europe', above n 10.

20 Council of Europe, *European Convention for the Protection of Human Rights and Fundamental Freedoms*, as amended by Protocols Nos. 11 and 14, 4 November 1950, ETS 5 (ECHR).

21 For instance, Australia does not have a national or regional human rights instrument.

22 E.g. according to an NGO report from Denmark, only 25 people received 'humanitarian residence' under section 9b of the Aliens Act, and it was due to their having life-threatening diseases which could not be treated in their home countries: M. Clante Bendixen, 'New New Practice: Somalis Lose Residence Permits after 4 Years', *Refugees: DK-Information on Refugees in Denmark*, 20 September 2016, <http://refugees.dk/en/news/2016/september/new-practice-somalis-lose-residence-permits-after-4-years/>.

23 See e.g. Migration Act 1958 (Cth), s 417.

24 Migration Act 1958 (Cth), s 417. See discussion in Liberty Victoria, *Playing God: The Immigration Minister's Unrestrained Power*, 2017, <https://libertyvictoria.org.au/content/playing-god-immigration-minister%E2%80%99s-unrestrained-power>.

authorities who have the right to control the criteria of membership in that state. As such, states typically require satisfaction of high thresholds of residence, integration and allegiance. The purpose of this chapter, though, is to go beyond the current legal framework for citizenship and question whether integrative links of a refugee should be relevant when a state is seeking to cease refugee status and/or return that person to their country of origin.

I start with the decision of the International Court of Justice in *Nottebohm* which held that 'nationality is a legal bond having as its basis a social fact of attachment, a genuine connection of existence, interest and sentiments, together with the existence of reciprocal rights and duties'.[25] A recognised refugee on a temporary residence permit may meet some of these indicators: they form a 'social fact of attachment'; and a 'genuine connection' with the asylum host state. However, there may not exist reciprocal rights and duties if that host state does not recognise the refugee as eligible to become part of the host society. For instance, recognised refugees on temporary protection visas in Australia have work rights but have no ability to apply for permanent protection and are not treated like citizens, nor are they able to apply for citizenship.[26]

However, as I argued in Chapter 5, the act of fleeing persecution is understood by some scholars as an act which breaks the bond between a refugee and their home country.[27] It is also accepted that a refugee lacks the effective nationality of their home state. To this, I underscore that recognised refugees who are resident in a host state *do* establish integrative links in a society. Because of these facts and concepts, it may in fact be possible to classify recognised refugees as having a type of *social* citizenship status within a host state.

In this context, I point to the analysis of other commentators on the meaning of residence, membership and citizenship. Whilst I recognise that there are marked differences between conceptions of citizenship, and that many nation states have introduced strict tests for citizenship, I focus here on those scholars who present a more cosmopolitan sense of citizenship as not merely a legal status but which can also include social membership. This is because I argue it best reflects the particular situation of long-term refugee residents in asylum host states.

A starting point for examining the social and political membership aspect of citizenship is the work of Linda Bosniak,[28] who recognises that citizenship is comprised of a legal status but also adds three other conceptual understandings: 'citizenship as rights', 'citizenship as political activity' and 'citizenship as a form of collective identity and sentiment'.[29] Rubenstein and Adler also interpret

25 *Nottebohm (Lichtenstein v Guatemala)*, judgement of 6 April 1955, ICJ Rep 1955, 4, 22.

26 For instance, they cannot work in the public service (such as a government agency), nor do they have the right to vote.

27 See discussion of refugeehood in Chapter 5 of this book. In the context of return, this is relevant because it may be the case that the refugee no longer considers the original country as their 'home'. Alternatively, the home country may not accept them back.

28 For instance, the introduction of 'citizenship tests' for resident immigrants, discussed in.

29 Bosniak, 'Citizenship Denationalized', above n 9, 456–88.

citizenship to include a legal status (which depends upon whom the state recognises as a citizen) but also recognise a second, broader view of citizenship as 'the collection of rights, duties, and opportunities for participation that define the extent of *sociopolitical membership* within a community'.[30]

I point to these understandings of social or political membership to argue that recognised refugees on temporary residence permits in a host state may form a close connection with that host state which gives rise to an identity which is 'citizen-like' (in terms of belonging in the absence of legal status and/or rights). That is, they may perceive themselves as members of the host state society – as 'Australians' or 'British' for instance – even though they have not been given a formal citizenship status in line with that social identity. In some cases, this self-perception and identity may be reciprocated, that is, the community of the asylum host state may also perceive the refugee residents as part of the community.[31] This may form part of a broader argument that they have a moral claim to citizenship. That is, although the Refugee Convention does not require the host state to action this by *granting the refugee citizenship*, that moral claim to citizenship should be considered in any cessation and deportation decisions.

This may mean that a form of social citizenship can develop without any reciprocal actions on the part of the state. This may be controversial, because many see citizenship as a form of social contract between two parties (i.e. the state and the citizen). However, is it sufficient if the community itself reciprocates instead of the government? In the case of long-term resident refugees, there may be a segment of society who do not see them as part of the host state community.[32] However, I would argue that integrative links should nevertheless be considered as part of a return decision given the strong arguments in favour of this, as set out in this chapter.

This link between asylum and citizenship has been canvassed in the literature on nationality. For instance, Luke Lee argues that through the grant of asylum, the refugee enters into a special legal relationship with the state of asylum similar to that of nationality.[33] Others have noted that the 'link between integration and

30 K. Rubenstein and D. Adler, 'International Citizenship: The Future of Nationality in a Globalized World' (2000) 7(2) *Indiana Journal of Global Legal Studies* 519, 522 (emphasis added).

31 For instance, an Australian Commonwealth Ombudsman report on long-term permanent residents noted that such residents 'have been here so long that they, and the communities they live in, *see them as Australians.* All have lived in Australia for more than 10 years, often much longer. They came as babies or children and have spent the bulk of their formative years, and all their adult years, in Australia. They have well-established family and community ties here, and often have children themselves': cited in Foster, above n 8, 502.

32 There is a vast literature on societal attitudes to migrants and refugees, but see e.g. H. Dempster and K. Hargrave, 'Understanding Public Attitudes towards Refugees and Migrants', *Chatham House Working Paper 512*, June 2017, <https://euagenda.eu/upload/publications/untitled-92767-ea.pdf>.

33 L.T. Lee, *Consular Law and Practice* (Oxford University Press, 3rd ed., 2015), 196: 'there are grounds for likening the status of a refugee to that of a national of the State of asylum, as regards protection. This special link was described by the Administrative Court of Munich:

naturalization is especially important in the case of refugees, who unlike other aliens, lack an effective nationality (they may be considered "a de facto stateless refugee"); a situation which is "abnormal and should not be regarded as permanent"'.[34]

The concept of what I call 'social citizenship' may also provide a useful framework in which to place such refugees. Matthew Gibney has discussed a similar concept, the 'principle of societal membership', which he says 'calls for an alignment between the reality of people's social existence – their level of effective integration into a society – and their legal status'.[35] A similar term, 'denizenship', has been used by other scholars to describe the status of persons who are non-citizens but are resident in a particular state.[36] Alexander Aleinikoff explains it as follows:

> It is increasingly suggested that lawful residents who participate in and contribute to the social and economic life of the community should be recognised, to some degree, as members of that community entitled to a set of rights and a guarantee of fair treatment. I will adopt the label 'denizenship' to describe this membership status of resident 'aliens'.[37]

These analytical frameworks are relevant to my discussion, as they provide a foundation for the argument that if a refugee on a temporary permit forms a social and/or economic link to the host state, this should be reflected in the law applied to that person at the end of that residence. It therefore appears clear from a conceptual perspective that those integrative links cannot be considered irrelevant by a decision maker in the deportation context.

It is not possible within the confines of this chapter to fully analyse all relevant legal questions about the conceptual links between national identity, membership and citizenship. However, the fact that some of the literature on this issue has interpreted citizenship broadly in this way is relevant to my analysis in this chapter. This is because refugees in an asylum host state may, over time, establish an

---

"Through the grant of asylum the refugee enters – according to the spirit of the Geneva Convention . . . into a special legal relationship with the State of asylum. *This relationship is similar to the legal advantages of nationality*"' [citing Verwaltungsgerichtshof München, Nr. 60 VIII 59, 4 Aug. 1959, trans. by Michael Reiterer, *The Protection of Refugees by Their State of Asylum* (Abhandlungen zu Flüchtlingsfragen Band, Vienna, Vol 16, 1983), 37–8] (emphasis added).

34 R. da Costa, 'Rights of Refugees in the Context of Integration: Legal Standards and Recommendations', UNHCR Legal and Protection Policy Research Series, 2006, 25 <www.unhcr.org/44bb90882.pdf>, citing A. Grahl-Madsen, *Commentary on the Refugee Convention 1951*, Articles 2–11, 13–37.

35 M. Gibney, 'The Rights of Non-Citizens to Membership', in C. Sawyer and B. Blitz (eds.), *Statelessness in the European Union: Displaced, Undocumented, Unwanted* (Cambridge University Press, 2011), 66.

36 See e.g. G. Kibreab, 'Citizenship Rights and Repatriation of Refugees' (2003) 37(1) *The International Migration Review* 24.

37 A. Aleinikoff, *Semblances of Sovereignty: The Constitution, the State and American Citizenship* (Harvard University Press, 2002), 147.

identity in that state that is akin to citizenship, which gives that refugee an expectation that this 'social' citizenship status should be considered prior to removal proceedings. This is addressed by leading US immigration scholar Joseph Carens, who argues that after a period, immigrants have a moral right to stay in a host state. In his piece 'On Belonging', Carens emphasises the 'moral importance of membership' and argues that

> [w]hatever their legal status, individuals who live in a society over an extended period of time become members of that society, as their lives intertwine with the lives of others there. These human bonds provide the basic contours of the rights that a state must guarantee; they cannot be regarded as a matter of political discretion. . . . As people stay longer, their moral claims grow stronger, and after a while they pass a threshold that entitles them to ***virtually the same legal status as citizens.*** Once people have been settled for an extended period – say, five years or so – they are morally entitled to the same legal rights (and ought to be subject to the same legal obligations) as citizens, except perhaps for the right to vote and the right to hold high public office.[38]

Rainer Bauböck also refers to the concept of refugees having 'de facto settlement' status and the need for a 'corrective mechanism' to recognise this. Specifically, he points to the existence of adjustment status mechanisms for certain categories of migrants as 'an acknowledgement that programmes designed for strictly temporary stay need a correct mechanism that takes *de facto* settlement into account'.[39] This is recognised to some extent in the adjustment mechanism for TPS holders in the US (discussed further later in the chapter).[40]

Indeed, there is some recognition of the implications of integrative links and the meaning of nationality in international jurisprudence. In this context, Article 12(4) of the ICCPR is relevant: it provides that '[n]o one shall be arbitrarily deprived of the right to enter his own country'.[41] Judge Cançado Trindade of the ICJ has asserted that Article 12(4) 'extends an unrestricted protection against expulsion to aliens who . . . have developed ***such a close relationship with the State of residence*** that [it] has practically become his "home country"'.[42] Further, the significance of social and political links to a state were addressed in the dissenting opinions in the UN Human Rights Committee decision in *Stewart v. Canada*.[43]

38 J. Carens, 'On Belonging: What We Owe People Who Stay' *Boston Review*, 1 June 2005, <http://bostonreview.net/carens-on-belonging> [emphasis added].

39 R. Bauböck, 'Temporary Migrants, Partial Citizenship and Hypermigration', in J. Shaw and I. Štiks, *Citizenship Rights* (Ashgate, 2013), 217.

40 Discussed later in this chapter.

41 UN General Assembly, *International Covenant on Civil and Political Rights*, 16 December 1966, United Nations, Treaty Series, vol. 999, p. 171, (ICCPR).

42 *Diallo Case (Republic of Guinea v Democratic Republic of the Congo)*, ICJ, 2010 (30 November 2010), separate opinion, [156] [emphasis added]. The judge noted that in this particular case, Mr Diallo came to the state of residence at the age of 17 and lived there for 30 years.

43 *Stewart v. Canada*, CCPR/C/58/D/538/1993, UN Human Rights Committee (HRC), 1 November 1996 1996) (*Stewart v Canada*).

The Committee, interestingly made direct reference to the concept of alienage, affirming that

> the concept "his own country" is not limited to nationality in a formal sense, that is, nationality acquired on birth or by conferral, it embraces, at the very least, an individual who, because of his special ties to or claims in relation to a given country cannot there be considered to be a mere alien.[44]

The Human Rights Committee in *Stewart v. Canada* ultimately found that there was no violation of Article 12 of the ICCPR.[45] What is important about this case for my discussion is that the minority took the view that one's 'own country' in Article 12(4) of the ICCPR is not limited to those who have 'formal links to that state'. Rather, the aim of Article 12(4) is to protect 'the strong *personal and emotional links* an individual may have with the territory where he lives and with the *social circumstances* obtaining in it'.[46] That is, an individual is not to be deprived of 'the web of relationships that form his or her social environment'.[47] As Michelle Foster notes, 'the balance of academic opinion favours the view that long-term residents who have acquired strong personal and emotional relationships to their country of residence fall within the ambit of "own country"'.[48]

This is relevant to refugees on temporary residence permits, as it suggests that there is some basis for considering the factual element of a refugee's stay in a host state – that is, the social, family and political links they have established during their residence period. This is justified because those links indicate that the refugee has acted in a way and may consider that the host state has become their 'home country'. As Alison Kesby has noted:

> It has therefore been argued that those who have been lawfully present for an extended period should be protected from expulsion on the basis of 'acquired rights' or 'legitimate expectations'. On this approach, the expression, 'his own country', requires matters such as 'long standing residence, close personal and family ties and intentions to remain (as well as the absence of such ties elsewhere)' to be considered. In the case of a non-national, the connection would need to be strong to support a finding that the country was 'his own', however, it would be open to an 'alien' to show such ties.[49]

44 *Stewart v. Canada*, 16 [12.4].

45 This is because it focused on the arbitrary nature of the measures that prevented individuals from acquiring formal links and this was not an issue in the particular case.

46 *Stewart v Canada*, Individual Opinion of Elizabeth Evatt and Cecilia Quiroga (co-signed by Francisco Urbina), 21 [5] (emphasis added).

47 Ibid.

48 Foster, above n 8, 519, citing Hurst Hannum, Manfred Nowak, Stig Jagerskiold, Rosalyn Higgins and Lewis Saideman.

49 A. Kesby, *The Right to Have Rights* (Oxford University Press, 2012), 24.

What is raised by this analysis is what constitutes 'long-standing residence', such as to satisfy a legal test for refugee integration for the purposes of the cessation and deportation decision. This is discussed later in this chapter.

In light of this theoretical analysis of membership and status, I now turn to examine the acquired rights framework set out in the Refugee Convention.

Social citizenship and the 1951 Refugee Convention – the acquired rights framework

It is important to discuss cessation and return against the framework of acquired rights of refugees under Articles 3 to 34 of the Refugee Convention (see Chapter 1). The level of rights and benefits which accrue to refugees under Articles 3 to 34 reflect the level of attachment that such refugees have to the asylum host state: the social and economic rights set out in the Convention adhere to a refugee as the status of the person becomes more settled, that is, the more integrated and greater recognised a refugee becomes, the more rights that refugee becomes entitled to under the Convention. As UNHCR has noted, the Refugee Convention places 'considerable emphasis on the integration of refugees' and 'enumerates a range of social and economic rights that are geared towards the process of integration'.[50] The importance of acquired rights in the context of cessation has also been mentioned by other commentators. For instance, Corey Johnson has noted that:

> the ability for a refugee to make an acquired rights claim to stay in a host country logically becomes more persuasive as the number of years the refugee has spent in the host country increases and ties to the country of origin deteriorate.[51]

All refugees, irrespective of their status under national law, are entitled to certain basic rights. These include the negative rights against *non-refoulement* (Article 33), along with discrimination as to 'race, religion or country of origin' (Article 3). To this can be added Article 31, the non-penalization provision, and Article 16(1), which entitles all refugees to free access to courts of law 'on the territory of all Contracting States'.

However, the spectrum of rights granted to those recognised refugees under the Convention differ according to the residential status. Some rights adhere to refugees who are merely 'present' in the jurisdiction of the state.[52] Further rights

50 UNHCR, *UNHCR Note on Refugee Integration in Central Europe*, 2009, 5.

51 C.R. Johnson, 'Ceased Circumstances and the End of Refugee Status the Use of Article 1 C5 in South Africa' Scalabrini Centre of Cape Town, August 2012, 13. See also L.N. Kingston, 'Bringing Rwandan Refugees "Home": The Cessation Clause, Statelessness, and Forced Repatriation' (2017) 29(3) *International Journal of Refugee Law* 417, 421.

52 Simple presence is expressed in the Refugee Convention by such terms as 'within' (Art. 4) or 'in' the territory without any requirement as to lawfulness of that presence.

accrue to those 'present in the territory', and increase as the refugee is 'lawfully' present or has 'lawful' stay.[53] For instance, once a refugee is 'lawfully staying' in a state, they have the right to be issued with travel documents to enable international travel (Article 28), the right to work (Article 17) and rights in respect to Social Security (Article 24) and housing (Article 21).

Further, the rights granted are comparative by reference to 'aliens generally in the same circumstances'[54] or 'the same treatment as nationals'.[55] For instance, the Refugee Convention requires that contracting states accord refugees the same treatment as is accorded to 'nationals' in relation to rationing,[56] elementary education[57] and social security.[58] As Vincent Chetail has noted:

> As a result of this progressive entitlement regime, the [1951] Geneva Convention provides for an incremental continuum of protection that depends on the intensity of the territorial bond between a refugee and his/her state of asylum. In sum, the longer the refugee remains in the territory of the state party, the broader the range of entitlements becomes.[59]

Taken together, the residence framework (those 'present' or 'staying') and comparators to 'aliens' and 'nationals' illustrates that the structure of entitlements in the Refuge Convention is predicated on the concept that refugees may become part of the host state society such that they should be treated on the same basis to that of nationals (see, for instance, Article 22 – Public Education; Article 23 – Public Relief and Article 24 – Labour Legislation and Social Security). That is, there is a level of equivalency between nationals and refugees in some provisions of the Refugee Convention. The question is what this equivalence of treatment means for the political membership/citizenship status of refugees and any cessation decision taken by the host state.

The UNHCR Executive Committee, in its Conclusion on Local Integration, has emphasised that states should give refugees a secure legal status and rights and entitlements set out in the Refugee Convention which are 'broadly commensurate with those enjoyed by its citizens'.[60] UNHCR has also recommended that alternatives to cessation should be considered for those 'with strong economic ties and all family and social links in the country of asylum, particularly

53 For example, refugees 'lawful staying' is referred to in Articles 15, 17, 19, 21, 23, 24 and 28.
54 See e.g. Refugee Convention, Article 21.
55 Ibid, Article 20.
56 Ibid.
57 Ibid, Article 22(1).
58 Ibid, Article 24.
59 V. Chetail, 'Are Refugee Rights Human Rights? An Unorthodox Questioning of the Relations between Refugee Law and Human Rights Law', in R. Rubio-Marín, *Human Rights and Immigration* (Oxford University Press, 2014), 42.
60 UNHCR Executive Committee, *Conclusion on Local Integration*, Number 104 (LVI) 2005, (d): '*Notes* that the 1951 Convention and its 1967 Protocol set out rights and minimum standards for the treatment of refugees that are *geared towards the process of integration*'.

when most ties in the country of origin have been lost'.[61] UNHCR notes that providing such refugees with an alternative residence status is not required by the Refugee Convention *per se* but is:

> consistent with the instrument's broad humanitarian purpose and with respect for previously acquired rights, as set out in Executive Committee Conclusion No. 69 and international human rights law standards.[62]

Further, Janet Reilly has argued that the acquired rights in the Convention 'set refugees on a path to citizenship'.[63] The implications of this are that, although Article 34 of the Refugee Convention does not oblige asylum host states to grant citizenship to refugees, the acquired rights framework reflects that such persons are given citizen-like benefits. If those are to be taken away upon cessation, then that should be a relevant consideration in cessation and return decisions.

I therefore use acquired rights as a framework for justifying reference by decision makers to integrative links in cessation and deportation decisions – this is because the acquired rights framework shows that the Refugee Convention foresees integration.

Of course, refugees are not simply refugees but are also entitled to human rights, which is the framework to which I now turn.

Human rights law, integrative links and return decisions

In addition to the acquired rights set out in the Refugee Convention, the International Covenant on Civil and Political Rights (ICCPR)[64] and ECHR[65] set out important rights which can provide a framework for considering integrative links. As discussed in Chapter 3 of this book, it is widely accepted that human rights law can be considered in interpreting *some* aspects of the refugee definition in Article 1A(2) of the Refugee Convention, such as the meaning of 'persecution' and 'particular social group'.[66] However, the use of human rights standards is less

61 UNHCR Conclusion 69, (e).

62 UNHCR Guidelines on international protection: cessation of refugee status under article 1 C(5) and (6) of the 1951 Convention relating to the status of refugees (the ceased circumstances clauses), 2003 para 22, citing article 12(4) of the ICCPR which declares that 'no one shall be arbitrarily deprived of the right to enter his own country' and Human Rights Committee General Comment Number 27, Article 12, 1999.

63 J.E. Reilly, 'Temporary Refugees: The Impact of US Policy on Civic Participation in Political Belonging among Libertarians in the United States' (2016) 35(3) *Refugee Survey Quarterly* 94, 96.

64 ICCPR, above n 42.

65 ECHR, above n 20.

66 See discussion in S. Meili, 'When Do Human Rights Treaties Help Asylum Seekers? A Study of Theory and Practice in Canadian Jurisprudence Since 1990' (2014) 51 *Osgoode Hall Law Journal* 627, 656; N. Bednar and M. Penland, 'Asylum's Interpretative Impasse: Interpreting "Persecution" and "Particular Social Group" Using International Human Rights Law' (2016) 26 *Minnesota Journal of International Law* (available at SSRN: https://ssrn.com/abstract=2879977).

widely utilised or accepted in relation to *other provisions* of the Refugee Convention. As I argued in Chapter 3, given the fact that Article 1C is part of the refugee definition, there appears to be no legal reason for failing to apply human rights law, an interpretative tool in relation to cessation, just as it is with Article 1A(2).

For the sake of completeness, I note that international human rights law can also be used as an interpretative tool in relation to domestic conceptions of alienage and citizenship.[67] However, for the purpose of this chapter, I focus on the former issue – the way in which human rights law should inform our interpretation of Article 1C(5) in relation to integrative links established by the refugee and the return decision which may follow cessation.

Relevant human rights standards relevant to integrative links

Family protection rights in the ICCPR and ECHR have significantly influenced jurisprudence on refugee returns, at least at the international level. Article 17 of the ICCPR sets out a protection against 'arbitrary or unlawful interference' with the family, and Article 23(1) affirms that the family is entitled to protection of the state as the fundamental unit of society. In a number of communications under the ICCPR, the UN Human Rights Committee has considered whether a decision by a state party to deport a long-term resident may be considered 'interference' with the family.[68] In *Nystrom*, the Human Rights Committee found that

> In light of the information made available before it, the Committee considers that the Minister's decision to deport the author has had irreparable consequences on the author, which was disproportionate to the legitimate aim of preventing the commission of further crimes, especially given the

67 In the Australian High Court case of *Koroitamana v Commonwealth*, Justice Kirby stated: 'I accept that the Australian constitutional notions of alienage and nationality are to be understood in the context of any universal principles of fundamental human rights applicable to and accepted by, the community of civilised nations': (2006) 227 CLR 31 at 50.

68 For instance, the UN Human Rights Committee in *Madafferi v Australia* (CCPR/C/81/D/1011/2001, 26 July 2004) considered the proposed deportation of an Italian national who had resided in Australia since 1989 where the applicant had married an Australian national and had four children (who were Australian nationals). The applicant was subject to a visa cancellation by the Minister for Immigration due to past criminal offences in Italy. The Committee found that the removal by Australia of Mr. Madafferi would, if implemented, constitute arbitrary interference with the family, contrary to Article 17 (1) (in conjunction with Article 23) of the ICCPR and a violation of Article 24(1) in relation to the four minor children due to a failure to provide them with the necessary measures of protection as minors. The Committee specified that: 'in cases where one part of a family must leave the territory of the State party while the other part would be entitled to remain, the relevant criteria for assessing whether or not the specific interference with family life can be objectively justified must be considered, on the one hand, in light of the significance of the State party's reasons for the removal of the person concerned and, on the other, the degree of hardship the family and its members would not count as a consequence of such removal': [9.8]. See also *Nystrom v. Australia, UN Human Rights Committee*, Communication No 1557/2007, UN Doc CCPR/C/102/D/1557/2007 (18 July 2011) [7.8] (*Nystrom*).

> important lapse of time, between the commission of offences considered by the Minister and the deportation. Given that the author's deportation is of a definite nature and that limited financial means exist for the author's family to visit him in Sweden or even be reunited with him in Sweden, the Committee concludes that the author's deportation constituted an arbitrary interference with his family in relation to the author, contrary to articles 17 and 23, paragraph 1 of the Covenant.[69]

Some guidance on integrative links and human rights principles can be gained from examining ECHR jurisprudence on the right to a family life and private life. As Alison Kesby notes, the European Court of Human Rights (ECtHR) 'has been particularly open to applicants where they are nationals of the state of residence in all but name such as where they have been born and have lived all of their life in the state in question and have established their family life there'.[70]

Article 8 of the ECHR, which protects family life, has been particularly influential in return cases.[71] For instance in *Beljoudi v. France*, a case involving an applicant who had committed criminal offences, the court took into account the impact of return on the applicant's family life. In this case the lengthy periods within which the applicant was physically present in France were noted.[72] The court took the view that:

> the deportation of a person from the country in which he has lived all his life to another country with which his only links are the formal ties of nationality may raise issues not only from the standpoint of respect for his family life but also in connection with respect to his private life.

Having regard to the effect of the deportation of the applicant on his marriage, the commission held that 'from the point of view of respect for the applicant's family life, . . . the decision to deport Mr Beldjoudi, if put into effect, would not be proportionate to the legitimate aim pursued and would therefore violate Article 8'.[73] Similarly, in *Üner v. Netherlands*, the court considered 'the solidity

69 *Nystrom* [7.11].

70 Kesby, above n 49, 26.

71 For a fuller discussion of the jurisprudence on this article, see D. Thym, 'Respect for Private and Family Life under Article 8 ECHR in Immigration Cases: A Human Right to Regularize Illegal Stay?' (2008) 57(1) *International and Comparative Law Quarterly* 87.

72 *Beldjoudi v. France*, 55/1990/246/317; 12083/86, European Court of Human Rights, 26 February 1992 [77]: 'he has spent his whole life – over forty years – in France, was educated in French and appears not to know Arabic. He does not seem to have any links with Algeria apart from that of nationality'.

73 *Beldjoudi v. France*, 55/1990/246/317; 12083/86, Council of Europe: European Court of Human Rights, 26 February 1992 Para 79. The Commission noted at para 78 that: 'Mrs Beldjoudi for her part was born in France of French parents, has always lived there and has French nationality. Were she to follow her husband after his deportation, she would have to settle abroad, presumably in Algeria, a State whose language she probably does not know. To be uprooted like this could cause her great difficulty in adapting, and there might be real

of social, cultural and family ties with the host country and with the country of destination'.[74]

The ECtHR has also considered integrative links as part of the right to a 'private life' under Article 8. For instance, in *Slivenko v. Latvia*,[75] the court noted that the applicants were 'removed from the country where they had developed, uninterruptedly since birth, the network of personal, social and economic relations that make up the private life of every human being'[76] and that this constituted a clear interference with their private life. In *Maslov v. Austria*, the Grand Chamber of the ECtHR found that 'the totality of social ties between settled migrants and the community in which they are living constitutes part of the concept of "private life" within the meaning of article 8'.[77]

Application to cessation under Article 1C(5)

How then to apply these human rights principles to cessation decisions under the Refugee Convention? Although family or private life considerations are not explicitly set out in Article 1C(5), I argue that family links by a resident refugee should be a relevant consideration in cessation decisions for a number of reasons. First, the principle of family unity is referred to in the preamble to the Refugee Convention. There is an argument that this can therefore be invoked to interpret the formal text of the Convention, such as Article 1C(5).[78] Further, this can be justified based on the broader argument that the Convention should be interpreted in light of its object and purpose[79] and against the factual context in which it now operates, that is, as a living instrument.[80] It is unclear whether the drafters of the Refugee Convention foresaw that states would introduce widespread use of temporary residence permits for recognised refugees or that refugees may be resident for many years and be subject to return. It is also justified because

---

practical or even legal obstacles, as was indeed acknowledged by the Government Commissioner before the Conseil d'Etat. . . . The interference in question might therefore imperil the unity or even the very existence of the marriage'.

74 *Üner v. Netherlands* (2007) 45 EHRR 14 [57]–[58].

75 *Slivenko v Latvia* (2004) 39 EHRR 24 (*Slivenko v Latvia*).

76 *Slivenko v Latvia*, [96].

77 *Maslov v Austria*, Application No 1638/03, judgement of the ECtHR of 23 June 2008, [63].

78 On the use of the preamble to interpret the text of the Convention, see J.C. Hathaway and M. Foster, *The Law of Refugee Status* (Cambridge University Press, 2nd ed., 2014), 10: 'As the UNHCR has explained, this "strong human rights language" in the Preamble indicates that "the aim of the drafters [was] to incorporate human rights values in the identification and treatment of refugees, thereby providing helpful guidance for the interpretation, in harmony with the Vienna Convention, of the provisions of the 1951 Convention"'. See also J.C. Hathaway, *The Rights of Refugees under International Law* (Cambridge University Press, 2005), 53 and on family unity: 533–60.

79 See discussion in Chapter 1 of this book.

80 See discussion of the need for a modern day interpretation of the Refugee Convention in Hathaway, *Rights of Refugees* above n 78, 63–5.

it is strongly arguable that human rights protections should be an interpretative tool in applying Article 1C,[81] a matter which has been specifically endorsed by UNHCR in relation to Article 1C(5).[82]

In light of the framework of acquired rights established by the 1951 Refugee Convention and the recognition of family and private life in human rights law, the next question to be examined is how this relates to social belonging/membership, residency and citizenship. That is, how does residency in a host state interact with social and political membership within that state and any 'social' citizenship status which may arise as a result of integrative links developed by a refugee during that stay?

Integration and return – implications for identity, membership and acts of citizenship

As discussed elsewhere in this book, the act by a refugee of fleeing their country of origin and claiming refugee status results in a severing of the political bond between that individual and their home state. Over time, as a refugee *establishes* links with their asylum host state, they also may increasingly *lose* their social links to their country of origin. The refugee definition in Article 1A(2) actually refers to this relationship to the country of origin in its reference to the refugee being 'able and willing' to return to their country of nationality.[83] The relationship of the refugee to their country of origin is also recognised in the compelling reasons exception to Article 1C(5). As I have argued in previous chapters, the test for Article 1C(5) cessation should be interpreted as different to Article 1A(2) recognition, and the cessation test should be one of 'effective protection'. I have also argued in Chapter 5 that there must be a restoration of protection in the country of origin.

Group-based cessation and integrative links

UNHCR has emphasised the significance of integrative links in cessation decisions involving the end of group-based refugee protection in a number of African nations. For instance, in its cessation determination relating to Rwanda in 2011, UNHCR noted:

> Many Rwandan refugees are long-term residents in their countries of asylum, one-third of them having been born in exile. Many refugees have established

81 This is discussed in this book in Chapter 2. But also see Hathaway, *Rights of Refugees*, above n 78, 53–4.

82 UNHCR, 'Note on the Cessation Clauses', UN Doc. EC/47/SC/CRP.30 (1997), 9: 'Human rights factors should be taken into account as well as previously acquired rights of refugees'.

83 Although, of course, this is linked to an objective requirement that the refugee be unable to return due to persecution for a Convention reason. The mere subjective desire of the refugee to being unable or unwilling to return is not sufficient.

> family ties through marriage to nationals of the country of asylum or third-country nationals residing there. Many are contributing to the local economy. After decades of exile, the links of these individuals with their country of origin have weakened considerably. In such cases, UNHCR considers local integration or an alternative legal status to be the most appropriate durable solution.[84]

One of the obstacles in the Rwandan cessation process is that many host states in the region stated that they faced significant challenges in accommodating the integration of refugees.[85] Writing on the status of Rwandan refugees in Zimbabwe, Sniderman notes that '[l]ocal integration through a permanent residence permit or Zimbabwean citizenship is virtually non-existent as a durable solution'.[86] Similar concerns have been raised by commentators in relation to the UNHCR cessation declaration in relation to Ethiopia. For instance, Yasmeen Siddiqui states that 9 years after the declaration, the cohort comprising of pre-1991 Ethiopian refugees do not have a secure legal status. She notes that the Ethiopian residual caseload is issued renewable identity cards under a confusing administrative process.[87]

The fact that cessation in such a context can lead to refugees living in limbo, with no permanent status or citizenship in any country, is of concern, as it indicates a legal gap in protection. Sniderman gives a clear example of this in relation to the cessation of protection for Ethiopians in 1999 where he points out that refugees who had lived in Ethiopia for over *30 years* had their refugee status removed but were not deported. This meant that they continued to live in a legal limbo, with the effect that cessation turned refugees into illegal migrants.[88] This has lead Gaim Kibreab to conclude that temporary protection in the Global South 'rarely translates into permanent status regardless of the amount of time that passes'.[89]

This analysis of group-based cessation indicates that, although UNHCR has emphasised the need for integrative links to be considered in cessation and return decisions, in effect, this may lead to ceased refugees simply continuing to live in the host state with no permanent or certain legal status. This illustrates the need to have a set of legal principles in place to guide decision makers as to how

84 UNHCR, 'Implementation of the Comprehensive Strategy for the Rwandan Refugee Situation, Including UNHCR's Recommendations on the Applicability of the "Ceased Circumstances" Cessation Clauses', 31 December 2011, [15], <www.refworld.org/docid/4f33a1642.html>.

85 Ibid [18].

86 A. Sniderman, 'Explaining Delayed Cessation: A Case Study of Rwandan Refugees in Zimbabwe' (2015) 27(4) *International Journal of Refugee Law* 607, 618.

87 Y. Siddiqui, 'Reviewing the Application of the Cessation Clause of the 1951 Convention Relating to the Status of Refugees in Africa', *Oxford Refugee Studies Centre, Working Paper Series No 76*, 34.

88 Sniderman, above n 86, 614.

89 G. Kibreab, *Refugees and Development in Africa: The Case of Eritrea* (Red Sea Press, 1987), as cited in Siddiqui, above n 87, 38. See also G. Kibreab, 'Displacement, Host Governments' Policies, and Constraints on the Construction of Sustainable Livelihoods', UNESCO, 2003, 59.

factual integration should be considered as part of cessation decisions. However, the large numbers of refugees at issue under group-based temporary protection and cessation may mean that requiring integrative links to be considered is not considered workable by many states (or indeed UNHCR).

What does this mean for the legal significance of the integrative links developed by a recognised refugee in the asylum host state? We can here obtain guidance by making some analogies between cessation of long-term refugee residents and other cohorts of migrants.

Case studies: deportation of long-term migrants

Many states have only commenced the use of cessation procedures comparatively recently. As a result, there is a lack of case law about the rights of long-term resident refugees who seek to argue against cessation and/or deportation by referring to their integrative links with their asylum host state.

Temporary protection status – USA

The legal problems which can be caused when a host state grants only temporary residence to protected persons is illustrated by the operation of the Temporary Protected Status (TPS) regime in the United States. TPS is granted to nationals of specifically designated countries that are facing ongoing armed conflict, environmental disaster, or extraordinary and temporary conditions.[90] TPS beneficiaries receive provisional protection against deportation but do not receive permanent legal status[91] and are provided with only limited routes to permanent residence. The TPS regime has been criticised due to the length of time which some TPS holders have been given a lawful status without any permanency. For example, some TPS holders from Somali and El Salvador have been in the United States for more than 20 years.[92] Some commentators have therefore labelled TPS status as 'permanent temporariness'.[93] This illustrates the uncertainty which is created by long-term temporary residency and the practical difficulties in

90 8 USC 1254, discussed in S. Legomsky, 'Refugees, Asylum and the Rule of Law in the USA', in S. Kneebone, *Refugees, Asylum Seekers and the Rule of Law: Comparative* Perspectives (Cambridge University Press, 2009), 136–8.

91 Department of Homeland and Security, *Temporary Protected Status*, U.S Citizenship and Immigration Services, <www.uscis.gov/humanitarian/temporary-protected-status>.

92 M. Messick and C. Bergero, *Temporary Protected Status in the United States: A Grant of Humanitarian Relief That Is Less Than Permanent*, Migration Policy Institute (2 July 2014), <www.migrationpolicy.org/article/temporary-protected-status-united-states-grant-humanitarian-relief-less-permanent>.

93 A.J. Bailey et al., '(Re)producing Salvadoran Transnational Geographies' (2000) 92 *Annals of the Association of American Geographers*, 125–44, as cited in Reilly, above n 63, 103.

attempting to deport such persons. There are two points to note here. In addition to the personal uncertainty caused to applicants from the extended use of TPS, it also appears to have led to legal uncertainty and increased use of litigation.[94] Given that immigration tribunals and courts in many countries have significant backlogs,[95] I would query whether it is desirable both as a matter of policy and of law, to have a situation where there are high levels of uncertainty in the community about the legal position of a large number of long-term residents and the impact this has on the already congested status determination systems in many asylum host states.

The second point to make about the TPS system is that the uncertainty inherent in the system is remedied to some extent by the availability to some of an 'adjustment of status' mechanism. US immigration law provides pathways for certain long-term residents to become lawful permanent residents under certain conditions.[96] Adjustment of status is an important procedure, as it allows an eligible applicant to become a lawful permanent resident of the United States without having to travel overseas and apply for an immigrant visa externally. One legal issue which is not entirely clear is whether TPS constitutes an admission for purpose of establishing eligibility for adjustment of status under Section 245(a) of the Immigration and Nationality Act. Of interest here are two decisions from the Ninth and Sixth Circuit, *Ramirez v. Brown*[97] and *Flores v. USCIS*,[98] holding that TPS *does* constitute an 'admission' for the purpose of establishing eligibility for adjustment of status under the Immigration and Nationality Act.[99] Interestingly, the court in *Ramirez* noted that:

> Because TPS confers an actual status on and provides a slew of benefits to an alien who satisfies rigorous eligibility requirements, it is different

94 See discussion of the legal uncertainty in litigation in the US relating to TPS in C. Mehta, 'Potential Adjustment of Status Options after the Termination of TPS', 22 January 2018, <http://blog.cyrusmehta.com/2018/01/potential-adjustment-of-status-options-after-the-termination-of-tps.html>.

95 For instance, as at 30 June 2018, US Immigration Courts had a backlog of 732,730 cases: L. Robbins, 'In Immigration Courts, It Is Judges vs. Justice Department' *New York Times*, 7 September 2018, <www.nytimes.com/2018/09/07/nyregion/nyc-immigration-judges-courts.html>. On the UK, see A. Travis, 'Half Asylum Claims "Non-Straightforward" and as a Result Face Long Delays' *The Guardian*, 29 November 2017, <www.theguardian.com/uk-news/2017/nov/28/half-of-asylum-claims-classed-as-non-straightforward-face-long-delays>.

96 Immigration and Nationality Act, s 209(2)(b) (refugees) and s 245 (non-immigrant). TPS recipients can potentially adjust their status within the United States through either a family-based I-130 petition or an I-140 employment-based petition for permanent residency.

97 852 F.3d 954 (9th Cir. 2017).

98 718 F.3d 548 (6th Cir. 2013).

99 For instance, the court in *Ramirez* held that 'interpreting § 1254a(f)(4) to confer a limited "admission" on TPS recipients is consistent with the purpose of TPS' (at 18).

> than other forms of temporary reprieve we ordinarily would not consider sufficient for 'admission'.[100]

However, there appears to be a great deal of uncertainty about how adjustment of status for TPS recipients is applied in different states within the US, with criteria varying quite significantly across judicial circuits. Thus, the USA example is a stark illustration of the need for a level of clarity and consistency in the law to deal with the residency rights of long-term immigrants and refugees.

I will now turn to a series of case studies relating to immigrants more generally, with a focus on examples from Europe and Australia. A number of jurisdictions have considered duration of stay as part of visa cancellation and deportation orders made after a migrant has committed a serious criminal offence. In this section of the chapter, I analyse these to see if they can provide any guidance for the criteria which should be applied to the return of refugees on temporary permits. Clearly, the Refugee Convention grants refugees a special status which no other instrument in international law grants to any other category of forced 'migrant'. Therefore, references to non-refugee examples below indicate how law can and should recognise the integration which a migrant has undertaken in practice.

Case studies on integration factors which should be considered

Many states around the world have legal provisions which state that a non-citizen resident may be subject to deportation if they commit a sufficiently serious criminal offence.[101] It is not possible to canvass all examples in the following section. Thus, I have used case studies from the EU and Australia to illustrate the type of considerations which are influential in such cases.

Australia

In Australia, integrative links are considered as part of 'good character' visa cancellation decisions under the Migration Act.[102] An important

100 *Ramirez v. Brown*, 852 F.3d 954 (9th Cir. 2017), 19.

101 New Zealand: Immigration Act 2009, s 161; United States: Immigration and Nationality Act, s 237; UK: Borders Act 2007, s 32 (note this section provides for automatic deportation, with certain exceptions set out in s 33); Canada: Immigration and Refugee Protection Act, s 36(1).

102 Migration Act Cth (1958), Section 501 which provides that a person does not pass the character test if they fall within any of the grounds specified in subsections 501(6)(a) to (d). These grounds can be grouped into 5 broad categories: substantial criminal record; conviction for immigration detention offences; association with persons suspected of engaging in criminal conduct; past and present criminal or general conduct; and significant risk of particular types of future conduct. Most of the cases involve individuals who commit an offence which carries with it a prison sentence of more than 12 months duration.

government document, called 'Ministerial Direction 65', provides guidance for decision makers carrying out visa cancellations on character grounds. This provides that decision makers must have regard to:

a How long the non-citizen has resided in Australia, including whether the non-citizen arrived as a young child, noting that:

i less weight should be given where the non-citizen began offending soon after arriving in Australia; and
ii more weight should be given to time the non-citizen has spent contributing positively to the Australian community.

b The strength, duration and nature of any family or social links with Australian citizens, Australian permanent residents and/or people who have an indefinite right to remain in Australia, including the effect of cancellation on the non-citizen's immediate family in Australia (where those family members are Australian citizens, permanent residents, or people who have a right to remain in Australia indefinitely).[103]

There are a large number of cases dealing with criminal deportation,[104] but here I would like to highlight the factors set out in one particular case, *Johnson*, where Justice French[105] set out a list of factors relevant to assessing whether a person has become a member of the Australian community for the purpose of absorption. The factors include:

1 The time that has elapsed since the person's entry into Australia;
2 The existence and timing of the formation of an intention to settle permanently in Australia;
3 The number and duration of absences;
4 Family or other close personal ties in Australia;
5 The presence of family members in Australia or the commitment of family members to come to Australia to join the person;
6 Employment history;
7 Economic ties, including property ownership;
8 Contribution to, and participation in, community activities;
9 Any criminal record.[106]

103 Ministerial Direction 65 Made under s499 Migration Act, 'Visa Refusal and Cancellation under s501 and Revocation of a Mandatory Cancellation of a Visa under s501CA', 22 December 2014, <www.homeaffairs.gov.au/visas/Documents/ministerial-direction-65.pdf>.

104 *Minister for Immigration and Multicultural and Indigenous Affairs v Nystrom* (2006) 228 CLR 566.

105 Justice French, acting in this case as a judge of the Federal Court of Australia, later became the Chief Justice of the High Court of Australia.

106 *Johnson* (2004) 136 FCR 494, 510.

European Union

The duration of stay and integrative links of a refugee are recognised in EU directives and case law. The 2003 Directive on the Status of Non-EU Nationals Who are Long-Term Residents provides that the status of 'long-term resident' should be awarded after a person has lived legally in an EU Member State for an uninterrupted period of 5 years.[107]

Enhanced protection against return

A recent decision of the CJEU in the joined case of *Applicant B and Votero*, handed down in 2018, illustrates how long-term residence is dealt with under EU law.[108] What is of interest to the discussion of integrative links in this chapter is that one of the applicants (a national of Greece) who had committed a criminal offence, challenged a removal decision on the basis that, as he had resided in Germany since the age of 3 and had no ties to Greece, he qualified for what is known as 'enhanced protection' against expulsion provided for in the EU Directive on Free Movement of Residence.[109] In the decision of the CJEU, the court noted that the protection against expulsion provided for in the EU Directive on Free Movement and Residence gradually increases in proportion to the *degree of integration* of the EU citizen in the host Member State. The court held that 'whether or not the enhanced protection provided for in Article 28(3)(a) of Directive 2004/38 is granted will still depend on the duration of residence and the degree of integration of the citizen concerned in the host Member State'.[110] The courts here adopted a holistic approach to the assessment of the individual situation: the court considered the strength of the integrative links forged with the host Member State as well as the criminal behaviour of the applicant.[111]

107 Council Directive 2003/109/EC of 25 November 2003 concerning the status of third-country nationals who are long-term residents OJ L 16, 23.1.2004, pp. 44–53. In 2011, the directive was amended to cover non-EU citizens, such as refugees or the stateless, who enjoy international protection. Note that the granting of this status is dependent upon the person having a stable and regular source of income, health insurance and, when required by the EU State, having complied with integration measures. The applicants must also not constitute a threat to public security or public policy. The United Kingdom, Ireland and Denmark have special arrangements for immigration and asylum policy, and the Directive on long-term resident status does not therefore apply in these countries.

108 Joined cases *C316/16 (Applicant B) and C424/16 (Vomero).*

109 Directive 2004/38/EC of the European Parliament and of the Council of 29 April 2004 on the right of citizens of the Union and their family members to move and reside freely within the territory of the Member States amending Regulation (EEC) No 1612/68 and repealing Directives 64/221/EEC, 68/360/EEC, 72/194/EEC, 73/148/EEC, 75/34/EEC, 75/35/EEC, 90/364/EEC, 90/365/EEC and 93/96/EEC, Official Journal of the European Communities, 30.4.2004, L 158/77 (hereinafter EU Directive on Free Movement and Residence).

110 *Land Baden-Württemberg (C-316/16) and Secretary of State for the Home Department v Franco Vomero (C-424/16)*, CJEU, 17 April 2018, [82] (*Vomero*).

111 *Vomero*, where the CJEU at [83] states: 'Article 28(3)(a) of Directive 2004/38 must be interpreted as meaning that, in the case of a Union citizen who is serving a custodial sentence

Recognising 'social citizenship': how integrative links should be considered in cessation and deportation of long-term refugee residents

The state practice summarised above indicates that the settlement status of long-term residents are recognised in the legal procedure in some jurisdictions (via consideration of their social and political integration). I argue that this should also be a consideration in cessation and deportation decisions.

I therefore recommend that integration by a refugee in an asylum host state should be considered in deportation decisions. This analysis is firmly anchored in the rights granted to refugees as they increase their links to the asylum host state (from being merely 'present' to 'lawfully present' and then 'lawfully staying' or 'resident' in a state) and in the social membership status of long-term resident refugees.

In terms of the duration of stay which will trigger this process, I note that some state practice and commentary on duration of stay appears to accept that a 5-year period is the point at which an asylum host state should consider granting a refugee permanency. For instance, the South African Refugees Act allows refugees to apply for permanent residence after 5 years of continuous residence in South Africa.[112] Similarly, UK law allows for refugees to apply for indefinite leave to remain after 5 years.[113] Academic commentary also seems to agree on a period of 5 years.[114] For instance, James Hathaway has noted that 'five years is not an unreasonable estimate of the earliest point at which repatriation may be said to be unviable from a psychosocial perspective'.[115] Interestingly, two EU Directives

---

and against whom an expulsion decision is adopted, the condition of having 'resided in the host Member State for the previous ten years' laid down in that provision may be satisfied where an overall assessment of the person's situation, taking into account all the relevant aspects, leads to the conclusion that, notwithstanding that detention, the integrative links between the person concerned and the host Member State have not been broken. Those aspects include, inter alia, the strength of the integrative links forged with the host Member State before the detention of the person concerned, the nature of the offence that resulted in the period of detention imposed, the circumstances in which that offence was committed and the conduct of the person concerned throughout the period of detention'.

112 Refugee Act 1998, South Africa, s 27(c): 'A refugee is entitled to apply for an immigration permit . . . after five years' continuous residence in the Republic from the date on which he or she was granted asylum, if the Standing Committee certifies that he or she will remain a refugee indefinitely'.

113 UK Home Office Guidance, 'Refugee Leave', 2 March 2017, <www.statewatch.org/news/2017/mar/uk-home-office-refugee-settlement-limits-policy-3-17.pdf>.

114 See e.g. Joseph Carens: 'Once people have been settled for an extended period – say, five years or so – they are morally entitled to the same legal rights (and ought to be subject to the same legal obligations) as citizens': J. Carens, 'On Belonging: What We Owe People Who Stay' *Boston Review*, 1 June 2005, <http://bostonreview.net/carens-on-belonging?>.

115 See e.g. J.C. Hathaway and R. Alexander Neve, 'Making International Refugee Law Relevant Again: A Proposal for Collectivized and Solution-Oriented Protection' (1997) 10 *Harvard Human Rights Journal* 115, 199. See also Joseph Carens: 'Once people have been settled for an extended period – say, five years or so – they are morally entitled to the same legal rights (and ought to be subject to the same legal obligations) as citizens': J. Carens, 'On Belonging: What We Owe People Who Stay' *Boston Review*, 1 June 2005, <http://bostonreview.net/carens-on-belonging?>.

on residence also place the marker at 5 years: the 2003 Directive on the Status of Non-EU Nationals who are Long-Term Residents states that the status of long-term resident should be awarded after a person has lived legally in an EU Member State for an uninterrupted period of 5 years. Additionally, the EU Directive on Free Movement and Residence provides that EU citizens who have resided legally for a continuous period of 5 years in a Member State (other than their own) will acquire a right of permanent residence in that state.[116] Although these directives are not explicitly applicable to refugees, these do provide further evidence that many states recognise that 5 years is the period after which some recognition of integrative status should take place. I also note that for many countries, refugees and other migrants need to wait 5 years before they become eligible for citizenship, so arguably these states have recognised that this is the length of time that it takes a person to integrate into a society.[117]

In light of the preceding, I argue that 5 years should be considered the point at which a grant of permanent residence should be considered by an asylum host state and that, if this is not done, the duration of stay by the refugee in the host state should be an influential factor in any cessation and return decision.

The reasonableness of return

The state practice discussed in this chapter reflects the use of principles such as 'enhanced protection against expulsion' and the concept of an 'absorbed person'. However, given that my analysis is concerned with *refugees*, it may be preferable to utilise an accepted concept from refugee law. One such concept which could be applied to an 'integrative links' situation is the 'reasonableness criterion' used as part of the Internal Flight Alternative (IFA) test.[118] Under this test, states may deny a person refugee status where that person has a well-founded fear of persecution in relation to a region within their country of origin, but can relocate to another area within their country of origin (where they will not face a well-founded fear of persecution).[119] Significantly, for the purpose of this chapter, most jurisdictions recognise that in order for IFA to be found in relation to a particular applicant, it must be 'reasonable' for that applicant to relocate. The

116 Hathaway and Neve, above n 115.

117 For instance, the minimum period of residence in order to apply for citizenship is 5 years in the UK, New Zealand and the Netherlands.

118 I note that James Hathaway and Michelle Foster advocated the use of 'Internal Protection Alternative': see J.C. Hathaway and M. Foster, 'Internal Protection/Relocation/Flight Alternative as an Aspect of Refugee Status Determination', in E. Feller, V. Türk and F. Nicholson (eds.), *Refugee Protection in International Law: UNHCR's Global Consultations on International Protection* (Cambridge University Press, 2003), 358, 382–3. However, as 'Internal Flight Alternative' is the term used by many states and jurisprudence I have used it here as the more commonly recognised terminology.

119 For a discussion of relocation and its interaction with cessation, see M. O'Sullivan, 'Territorial Protection: Cessation and Internal Protection Alternative Compared', in S. Juss (ed.), *Ashgate Commentary on Migration Law and Theory* (Ashgate, 2013).

reasonableness criterion is reflected in the EU Qualification Directive[120] and is used in IFA decisions in a number of state parties to the Convention, including Austria, Denmark, USA, Canada, UK, the Netherlands, France and Germany.[121] UNHCR has also endorsed a 'reasonableness' criterion for relocation:

> The fear of being persecuted need not always extend to the whole territory of the refugee's country of nationality. Thus in ethnic clashes or in cases of grave disturbances involving civil war conditions, persecution of a specific ethnic or national group may occur in only one part of the country. In such situations, a person will not be excluded from refugee status merely because he could have sought refuge in another part of the same country, if under all the circumstances it would not have been reasonable to expect him to do so.[122]

As noted earlier, refugees who are subjected to a cessation decision may have stayed in a host state for a significant period of time. During this period, circumstances in the refugee's country of origin may have substantially changed – there may be a different social and economic structure and the refugee may no longer have family, friends or employment in his or her country of origin. In many cases, due to extended (and sometimes continuing) armed conflict within the country, the refugee's former home may also have been destroyed or taken over, and local communities and other support networks may no longer be functioning.[123] In such situations, it is arguable that the return of a refugee who has been residing in an asylum host state for a number of years and who has integrated to some extent in the country of asylum may be viewed as 'relocating' back to their country of origin.

Similar parallels have been made by UNHCR in relation to the cessation and IFA provisions of the EU Qualification Directive. UNHCR note that cessation

120 Article 8(1), *Directive 2011/95/EU of the European Parliament and of the Council of 13 December 2011 on Standards for the Qualification of Third-Country Nationals or Stateless Persons as Beneficiaries of International Protection, for a Uniform Status for Refugees or for Persons Eligible for Subsidiary Protection, and for the Content of the Protection Granted (recast)*, [2011] OJ L 337/9.

121 See discussion in H. Storey, 'The Internal Flight Alternative Test: The Jurisprudence Re-Examined' (1998) 10 *International Journal of Refugee Law* 499, 511.

122 UNHCR, *Handbook on Procedures and Criteria for Determining Refugee Status under the 1951 Convention and the 1967 Protocol Relating to the Status of Refugees*, HCR/IP/4/Rev. 1, 1979, Reedited, Geneva, January 1992, [135] (hereinafter UNHCR *Handbook*) [91]. This was referred to by Lord Bingham in the leading UK case on IFA: *Januzi v Secretary of State for the Home Department* [2006] 2 AC 426 at 440.

123 For instance, as of May 2007, there were approximately 20,000 compensation claims before Kosovo courts arising from the destruction of property in 1999 and 2000 (see Centre on Housing Rights and Eviction, 'Property Return and Restitution: Kosovo-Prepared for Review of Covenant Law Issues in Kosovo by the UN Committee on Economic, Social and Cultural Rights', 2008, <www2.ohchr.org/english/bodies/cescr/docs/info-ngos/COHREUNMIK.pdf>. See also Kosovo: UNHCR, *Update on Kosovo Crisis*, 1999, <www.unhcr.org/3ae6b80f48.html>.

and relocation are both premised on a *change of place of residence*, that IFA relates to the availability of a relocation alternative within the country of origin, whereas the application of the 'ceased circumstances' clause refers the person to the protection of the country of origin and thereby may imply a return to that country. UNHCR notes that '[g]iven these similarities, the broad understanding of the term "protection" in the context of internal protection is also relevant for the application of the "ceased circumstances" clause'.[124]

Thus, I would argue that if a host state wishes to deport a refugee back to their country of origin then they should consider whether it is reasonable to do so, arguing by analogy to IFA. I would also point out that a 'reasonableness' test is also applied in other jurisdictions in relation to return of certain immigrants. For instance, section 117B(6) of the UK Nationality Immigration and Asylum Act 2002, provides that where the applicant is a child who is a British citizen or has been residing in the UK for a continuous period of 7 years or more, the public interest does *not* require removal if it would not be *reasonable* to expect the child to leave the UK.[125]

Counterarguments to my integrative links criterion

There are a number of arguments which could be raised in response to my analysis. First, some may argue that this represents an overly inclusive approach to the refugee definition in the Refugee Convention and that it is preferable to adopt a practical interpretation of the law. This is particularly so given the increasingly hostile environment in which many refugees must make a claim. Thus, although a legal argument can be raised that the level of integration in an asylum host state should be a relevant consideration in any deportation decision, I must also consider the implications of making such an argument. That is, requiring an asylum host state to consider integration may deter such states from granting refugees any sort of protection in the first instance. This may have an unwanted flow-on effect: that such states choose to deflect refugees or set up offshore processing (as has been the case in Australia). I acknowledge that my test may have unforeseen or unintended consequences in that it may motivate states to increase non-admission policies or give refugees a status other than refugee status (to avoid application of any robust cessation test). That is, it may be said that if the test for cessation is so strict that it makes it virtually impossible for states to return those who are no longer refugees under the law, then states may be unwilling to grant refugee status and, instead, give a diluted status or, indeed, not allow refugees to apply for protection in the first instance. This is demonstrated by the statement by Hon. Mr E. Mwambulukutu, Deputy Minister for

124 'UNHCR Statement on the "Ceased Circumstances" Clause of the EC Qualification Directive' (2008), 15, <www.unhcr.org/refworld/docid/48a2f0782.html> (emphasis added).

125 A similar provision is also set out in paragraph 276ADE(1)(iv) of the Immigration Rules, and s117C(5) of the 2002 Act. This reasonableness criterion was discussed in *KO (Nigeria) and Others v Secretary of State for the Home Department* [2018] UKSC 53.

Home Affairs of the United Republic of Tanzania, to the 48th session of the UNHCR Executive Committee:

> Governments have become more reluctant to grant asylum to refugees where protection is perceived as a way of obtaining permanent stay in a country which on strictly humanitarian grounds, has volunteered to host refugees.[126]

Sniderman has also raised a concern that states may recognise fewer asylum seekers as refugees if refugee status amounts to permanent residency, noting that '[i]f cessation is not regarded as a viable pathway for states to reduce their refugee caseloads – states may pursue worse alternatives'.[127]

My proposal has considered this reality by setting a threshold on the required duration of stay (5 years) and by acknowledging that states should still retain their legal and moral claim to decide whether to grant a refugee citizenship. I have also presented a compromise position by advocating for the *consideration* by the state of that integration of a refugee via application of a reasonableness test. What my analysis does is to recognise that the law must to some extent at least reflect the practical integration of a refugee in the host state.

A second counterargument may be that the formation of integrated links by a refugee should not be seen to give rise to a *right not to be expelled* after a particular length of time. This is an important right for states to maintain, particularly if a refugee who has formed integrated links commits a serious criminal act. In such a case, integrative links would be a consideration (as would *non-refoulement*) but would not of themselves prevent such a person being deported. Rather, the integrated links would simply form a relevant consideration that should be taken into account in a deportation decision. This may depend on whether the long-term resident refugee can be equated with a citizen in terms of participation in the asylum host a community.

Thirdly, I recognise that my integrative links framework is very public in nature. It may work to disadvantage women who may not participate as publicly in the community (for cultural reasons).[128] That is, that it may privilege male-dominated 'public' activities over the activities of women, which largely take place in the 'private' sphere. As Heaven Crawley has acknowledged:

> the dominant interpretation of refugee law has evolved through an examination of male asylum applicants and their activities. It is men who have been

126 Statement by Hon. Mr E. Mwambulukutu, Deputy Minister for Home Affairs of the United Republic of Tanzania, to the 48th Session, 15 Oct. 1997, 6, cited in M. Barutciski, 'Involuntary Pepatriation When Refugee Protection Is No Longer Necessary: Moving Forward after the 48th Session of the Executive Committee. (United Nations High Commissioner for Refugees)' (1998) 10(1–2) *International Journal of Refugee Law* 236, 252 (footnote 64).

127 Sniderman, above n 87, 614.

128 I thank my research assistant, Aisha Ismail, for alerting me to the fact that my 'integrative links' framework may have gender implications.

> considered the principal agents of political resistance and therefore the legitimate beneficiaries of protection resulting from persecution.[129]

This problem can be addressed by highlighting that it is not only 'public' manifestations of belonging which will constitute integrative links and that the gender dimensions of this test could be raised with decision makers by inclusion of instructions in relevant gender guidelines.

Conclusions – an integrative links test

In summary, I argue that after a significant amount of time has elapsed (5 years or more), the social and/or political integration established by refugees must be reflected in law to the effect that such persons cannot be deported from a host state without that host state taking into account the integrative links the refugee has established. There should be flexibility within the system to adjust the status of such persons.

This is justified on a number of legal bases. First, a significant period of residence in an asylum host state may affect the capacity of refugees to reintegrate into their home country. Thus, although integrative links are not explicitly mentioned in Article 1C(5) of the Refugee Convention, it does link to the terms used in Article 1C(5) about the refugee no longer being able to 'continue to refuse to avail himself of the protection of the country of his nationality'. Second, it is arguable that persons who have lived in a host state for many years (5–20 years) have a right, as a matter of both law and morality, to claim membership of a society and therefore to at least be able to claim a pathway to citizenship. Third, there is an argument that Article 1C should be interpreted in light of human rights principles, as is Article 1A(2). This is justified as a general proposition, but also because Article 1C(5) is part of the refugee definition and utilises similar principles to that of Article 1A(2) and linked to it via the terms 'persecution' and 'protection'. Finally, whilst it is recognised that the cessation clauses pursue a legitimate aim – to return persons who are no longer refugees back to their country of origin – this must be considered in light of individual circumstances and be proportionate to this aim. That is, the decision maker must bear in mind the hardship which may result to an individual resulting from cessation. In this respect, decision makers may consider whether a fair balance has been struck between the rights of the individual and the interests of the community.

My recommendations are therefore that:

- Residence of over 5 years by a recognised refugee[130] should give rise to 'enhanced protection' against deportation.

129 H. Crawley, '[En]gendering International Refugee Protection: Are We There Yet', in B. Burson and D.J. Cantor (eds.), *Human Rights and the Refugee Definition: Comparative Legal Practice and Theory* (Brill, 2016), 322, 323.

130 Under my approach, the 5 years would operate as of the date of domestic recognition of refugee status.

- Where cessation is utilised to revoke a person's refugee status, states wishing to return such a (former) refugee should consider the integrative links which the person has established in the asylum host state and the 'reasonableness' of that return.
- These considerations should include family ties, but also the duration of stay and the integrative links made by the refugee (discussed earlier in this chapter). In relation to the duration of stay, particular regard should be made to whether that stay was during the person's formative years (1–18 years of age).

As detailed earlier, there is a significant lack of clarity and consistency in state practice in relation to the standards to be applied when ceasing the status of refugees who have been resident in an asylum host state for significant periods of time. This chapter has presented one model for filling this gap in the law.

8 Conclusions

Cessation of refugee status is an increasingly important aspect of global refugee law and policy. It raises a central debate in refugee law about the scope and meaning of 'persecution' and 'protection' in the Refugee Convention and the relationship between these two important concepts in international refugee law. The question at the heart of this book, and indeed international refugee law more generally, is who is to be protected and upon what basis? Specifically, when refugee status is granted, what criteria should be used to withdraw that status?

As established in the analysis in preceding chapters, cessation raises complex legal and humanitarian questions, as it typically involves the revocation of refugee status from a person who has been resident in an asylum host state for a number of years. In this book, I have attempted to set out a legal test which is consistent with the Refugee Convention. However, for policy reasons, I also advocate for a legal test for cessation which is pragmatic – that states will accept. Thus, I have attempted to take a principled yet pragmatic approach to the obligation of states to naturalise resident refugees by recommending that integrative links be a relevant consideration in deportation decisions, rather than imposing a direct obligation on states to grant refugees citizenship.

As explained in Chapter 2, there is a tension between use of time-limited visas and the rights which accrue to refugees under Articles 3 to 34 of the Convention, particularly Article 34 dealing with naturalisation and assimilation of refugees. I argue that, when viewed in the context of the Refugee Convention as a whole, and its function as an instrument of human rights protection, the Convention *does* recognise that states should attempt to grant some form of lasting protection and security to refugees without constant review of status. Such an interpretation is consistent with the aim of providing refugees with a durable solution to their plight. It also accords with the nature of the rights which accrue to refugees under Articles 3–34, in that these are linked to the level of attachment that refugees have to the asylum host state. That is, the more integrated and greater recognised a refugee becomes, the more rights that refugee must be granted under the Convention. The fact that the Convention sets out a suite of rights which are commensurate with integration and legal acceptance in the asylum host state and which are, for the most part, similar to rights and benefits given to citizens and permanent residents, supports the notion that the Convention places great importance on a level of integration, stability and security of residence.

Against this background, this book discussed the criteria which should be utilised in applying cessation to individualised time-limited visas. Answering this question and achieving a principled interpretation of the Refugee Convention in the contemporary landscape is becoming increasingly complex due to the various, and sometimes conflicting, conceptions of 'protection' which are utilised by state parties to the Convention. I argue that persecution and protection, whilst linked in the refugee definition, are two very different concepts under cessation, and indeed under international refugee law more broadly. The concept of 'protection' in cessation decisions is a much wider and different concept to that of persecution, in that it involves positive attributes such as, *inter alia*, the provision of physical security and safety; the existence of a functioning government and basic administrative structures, including a functioning legal and judicial system; and an adequate infrastructure to enable residents to exercise their rights. As such, this book questioned whether it is possible for cessation to be satisfied where the refugee is being returned to a state where there is an ongoing armed conflict or where protection is being provided by a non-state actor.

The continuing and protracted human rights and security problems in Iraq, Afghanistan and Somalia provide an important illustration of some of the complexities, both legal and political, that arise in deciding the criteria upon which refugee status should be ceased. Despite concerted efforts to achieve peace and democratisation in these countries, they continue to suffer from protracted civil conflict, political instability and systemic economic problems. The situations in these three countries illustrate that cessation of refugee status should be based on criteria which are broader than mere absence of persecution. In this respect, cessation involves questions not only about refugee law but also geo-political questions about assessing the likely developments in the country situation in the future. For instance, what will be the likely effect of the withdrawal of multinational troops and other international actors upon the durability of change in the country? Are there security and socio-economic factors which may affect the country's future stability? In assessing such country conditions, the volatility caused by armed conflict in a country will militate against application of cessation under Article 1C(5).

In answering these questions, one must focus upon the terms and function of cessation and its relationship to other articles in the Refugee Convention. Thus, in Chapter 2, I argued that a recognised refugee who is to be subject to cessation is in a different legal position to that of an asylum seeker applying for refugee status as part of an initial procedure. A recognised refugee has been found by state authorities to have a well-founded fear of persecution, has been given rights in accordance with that status and has integrated (at least to some extent) in the host state. This must be reflected in the cessation criteria.

Thus, the central argument of this book is that cessation under Article 1C(5) imposes different criteria to that of recognition of refugee status. That is, that Article 1C(5) is not the 'mirror image' of Article 1A(2). This arises from the wording of Article 1C(5), its purpose and its relationship with other articles in the Convention. Significantly, Article 1C(5) refers to the '*circumstances in connection with which*' a person has been recognised as a refugee. The criteria in Article 1C(5) are therefore broader than the reasons for recognition of refugee status under Article 1A(2). I argue therefore that use of Article 1C(5) is not appropriate where there is merely an absence of fear of persecution in the refugee's country of nationality within the meaning of Article 1A(2). Rather it is necessary to prove that objective, effective protection is available in the country of origin encompassing criteria such as human rights protections, the rule of law and the absence of armed conflict.

It is also widely recognised that the standard required for Article 1C(5) is that the changes in country conditions are 'fundamental, stable and durable'. I argued that changes cannot meet this standard if there continue to be violations of basic human rights, armed conflict and an absence of basic socio-economic infrastructure in the country of origin. Further, cessation involves the withdrawal of the 'acquired rights' given to refugees lawfully present in the country of asylum and as such must be applied with caution. The fact that refugees have been recognised as such, and given a status, places recognised refugees in a different legal position to asylum seekers lodging an initial application for refugee status, and this must be reflected in the criteria for cessation. Specifically, both refugee status itself and the acquired rights associated with such status should not be withdrawn from a recognised refugee without sufficiently clear reasons, that is, satisfaction of the criteria set out in Article 1C of the Convention, as interpreted in this book. As such, I have critiqued the narrow interpretation of cessation by courts in Australia and the EU. I particularly question the approach of the Australian High Court which requires refugees to reprove their refugee status under Article 1A(2) in order to obtain a permanent protection visa.

Related to this, and due to the nature of refugeehood as involving the relationship between the individual and state, the mere fact that a non-state body may be *able* to provide protection in a region or country is not sufficient to constitute 'protection' under the Refugee Convention. Thus, non-state actors should not be viewed as sufficient actors of protection under international refugee law. If protection is provided by a temporary, transitional non-state entity, there is a risk that refugees will be returned to a country where they will be at risk of persecution contrary to the principle of *non-refoulement*. This is particularly so in relation to clans and militias who have obtained political control of a certain part of a state. Such political control and the provision of security to individuals should not be equated with the high level of 'protection' required for the purposes of international refugee law. Likewise, the presence of multinational troops should not be viewed as providing such protection, particularly where there is an ongoing armed conflict occurring within the state in question (such as Iraq and Afghanistan). Thus, a broad interpretation of non-state actors which includes 'parties' and 'international organizations', such as set out in Article 7(1) of the EU Qualification Directive is not justifiable on a principled level, nor advisable in practice. This is particularly so in cessation cases where persecution of an individual (via recognition of refugee status) has already shown to have occurred, and the asylum host state is attempting to return the refugee to that country of origin based on an alleged change in circumstances.

In terms of procedural requirements, I have argued that cessation must be formally invoked by a state and requires the state to assume the burden of demonstrating a 'fundamental, stable and durable' change in the circumstances of the country of origin. I also argue for a liberal approach to be taken to the consideration of past persecution in cessation decisions. Thus, despite any change of circumstances in the country of origin which mean that the reason for the previous persecution has been removed, the fact that past persecution has taken place has evidentiary value in assessing any new claims of persecution (even if the link to the past persecution is only partial). In assessing the relationship between past persecution and cessation of refugee status, decision makers must take an approach which fully reflects the long-term effects of past persecution. In the context of Article 4(4) of the EU Qualification Directive, it should be borne in mind that past persecution should not and cannot be cleanly separated from the consideration of future persecution and the *fact* that past persecution has occurred may be of evidential value to findings on future persecution, even if the *reasons* or *grounds* for that persecution are not the same.

I recognise that given the current climate of restrictionism in refugee law and policy, there may be resistance to a more liberal interpretation of cessation which imposes a threshold of 'effective protection', rather than the narrower requirement of absence of persecution. However, in making conclusions on these legal issues, the nature of the act of cessation should be borne in mind. Cessation is a serious decision which takes away refugee status from a recognised refugee. As UNHCR has emphasised, as a result of this, cessation provisions must be exercised with great caution.[1] Thus, given the seriousness of cessation and the risk of return of refugees in breach of the *non-refoulement* principle, I submit that the 'effective protection' test is reflective of a good faith, purposive interpretation of the Convention and that a more liberal interpretation is called for than that advocated by certain states.

Given the preceding, what is the significance of this analysis for international refugee law more broadly?

The arguments put forward in this book have practical implications for the return of asylum seekers and refugees to situations of ongoing conflict and post-conflict situations and is therefore highly pertinent to the future development of international refugee law. The use of Article 1C(5) by states to date is of concern in this context, as the clause has been largely applied to refugees from Iraq and Afghanistan – countries which continue to be in a situation of civil conflict and

1 UNHCR, 'Guidelines on International Protection: Cessation of Refugee Status under Article 1C(5) and (6) of the 1951 Convention Relating to the Status of Refugees (the "Ceased Circumstances" Clauses)', HCR/GIP/03/03, 10 February 2003 [7]; UNHCR, Executive Committee Conclusion No. 69, *Cessation of Status*, U.N. GAOR, 47th Sess. (1992), Preamble, [4].

face ongoing security concerns and political volatility. The continuing security problems in Afghanistan in particular illustrate the importance of applying cessation criteria which include requirements of stability and durability of change so as to ensure that refugees are not sent back to their country of nationality in breach of the *non-refoulement* principle under Article 33 of the Convention.

In this book I have highlighted some of the legal and practical issues which arise when states attempt to utilise the cessation provisions under Article 1C(5) of the 1951 Refugee Convention. There are a number of future research topics which could draw on and develop the analysis presented in this book.

First, further work could be carried out to clarify the relationship between refugee status and complementary protection. As noted in Chapter 4 of this book, the CJEU in *Abdulla* insisted on the strict separation of the criteria for cessation and complementary protection and held that the cessation criteria did not include 'serious harm'. This raises a broader and serious issue about how refugee status and complementary protection should be defined in relation to each other. It is important to note that the stated purpose of the Qualification Directive is not to *replace* international refugee law but to provide regional guidelines on its interpretation. It is therefore essential to maintain the legitimacy of the Refugee Convention and to give full effect to the refugee definition. Whilst it is acknowledged that the criteria for complementary protection must be demarcated to some extent from that of refugee status, in order to recognise the special nature of refugee status and the 1951 Refugee Convention, the complementary protection criteria must not be used as a means of restricting the operation of the refugee definition and its associated protections.

Second, further consideration should be given to the operation of individualised temporary permits and visas to ensure that they operate humanely and according to the principles set out in the 1951 Refugee Convention. I highlight in particular here the use of 'rolling' temporary protection visas in Australia. The use of such visas requires further study, given the Convention emphasises principles of integration, stability and security of residence for refugees in the rights set out in Articles 3–34 of the Convention, and particularly Article 34. As I argue in this book, Article 1C(5) of the Convention arguably does not justify the use of protection visas or permits which are granted on a continually renewable basis with no avenue for permanency. Here the recognition of the principle of human dignity in Article 1 of the EU Charter of Fundamental Rights could provide a framework for further analysis of the issues discussed in this book, particularly in relation to the use of 'rolling' renewable resident permits and the use of cessation against refugees who have been resident in host states for lengthy periods.[2]

Finally, it is important to consider more broadly the implications of the preceding for international refugee law and how refugee law is interpreted across jurisdictions. One important aspect of interpretation of the Refugee Convention

2 European Union, *Charter of Fundamental Rights of the European Union*, 26 October 2012, 2012/C 326/02, Article 1: 'Human dignity is inviolable. It must be respected and protected'.

is consistency between jurisdictions, which has been a problem in the area of refugee law and practice. Some commentators and courts have highlighted the need to ensure a level of consensus in interpretation of the Refugee Convention.[3] In one oft-cited comment, Lord Steyn of the House of Lords emphasised the need to give the Refugee Convention an 'independent meaning' derived from the sources set out in the VCLT and 'without taking colour from distinctive features of the legal system of any individual contracting state'.[4] Lord Steyn then noted that '[i]n principle therefore there can only be one true interpretation of a treaty'.[5]

However, this goal has been difficult to reach in practice. Many commentators have pointed to the lack of consistency between jurisdictions in relation to interpretation of the Convention.[6] This lack of consistency can be seen in the different tests used for key aspects of the refugee definition, such as the meaning of 'particular social group',[7] and the interpretation of exclusion clauses under Article 1F.[8] It has been noted by some commentators that there is generally a good level of dialogue between the courts of Australia, UK, New Zealand and Canada, primarily due to their shared legal and political history.[9] On the other hand, there appears to be some obstacles to judicial dialogue, particularly within the EU. For instance, Hélène Lambert has pointed to 'the lack of a transnational European legal dialogue in French and British asylum jurisprudence'.[10]

A related problem is that many states do not endorse the legal or country information guidelines issued by UNHCR, which would ensure a greater level of consensus across jurisdictions. As discussed in Chapter 1, UNHCR tends to have a central role in group-based cessation due to their issuance of general declarations on the 'ceased circumstances' clause. However, as discussed in this book, the position of UNHCR on key aspects of the interpretation of Article 1C(5) has not been considered or endorsed in leading jurisprudence in Australia and the EU. I note here that the UNHCR Handbook, guidelines and other advisory opinions of UNHCR are not legally binding on states parties to the Refugee Convention.

3 See e.g. A. North and J. Chia, 'Towards Convergence in the Interpretation of the Refugee Convention: A Proposal for the Establishment of an International Judicial Commission for Refugees', in J. McAdam (ed.), *Forced Migration, Human Rights and Security* (Hart Publishing, 2008). See also *R. v. Secretary of State for the Home Department, Ex parte Adan; R. v. Secretary of State for the Home Department Ex parte Aitseguer* [2001] 2 A.C. 477 at 516 (Lord Steyn) (*Adan* 2001).

4 *Adan* 2001, 516 (Lord Steyn).

5 Ibid.

6 See e.g. H. Lambert, 'Transnational Judicial Dialogue, Harmonization and the Common European Asylum System' (2009) 58(3) *International and Comparative Law Quarterly* 519; North and Chia, above n 3, 225–61.

7 See North and Chia, above n 3, 230–2.

8 Ibid 232–3.

9 See Hathaway, Rights of Refugees, above n 2, 1–2 (citations omitted).

10 H. Lambert, 'Transnational Judicial Dialogue, Harmonization and the Common European Asylum System' (2009) 58(3) *International and Comparative Law Quarterly* 519, 540.

As Jane McAdam has noted, UNHCR's supervisory role under Articles 35 and 36 of the Refugee Convention:

> does not extend to a mandate to provide authoritative rulings or opinions on the meaning of particular treaty terms, and accordingly the UNHCR can only issue *guidance* on the 1951 Convention's interpretation through the UNHCR *Handbook on Procedures*, UNHCR guidelines, and its notes on international protection.[11]

Hathaway and Foster have also queried the use of UNHCR documents as subsequent agreement:

> In truth, most policy documents issued by the UNHCR are produced by the agency without the sort of active deliberation and agreement of state parties that would ordinarily be expected of a "subsequent agreement" between the parties. . . . Refugee case law has thus sensibly refrained from assigning any particular interpretive status to the UNHCR's published positions, even as it has clearly recognised the frequent value of the agency's advice in the interpretive process.[12]

Naturally, there will always be a certain level of difference between the interpretation of the Refugee Convention in national jurisdictions due to varying constitutional and administrative structures and political imperatives.[13] However, there are strong arguments in favour of states endorsing and applying this international UNHCR guidance, in light of the need for better levels of consistency noted earlier. It is also important because when domestic courts do look to each other for guidance on interpretation of the Refugee Convention, this cross-fertilisation of jurisprudence is informed by input from UNHCR.

The issue of consistency is a particularly pertinent one for EU asylum law, which has formulated harmonised directives on refugee laws and procedures via the EU Common European Asylum System. Here, the case law on cessation discussed in Chapter 4 raises some concerns about regionalisation of refugee law in the EU. Although the EU Qualification Directive is explicitly stated to be based on the 1951 Refugee Convention, and all EU Member States are signatories to

11 J. McAdam, 'Interpretation of the 1951 Convention', in A. Zimmermann (ed.), *The 1951 Convention Relating to the Status of Refugees and Its 1967 Protocol: A Commentary* (Oxford University Press, 2011), 79 (emphasis in original).

12 J.C. Hathaway and M. Foster, *The Law of Refugee Status* (Cambridge University Press, 2nd ed., 2014), 10. In noting this, Hathaway and Foster do also state that '[w]hilst we agree that the UNHCR's views are not binding on states parties as a matter of treaty interpretation, we nonetheless believe that serious engagement with UNHCR advice is to be expected, in particular given the duty of state parties under Art. 35 of the Convention to cooperate with the UNHCR in the exercise of its supervisory functions' (at 10).

13 This issue is discussed in S. Kneebone (ed.), *Refugees, Asylum Seekers and the Rule of Law: Comparative Perspectives* (Cambridge University Press, 2009).

that Convention, the role of the CJEU in ensuring that EU asylum law is consistent with international refugee law requires further consideration.

The preliminary ruling procedure which operates between national courts and the CJEU is an important tool for promoting harmonisation of standards between EU Member States.[14] Its role is also important given that there is no international refugee court or other supervisory body which has the power to make orders in relation to the adherence by states to the Refugee Convention.[15] In this light, the CJEU is poised to take an influential role in the shaping of EU refugee law, and in turn, international refugee law.

However, there are a number of concerns with the way in which the CJEU consider the 1951 Convention. One of these is that current CJEU procedure does not give a formal intervention or *amicus curiae* role to UNHCR. This is a serious impediment to ensuring that EU asylum law accords with the 1951 Convention.[16] This is of particular concern because the CJEU is a supra-national and therefore highly influential regional court. It would be highly undesirable for the court to develop its refugee jurisprudence without reference to current international refugee legal standards. If this occurs, the harmonisation of EU refugee law may fragment the international nature of the Convention. Thus, I recommend that CJEU procedures relating to the intervention by a third party in cases involving refugee matters should be amended to allow for a formal intervention right by UNHCR. Further, due to the fact that the EU Qualification Directive is said to codify the Refugee Convention, I argue that the CJEU must consider not only the provisions of the Directives but also the way in which the equivalent provisions have been interpreted in international law, including UNHCR opinion and academic commentary. In that way, European asylum law can contribute to both a fully harmonised European system, and, perhaps more importantly, to a truly universal understanding of refugee protection.

A further policy implication of using cessation, particularly in light of EU proposals to introduce status review mechanisms, is that it raises significant resource problems (it requires significant administrative and judicial resources). Thus, frequent use of status reviews may serve to exacerbate already existing backlogs of asylum processing in states.

This book has explored the legal issues arising from the application of Article 1C(5) of the Refugee Convention, the concepts of persecution and protection under international refugee law and, more broadly, what it means to be a refugee. I have set out an interpretation of protection in international refugee law which I hope reflects both a principled and pragmatic approach to the issue, and one which advances the core purpose of the Convention – the protection of refugees.

14 The Court of Justice of the European Union (CJEU) is given jurisdiction to deal with requests for preliminary rulings from national courts and tribunals under Article 267 of the Treaty on the Functioning of the European Union (TFEU).

15 See a similar point made by Jane McAdam, above n 11, 77. See also North and Chia, above n 3, 225–61.

16 See discussion of this in Chapters 3 through 5 of this book.

Appendices

Appendix 1

Excerpts from the 1951 Refugee Convention

Article 1A(2)

As a result of events occurring before 1 January 1951 and owing to well-founded fear of being persecuted for reasons of race, religion, nationality, membership of a particular social group or political opinion, is outside the country of his nationality and is unable or, owing to such fear, is unwilling to avail himself of the protection of that country; or who, not having a nationality and being outside the country of his former habitual residence as a result of such events, is unable or, owing to such fear, is unwilling to return to it.

In the case of a person who has more than one nationality, the term 'the country of his nationality' shall mean each of the countries of which he is a national, and a person shall not be deemed to be lacking the protection of the country of his nationality if, without any valid reason based on well-founded fear, he has not availed himself of the protection of one of the countries of which he is a national.

Article 1C

This Convention shall cease to apply to any person falling under the terms of section A if:

1. He has voluntarily re-availed himself of the protection of the country of his nationality; or
2. Having lost his nationality, he has voluntarily re-acquired it, or
3. He has acquired a new nationality, and enjoys the protection of the country of his new nationality; or
4. He has voluntarily re-established himself in the country which he left or outside which he remained owing to fear of persecution; or
5. He can no longer, because the circumstances in connexion with which he has been recognized as a refugee have ceased to exist, continue to refuse to avail himself of the protection of the country of his nationality;
   Provided that this paragraph shall not apply to a refugee falling under section A(1) of this article who is able to invoke compelling reasons arising out of previous persecution for refusing to avail himself of the protection of the country of nationality;

6 Being a person who has no nationality he is, because of the circumstances in connexion with which he has been recognized as a refugee have ceased to exist, able to return to the country of his former habitual residence;

Provided that this paragraph shall not apply to a refugee falling under section A(1) of this article who is able to invoke compelling reasons arising out of previous persecution for refusing to return to the country of his former habitual residence.

Article 33

1 No Contracting State shall expel or return ('refouler') a refugee in any manner whatsoever to the frontiers of territories where his life or freedom would be threatened on account of his race, religion, nationality, membership of a particular social group or political opinion.
2 The benefit of the present provision may not, however, be claimed by a refugee whom there are reasonable grounds for regarding as a danger to the security of the country in which he is, or who, having been convicted by a final judgment of a particularly serious crime, constitutes a danger to the community of that country.

Article 34

The Contracting States shall as far as possible facilitate the assimilation and naturalization of refugees. They shall in particular make every effort to expedite naturalization proceedings and to reduce as far as possible the charges and costs of such proceedings.

Appendix 2

Excerpts from the 2011 EU Qualification Directive

Article 7

Actors of protection

1 Protection against persecution or serious harm can only be provided by:

a the State; or
b parties or organisations, including international organisations, controlling the State or a substantial part of the territory of the State;

provided they are willing and able to offer protection in accordance with paragraph 2.

2 Protection against persecution or serious harm must be effective and of a non-temporary nature. Such protection is generally provided when the actors mentioned under points (a) and (b) of paragraph 1 take reasonable steps to prevent the persecution or suffering of serious harm, inter alia, by operating an effective legal system for the detection, prosecution and punishment of acts constituting persecution or serious harm, and when the applicant has access to such protection.

3 When assessing whether an international organisation controls a State or a substantial part of its territory and provides protection as described in paragraph 2, Member States shall take into account any guidance which may be provided in relevant Union acts.

Article 8

Internal protection

1 As part of the assessment of the application for international protection, Member States may determine that an applicant is not in need of international protection if in a part of the country of origin, he or she:

a has no well-founded fear of being persecuted or is not at real risk of suffering serious harm; or

- b has access to protection against persecution or serious harm as defined in Article 7;

and he or she can safely and legally travel to and gain admittance to that part of the country and can reasonably be expected to settle there.

2 In examining whether an applicant has a well-founded fear of being persecuted or is at real risk of suffering serious harm, or has access to protection against persecution or serious harm in a part of the country of origin in accordance with paragraph 1, Member States shall at the time of taking the decision on the application have regard to the general circumstances prevailing in that part of the country and to the personal circumstances of the applicant in accordance with Article 4. To that end, Member States shall ensure that precise and up-to-date information is obtained from relevant sources, such as the United Nations High Commissioner for Refugees and the European Asylum Support Office.

Article 11

Cessation

1 A third-country national or a stateless person shall cease to be a refugee if he or she:

- a has voluntarily re-availed himself or herself of the protection of the country of nationality; or
- b having lost his or her nationality, has voluntarily re-acquired it; or
- c has acquired a new nationality, and enjoys the protection of the country of his or her new nationality; or
- d has voluntarily re-established himself or herself in the country which he or she left or outside which he or she remained owing to fear of persecution; or
- e can no longer, because the circumstances in connection with which he or she has been recognised as a refugee have ceased to exist, continue to refuse to avail himself or herself of the protection of the country of nationality; or
- f being a stateless person, he or she is able, because the circumstances in connection with which he or she has been recognised as a refugee have ceased to exist, to return to the country of former habitual residence.

2 In considering points (e) and (f) of paragraph 1, Member States shall have regard to whether the change of circumstances is of such a significant and non-temporary nature that the refugee's fear of persecution can no longer be regarded as well-founded.

3 Points (e) and (f) of paragraph 1 shall not apply to a refugee who is able to invoke compelling reasons arising out of previous persecution for refusing to avail himself or herself of the protection of the country of nationality or, being a stateless person, of the country of former habitual residence.

Article 14(1)

Revocation of, ending of or refusal to renew refugee status

1 Concerning applications for international protection filed after the entry into force of Directive 2004/83/EC, Member States shall revoke, end or refuse to renew the refugee status of a third-country national or a stateless person granted by a governmental, administrative, judicial or quasi-judicial body if he or she has ceased to be a refugee in accordance with Article 11 . . .

QUALIFICATION FOR SUBSIDIARY PROTECTION

Article 15

Serious harm

Serious harm consists of:

a the death penalty or execution; or
b torture or inhuman or degrading treatment or punishment of an applicant in the country of origin; or
c serious and individual threat to a civilian's life or person by reason of indiscriminate violence in situations of international or internal armed conflict.

Article 24

Residence permits

1 As soon as possible after international protection has been granted, Member States shall issue to beneficiaries of refugee status a residence permit which must be valid for at least 3 years and renewable, unless compelling reasons of national security or public order otherwise require, and without prejudice to Article 21(3).
Without prejudice to Article 23(1), the residence permit to be issued to the family members of the beneficiaries of refugee status may be valid for less than 3 years and renewable.
2 As soon as possible after international protection has been granted, Member States shall issue to beneficiaries of subsidiary protection status and their family members a renewable residence permit which must be valid for at least 1 year and, in case of renewal, for at least 2 years, unless compelling reasons of national security or public order otherwise require.

Appendix 3

Questions referred to the European Court of Justice in *Abdulla*[1]

1 Is Article 11(1)(e) of [the] Directive . . . to be interpreted as meaning that – apart from the second clause of Article 1(C)(5) of the [Geneva] Convention – refugee status ceases to exist if the refugee's well-founded fear of persecution within the terms of Article 2(c) of that directive, on the basis of which refugee status was granted, no longer exists and he also has no other reason to fear persecution within the terms of Article 2(c) of [that directive]?

2 If Question 1 is to be answered in the negative: does the cessation of refugee status under Article 11(1)(e) of [the] Directive also require that, in the country of the refugee's nationality,

- a an actor of protection within the meaning of Article 7(1) of [the Directive] be present, and is it sufficient in that regard if protection can be assured only with the help of multinational troops,
- b the refugee should not be threatened with serious harm, within the meaning of Article 15 of [the Directive], which leads to the granting of subsidiary protection under Article 18 of that directive, and/or
- c the security situation be stable and the general living conditions ensure a minimum standard of living?

3 In a situation in which the previous circumstances, on the basis of which the person concerned was granted refugee status, have ceased to exist, are new, different circumstances founding persecution to be:

- a measured against the standard of probability applied for recognising refugee status, or is another standard to be applied in favour of the person concerned, and/or
- b assessed having regard to the relaxation of the burden of proof under Article 4(4) of [the] Directive . . . ?

1 *Case C-179/08, Dier Jamal v Federal Republic of Germany; Case C-178/08, Ahmed Adem and Hamrin Mosa Rashi v Federal Republic of Germany; Case C-177/08, Khoshnaw Abdullah v Federal Republic of Germany; Case C-176/08, Kamil Hasan v Federal Republic of Germany; Case C-175/08, Aydin Salahadin Abdulla v Federal Republic of Germany* [2008] OJ C 197/3.

Appendix 4

Excerpts from proposal for a regulation of the European Parliament to amend the Qualification Directive

Proposal for a Regulation of the European Parliament and of the Council on standards for the qualification of third-country nationals or stateless persons as beneficiaries of international protection, for a uniform status for refugees or for persons eligible for subsidiary protection and for the content of the protection granted and amending Council Directive 2003/109/EC of 25 November 2003 concerning the status of third-country nationals who are long-term residents 13.7.2016, COM/2016/0466 final – 2016/0223 (COD).

Article 11 cessation

1 A third-country national or a stateless person shall cease to be a refugee where one or more of the following apply:

- a the person has voluntarily re-availed himself or herself of the protection of the country of nationality;
- b having lost his or her nationality, the person has voluntarily re-acquired it;
- c the person has acquired a new nationality, and enjoys the protection of the country of his or her new nationality;
- d the person has voluntarily re-established himself or herself in the country which he or she left or outside which he or she remained owing to fear of persecution;
- e the person can no longer, because the circumstances in connection with which he or she has been recognised as a refugee have ceased to exist, continue to refuse to avail himself or herself of the protection of the country of nationality;
- f being a stateless person, the person is able, because the circumstances in connection with which he or she has been recognised as a refugee have ceased to exist, to return to the country of former habitual residence.

Points (e) and (f) shall not apply to a refugee who is able to invoke compelling reasons arising out of previous persecution for refusing to avail himself or herself of the protection of the country of nationality or, being a stateless person, of the country of former habitual residence.

2 When points (e) and (f) of paragraph 1 apply, the determining authority

- g shall have regard to whether the change of circumstances is of such a significant and non-temporary nature that the refugee's fear of persecution can no longer be regarded as well-founded;
- h shall base itself on precise and up-to-date information obtained from all relevant sources, including Union level country of origin information and common analysis of country of origin information referred to in Articles 8 and 10 of the Regulation (EU) No XXX/XX [Regulation on the European Union Agency for Asylum] or information and guidance issued by the United Nations High Commissioner for Refugee.

Bibliography

Books, chapters and articles

Albert, M. 'Governance and Prima Facie Refugee Status Determination: Clarifying the Boundaries of Temporary Protection, Group Determination, and Mass Influx' (2010) 29(1) *Refugee Survey Quarterly* 61.

Aleinikoff, T.A. 'State Centred Refugee Law: From Resettlement to Containment' (1992–1993) 14(1) *Michigan Journal of International* 120.

——— *Semblances of Sovereignty: The Constitution, the State and American Citizenship* (Harvard University Press, 2002).

Barnett, L. 'Global Governance and the Evolution of the International Refugee Regime' (2002) 14(2&3) *International Journal of Refugee Law* 238.

Battjes, H. *European Asylum Law and International Law* (Martinus Nijhoff, 2006).

Bonoan, R. 'Cessation of Refugee Status: A Guide for Determining When Internal Displacement Ends?' (2002) 17 *Forced Migration Review* 8.

Bosniak, L. 'Citizenship Denationalized' (2000) 7 *Indiana Journal of Global Legal Studies* 447.

Bradley, M. 'The Conditions of Just Return: State Responsibility and Restitution for Refugees', University of Oxford Refugee Studies Centre Working Paper Series, RSC Working Paper No. 21, March 2005, <www.rsc.ox.ac.uk/publications/working-papers/RSCworkingpaper21.pdf>

Broberg, M. and Fenger, N. *Preliminary References to the European Court of Justice* (Oxford University Press, 2010).

Burson, B. and Cantor, D. *Human Rights and the Refugee Definition: Comparative Legal Practice and Theory* (Brill, 2016).

Chimni, B.S. 'From Resettlement to Involuntary Repatriation: Towards a Critical History of Durable Solutions to Refugee Problems' (2004) 23 *Refugee Survey Quarterly* 55.

Clapham, A. *Human Rights Obligations of Non-State Actors* (Oxford University Press, 2006).

Crock, M., 'Judging Refugees: The Clash of Power and Institutions in the Development of Australian Refugee Law' (2004) 26(1) *Sydney Law Review* 51.

Cwik, M.E. 'Forced to Flee and Forced to Repatriate: How the Cessation Clause of Article 1C(5) and (6) of the 1951 Refugee Convention Operates in International Law and Practice [Notes]' (2011) 44(3) *Vanderbilt Journal of Transnational Law* 711.

Davies, S.E. *Legitimising Rejection: International Refugee Law in Southeast Asia* (Martinus Nijhoff, 2008).

Dicker, N. and Mansfield, J. 'Filling the Protection Gap: Current Trends in Complementary Protection in Canada, Mexico and Australia', *UNHCR New Issues in Refugee Research*, Research Paper No. 238, May 2012.

Durieux, J.-F. 'Of War, Flows, Laws and Flaws: A Reply to Hugo Storey' (2012) 31(3) *Refugee Survey Quarterly* 161.

Edwards, A. 'Tampering with Refugee Protection: The Case of Australia' (2003) 15(2) *International Journal of Refugee Law* 192.

Errera, R. 'Cessation and Assessment of New Circumstances: A Comment on *Abdulla*, CJEU, 2 March 2010' (2011) 23(3) *International Journal of Refugee Law* 521.

Esmaeili, H. and Wells, B. 'The Temporary Refugees: Australia's Legal Response to the Arrival of Iraqi and Afghan Boat-People' (2000) 23(3) *University of New South Wales Law Journal* 224.

Feller, E. 'International Refugee Protection 50 Years On: The Protection Challenges of the Past, Present and Future' (2001) 83(843) *International Review of the Red Cross* 581.

Feller, E., Türk, V. and Nicholson, F. (eds.) *Refugee Protection in International Law: UNHCR's Global Consultations on International Protection* (Cambridge University Press, 2003).

Fitzpatrick, J. 'Flight from Asylum: Trends toward Temporary "Refuge" and Local Responses to Forced Migrations' (1994–1995) 35(13) *Virginia Journal of International Law* 13.

——— 'The End of Protection: Legal Standards for Cessation of Refugee Status and Withdrawal of Temporary Protection' (1999) 13(3) *Georgetown Immigration Law Journal* 343.

——— 'Temporary Protection of Refugees: Elements of a Formalized Regime' (2000) 94(2) *The American Journal of International Law* 279.

——— 'Current Issues in Cessation of Protection under Article 1 C of the 1951 Convention and Article I.4 of the 1969 OAU Convention, UNHCR Background Paper for Expert Roundtable Discussion on Cessation (2001).

Fortin, A. 'The Meaning of "Protection" in the Refugee Definition' (2001) 12(4) *International Journal of Refugee Law* 548.

Foster, M. *International Refugee Law and Socio-Economic Rights: Refuge from Deprivation* (Cambridge University Press, 2007).

——— 'An "Alien" by the Barest of Threads': The Legality of the Deportation of Long-Term Residents from Australia' (2009) 33(2) *Melbourne University Law Review* 483.

Gibney, M. 'Liberal Democratic States and Responsibilities to Refugees' (1999) 93 *American Political Science Review* 169.

——— 'Between Control and Humanitarianism: Temporary Protection in Contemporary Europe' (2000) 14 *Georgetown Immigration Law Journal* 689.

——— *The Ethics and Politics of Asylum: Liberal Democracy and the Response to Refugees* (Cambridge University Press, 2004).

Goodwin-Gill, G. *The Refugee in International Law* (Oxford University Press, 1996).

——— 'The Extraterriorial Processing of Claims to Asylum or Protection: The Legal Responsibilities of States and International Organisations' (2008) 9 *UTS Law Review* 26.

——— 'The Politics of Refugee Protection' (2008) 27(1) *Refugee Survey Quarterly* 8.

Goodwin-Gill, G. and Lambert, H. (eds.) *The Limits of Transnational Law: Refugee Law, Policy Harmonization and Judicial Dialogue in the European Union* (Cambridge University Press, 2010).

Goodwin-Gill, G. and McAdam, J. *The Refugee in International Law* (Oxford University Press, 3rd ed., 2007).
Grahl-Madsen, A. *The Status of Refugees in International Law* (A.W. Sijthoff-Leyden, Vol. 1, 1966).
Guild, E. 'The Europeanisation of Europe's Asylum Policy' (2006) 18 *International Journal of Refugee Law* 630.
Haddad, E. *The Refugee in International Society: Between Sovereigns* (Cambridge University Press, 2008).
Hailbronner, K. (ed.) *EU Immigration and Asylum Law: Commentary on EU Regulations and Directives* (CH Beck, Hart, Nomos, 2010).
Hathaway, J.C. 'The Evolution of Refugee Status' (1984) 33 *International and Comparative Law Quarterly* 350.
——— 'A Reconsideration of the Underlying Premise of Refugee Law' (1990) 31 *Harvard International Law Journal* 129.
——— *The Law of Refugee Status* (Butterworths, Canada, 1991).
——— 'The Meaning of Repatriation' (1997) 9 *International Journal of Refugee Law* 551.
——— (ed.) *Reconceiving International Refugee Law* (Martinus Nijhoff, The Hague, 1997).
——— 'The Right of States to Repatriate Former Refugees' (2005) 20 *Ohio State Journal of Dispute Resolution* 175.
——— *The Rights of Refugees under International Law* (Cambridge University Press, 2005).
——— 'Why Refugee Law Still Matters' (2007) 8 *Melbourne Journal of International Law* 89.
——— 'EU Accountability to International Law: The Case of Asylum' (2011) 33(1) *Michigan Journal of International Law* 1.
Hathaway, J.C. and Foster, M. *The Law of Refugee Status* (Cambridge University Press, 2nd ed., 2014).
Hathaway, J.C. and Neve, R.A. 'Making International Refugee Law Relevant Again: A Proposal for Collectivised and Solution-Oriented Protection' (1997) 10 *Harvard Human Rights Journal* 115.
Hathaway, J.C. and Storey, H. 'What Is the Meaning of State Protection in Refugee Law? A Debate' (2016) 28(3) *International Journal of Refugee Law* 480.
Holzer, V. 'The 1951 Refugee Convention and the Protection of People Fleeing Armed Conflict and Other Situations of Violence', *UNHCR Legal and Protection Policy Research Series*, September 2012, PPLA/2012/05.
Hurwitz, A. *The Collective Responsibility of States to Protect Refugees* (Oxford University Press, 2009).
Jackson, I. *The Refugee Concept in Group Situations* (Martinus Nijhoff, The Hague, 1999).
Johnson, C. 'Ceased Circumstances and the End of Refugee Status: The Use of Article 1C5 in South Africa', Scalabrini Centre of Cape Town, August 2012.
Kälin, W. 'Non-State Agents of Persecution' (2000–2001) 15 *Georgetown Immigration Law Journal* 415.
Karavias, M. 'Non-State Actors in Control of Territory as "Actors of Protection" in International Refugee Law' (2014) 2 *Revue Belge De Droit International* 487.
Kelley, N. 'Internal Flight/Relocation/Protection Alternative: Is It Reasonable?' (2002) 14 *International Journal of Refugee Law* 4.

Kerber, K. 'The Temporary Protection Directive' (2002) 4 *European Journal of Migration and Law* 193.

Kesby, A. *The Right to Have Rights Citizenship, Humanity, and International Law* (Oxford University Press, 2012).

Kibreab, G. 'Displacement, Host Governments' Policies, and Constraints on the Construction of Sustainable Livelihoods', UNESCO, 2003.

Kingston, L.N. 'Bringing Rwandan Refugees "Home": The Cessation Clause, Statelessness, and Forced Repatriation' (2017) 29(3) *International Journal of Refugee Law* 417.

Kjaerum, M. 'Temporary Protection in Europe in the 1990s' (1994) 6 *International Journal of Refugee Law* 444.

Kneebone, S. 'Moving beyond the State: Refugees, Accountability and Protection', in Kneebone, S. (ed.) *The Refugees Convention 50 Years On: Globalisation and International Law* (Ashgate, 2003).

——— 'Strangers at the Gate: Refugees, Citizenship and Nationality' (2004) 10 *Australian Journal of Human Rights* 33.

——— 'Moving beyond the State: Refugees, Accountability and Protection', in Kneebone, S. (ed.) *The Refugees Convention 50 Years On: Globalisation and International Law* (Ashgate, 2003).

——— 'What We Have Done with the Refugee Convention: The Australian Way' (2005) 2 *Law in Context* 83.

——— 'The Pacific Plan: The Provision of "Effective Protection"?' (2006) 18 *International Journal of Refugee Law* 696.

——— (ed.) *Refugees, Asylum Seekers and the Rule of Law: Comparative Perspectives* (Cambridge University Press, 2009).

Koser, K. and Black, R. 'Limits to Harmonization: The "Temporary Protection" of Refugees in the European Union' (1999) 37 *International Migration* 521.

Lambert, H. 'The Conceptualisation of Persecution by the House of Lords: *Horvath v. Secretary of State for the Home Department*' (2001) 13(4) *International Journal of Refugee Law* 16.

——— 'The EU Asylum Qualification Directive, Its Impact on the Jurisprudence of the United Kingdom and International Law' (2006) 55(1) *International and Comparative Law Quarterly* 161.

——— 'International Refugee Law: Dominant and Emerging Approaches', in D. Armstrong (ed.) *Handbook of International Law* (Routledge, 2009) 344.

——— 'Transnational Judicial Dialogue, Harmonization and the Common European Asylum System' (2009) 58(3) *International and Comparative Law Quarterly* 519.

Lambert, H. and Farrell, T. 'The Changing Character of Armed Conflict and the Implications for Refugee Protection Jurisprudence' (2010) 22(2) *International Journal of Refugee Law* 237.

Lee, L. *Consular Law and Practice* (Oxford University Press, 3rd ed., 2015).

Lewis, C. 'UNHCR's Contribution to the Development of International Refugee Law: Its Foundations and Evolution' (2005) 17 *International Journal of Refugee Law* 67.

Leydet, D. 'Citizenship', in E.N. Zalta (ed.) *The Stanford Encyclopedia of Philosophy* (Fall 2017 ed.), <https://plato.stanford.edu/archives/fall2017/entries/citizenship/>

Maley, W. 'Australian's New Afghan Refugees: Context and Challenges' Refugee Council of Australia, undated, <www.refugee.council.org.au/html/resources/agmAfghan.html>

——— 'On the Position of the Hazara Minority in Afghanistan', 7 December 2011, <http://bmrsg.org.au/wp-content/uploads/2011/10/Maley-Hazaras-Opinion-Updated2.pdf>

Mansouri, F. et al. 'Temporary Protection and the Refugee Convention in Australia, Denmark, and Germany' (2009) 26(1) *Refuge* 135.

Marx, R. 'The Criteria of Applying the "Internal Flight Alternative" Test in National Refugee Status Determination Procedures' (2002) 14 *International Journal of Refugee Law* 179.

Mathew, P. 'Current Development: Australian Refugee Protection in the Wake of the Tampa' (2002) 96(3) *American Journal of International Law* 661.

McAdam, J. *Complementary Protection in International Refugee Law* (Oxford University Press, 2007).

——— 'Australian Complementary Protection: A Step-by-Step Approach' (2011) 33 *Sydney Law Review* 687.

McMillan, K. 'Uganda's Invocation of Cessation Regarding Its Rwandan Refugee Caseload: Lessons for International Protection' (2012) 24(2) *International Journal of Refugee Law* 231.

Meili, S. 'When Do Human Rights Treaties Help Asylum Seekers? A Study of Theory and Practice in Canadian Jurisprudence Since 1990' (2014) 51 *Osgoode Hall Law Journal* 627.

Mertus, J. The State and the Post-Cold War Refugee Regime: New Models, New Questions' (1998) 20 *Michigan Journal of International Law* 59.

University of Michigan Law School, 'The Michigan Guidelines on the Internal Protection Alternative' (1999) 21 *Michigan Journal of International Law* 134.

Milner, D. 'Exemption from Cessation of Refugee Status in the Second Sentence of Article 1C(5)/(6) of the 1951 Refugee Convention' (2004) 16(1) *International Journal of Refugee Law* 91.

Nathwani, N. *Rethinking Refugee Law* (Martinus Nijhoff, 2003).

Nihman, J.E. 'Non-State Actors and the International Rule of Law: Revisiting the "Realist Theory" of International Legal Personality', Amsterdam Centre for International Law Research Paper Series, 2010, <http://ssrn.com/abstract=15225020>

O'Sullivan, M. 'Before the High Court: *Minister for Immigration v QAAH*: Cessation of Refugee Status' (2006) 28(2) *Sydney Law Review* 359.

——— 'Withdrawing Protection under Article 1 C (5) of the 1951 Convention: Lessons from Australia' (2008) 20(4) *International Journal of Refugee Law* 586.

——— 'Acting the Part: Can Non-State Entities Provide Protection under International Refugee Law?' (2012) 24(1) *International Journal of Refugee Law* 85.

Persaud, S. Protecting Refugees and Asylum Seekers Under the International Covenant on Civil and Political Rights, *UNHCR New Issues in Refugee Research*, Research Paper No. 132 2006, <www.unhcr.org/4552f0d82.html>

Price, M.E. 'Persecution Complex: Justifying Asylum Law's Preference for Persecuted People' (2006) 47 *Harvard International Law Journal* 413.

Reilly, J.E. 'Temporary Refugees: The Impact of US Policy on Civic Participation and Political Belonging among Liberians in the United States' (2016) 35(3) *Refugee Survey Quarterly* 94.

Rotberg, R. *State Failure and State Weakness in a Time of Terror* (World Peace Foundation; Brookings Institution Press, 2003).

Rubio-Marín, R. *Human Rights and Immigration* (Oxford University Press, 2014).

Schloenhardt, A. 'Australia and the Boat-People: 25 Years of Unauthorized Arrivals' (2000) 23 *University of New South Wales Law Journal* 33.

Shacknove, A. 'Who Is a Refugee?' (1985) 95 *Ethics* 274.

Shaw, J. and Štiks, I. *Citizenship Rights* (Ashgate, 2013).

Siddiqui, Y. 'Reviewing the Application of the Cessation Clause of the 1951 Convention Relating to the Status of Refugees in Africa', University of Oxford Working Paper 76, August 2011.

Sidorenko, O.F. *The Common European Asylum System: Background, Current State of Affairs, Future Direction* (T.M.C. Asser Press, 2007).

Sniderman, A. 'Explaining Delayed Cessation: A Case Study of Rwandan Refugees in Zimbabwe' (2015) 27(4) *International Journal of Refugee Law* 607.

Sopf, D. 'Temporary Protection in Europe after 1990: The "Right to Remain" of Genuine Convention Refugees' (2001) 6 *Washington University Journal of Law and Policy* 109.

Storey, H. 'The Internal Flight Alternative Test: The Jurisprudence Re-Examined' (1998) 10 *International Journal of Refugee Law* 499.

——— 'EU Qualification Directive: A Brave New World?' (2008) 20 *International Journal of Refugee Law* 1.

——— 'Armed Conflict in Asylum Law: The "War-Flaw"' (2012) 31(2) *Refugee Survey Quarterly* 1.

——— 'The Law of Refugee Status, 2nd edition: Paradigm Lost?' (2015) 27(2) *International Journal of Refugee Law* 348.

——— 'The Meaning of "Protection" within the Refugee Definition' (2016) 35(3) *Refugee Survey Quarterly* 1.

Storey, H. and Wallace, R. 'War and Peace in Refugee Law Jurisprudence' (2001) 95(2) *American Journal of International Law* 349.

Tarwater, J.R. 'Analysis and Case Studies of the "Ceased Circumstances" Cessation Clause of the 1951 Refugee Convention' (2001) 15(3) *Georgetown Immigration Law Journal* 563.

Taylor, S. 'Protection or Prevention: A Close Look at the Temporary Safe Haven Visa Class' (2000) 23(3) *University of New South Wales Law Journal* 75.

Türk, V. 'Protection Gaps in Europe? Persons Fleeing the Indiscriminate Effects of Generalized Violence', 18 January 2011, <www.unhcr.org/refworld/docid/4d37d8402.html>

UNHCR 'The International Protection of Refugees: Interpreting Article 1 of the 1951 Convention Relating to the Status of Refugees' (2001) 20(3) *Refugee Survey Quarterly* 77.

Van Selm-Thorburn, J. *Refugee Protection in Europe: Lessons of the Yugoslav Crisis* (Martinus Nijhoff, 1998).

Walker, K. 'Defending the 1951 Convention Definition of Refugee' (2003) 17 *Georgetown Immigration Law Journal* 583.

Walzer, M. 'The Moral Standing of States: A Response to Four Critics' (1980) 9(3) *Philosophy and Public Affairs* 209.

Weis, P. *Nationality and Statelessness in International Law* (Sijthoff and Noordhoff, 2nd ed., 1979).

Wood, T. and McAdam, J. 'Australian Asylum Policy All at Sea: An Analysis of *Plaintiff M70/2011 v Minister for Immigration and Citizenship* and the Australia: Malaysia Arrangement' (2012) 61 *International and Comparative Law Quarterly* 274.

Zieck, M. 'Vanishing Points of the Refugee Law Regime: Response to James Hathaway' (2005) 20 *Ohio State Journal of Dispute Resolution* 217.

Ziegler, R. *The Voting Rights of Refugees* (Cambridge University Press, 2017).

Zimmerman, A. (ed.) *The 1951 Convention Relating to the Status of Refugees and Its 1967 Protocol: A Commentary* (Oxford University Press, 2011).

Zwaan, K. (ed.) *The Qualification Directive: Central Themes, Problem Issues, and Implementation in Selected Member States* (Wolf Legal Publishers, 2007).

Treaties and declarations

Convention for the Protection of Human Rights and Fundamental Freedoms, 4 November 1950, ETS No. 005.

Convention Governing the Specific Aspects of Refugee Problems in Africa, 10 September 1969, 1001 U.N.T.S. 45.

Convention Relating to the Status of Refugees, 28 July 1951, 189 UNTS 150.

International Covenant on Civil and Political Rights, 16 December 1966, 999 UNTS 171.

Protocol Relating to the Status of Refugees, 4 October 1967, 606 UNTS 267.

Statute of the Office of the United Nations High Commissioner for Refugees, 14 December 1950, A/RES/428(V).

Treaty on the Functioning of the European Union (Consolidated Version), 9 May 2008, [2008] OJ C 115/47.

Vienna Convention on the Law of Treaties, 23 May 1969, 155 U.N.T.S. 331.

UN documents

Ad Hoc Committee on Statelessness and Related Problems, Memorandum from the Secretariat of the International Refugee Organization, UN Doc. E/AC.32/L.16 (1950).

Conference of Plenipotentiaries, Texts of the Draft Convention and the Draft Protocol to Be Considered by the Conference, UN Doc. A/CONF.2/1 (1951).

Conference of Plenipotentiaries, 1951 Refugee Convention Israel: Amendment to Article 1, UN Doc. A/CONF.2/81 (1951).

——— Israel: Amendment to Article 1, UN Doc. A/CONF.2/82/Rev.1 (1951).

——— 20th Meeting, UN Doc. A/CONF.2/SR.20 (1951).

——— 23rd Meeting, UN Doc. A/CONF.2/SR.23 (1951).

——— 28th Meeting, UN Doc. A/CONF.2/SR.28 (1951).

Report of the Meeting of the Expert Group on Temporary Refuge in Situations of Large-Scale Influx, Geneva, 21–24 April 1981, EC/SCP/16.

United Nations Assistance Mission in Afghanistan (UNAMA) and the UN Office of the High Commissioner for Human Rights, 'Afghanistan Mid-Year Report 2012: Protection of Civilians in Armed Conflict', Kabul, Afghanistan, July 2012, <www.ohchr.org/Documents/Countries/AF/UNAMAMidYearReport2012.pdf>

United Nations Assistance Mission for Iraq (UNAMI), Report on Human Rights in Iraq: 2011, May 2012, <www.unhcr.org/refworld/docid/4fc726582.html>

United Nations High Commissioner for Refugees (UNHCR) 'Discussion Note on the Application of the "Ceased Circumstances" Cessation Clauses in the 1951 Convention', EC/SCP/1992/CRP.1, 20 December 1991.

——— Handbook on Procedures and Criteria for Determining Refugee Status under the 1951 Convention and the 1967 Protocol Relating to the Status of Refugees, HCR/IP/4/Rev.1, 1979, Reedited, Geneva, January 1992.

——— Report of the International Meeting on Humanitarian Aid to Victims of the Conflict in the Former Yugoslavia, 10 August 1992, HCR/IMFY/1992/4, <www.unhcr.org/refworld/docid/3ae68f3fc.html>
——— Note on International Protection (Submitted by the High Commissioner), 7 September 1994, A/AC.96/830, <www.unhcr.org/refworld/docid/3f0a935f2.html>
——— Note on the Cessation Clauses, EC/47/SC/CRP.30, 30 May 1997.
——— The Cessation Clauses: Guidelines on Their Application (1999), <www.unhcr.org/refworld/pdfid/3c06138c4.pdf>
——— Position Paper on Relocating Internally as a Reasonable Alternative to Seeking Asylum (The So-Called "Internal Flight Alternative" or "Relocation Principle") (1999) UNHCR Refworld, <www.unhcr.org/refworld/docid/3ae6b336c.html>
——— Complementary Forms of Protection: Their Nature and Relationship to the International Refugee Protection Regime, 9 June 2000, EC/50/SC/CRP.18, <www.unhcr.org/refworld/docid/47fdfb491a.html>
——— Global Consultations on International Protection, 2nd Meeting, Asylum Processes (Fair and Efficient Asylum Procedures), EC/GC/01/12 (2001).
——— Guidelines on International Protection: Cessation of Refugee Status under Article 1C(5) and (6) of the 1951 Convention Relating to the Status of Refugees (HCR/GIP/03/03), 10 February 2003.
——— Framework for Durable Solutions for Refugees and Persons of Concern, Core Group on Durable Solutions, UNHCR Geneva, May 2003.
——— Annotated Comments on the EC Council Directive 2004/83/EC of 29 April 2004 on Minimum Standards for the Qualification and Status of Third Country Nationals or Stateless Persons as Refugees or as Persons Who Otherwise Need International Protection and the Content of the Protection granted (OJ L 304/12 of 30.9.2004), 28 January 2005.
——— '*Minister for Immigration and Multicultural and Indigenous Affairs v. QAAH of 2004*: Outline of Submissions on Behalf of the Office of the United Nations High Commissioner for Refugees (as Amicus Curiae)', 8 June 2006, Published in (2007) 19(2) *International Journal of Refugee Law* 360–371.
——— Asylum in the European Union: A Study of the Implementation of the Qualification Directive, November 2007, <www.unhcr.org/refworld/docid/473050632.html>
——— 'UNHCR Statement on the "Ceased Circumstances" Clause of the EC Qualification Directive' (2008), <www.unhcr.org/refworld/docid/48a2f0782.html>
——— 'Eligibility Guidelines for Assessing the International Protection Needs of Iraqi Asylum-Seekers', April 2009.
——— 'Eligibility Guidelines for Assessing the International Protection Needs of Asylum-Seekers from Afghanistan', 17 December 2010, HCR/EG/AFG/10/04, <www.unhcr.org/refworld/docid/4d0b55c92.html>
——— 'UNHCR Comments on the European Commission's proposal for a Directive of the European Parliament and of the Council on minimum Standards for the Qualification and Status of Third Country Nationals or Stateless Persons as Beneficiaries of International Protection and the Content of the Protection Granted (COM(2009)551, 21 October 2009)' July 2010 </www.unhcr.org/4c5037f99.pdf>
——— *Note on Suspension of "General Cessation" Declarations in Respect of Particular Persons or Groups Based on Acquired Rights to Family Unity*, December 2011 www.refworld.org/docid/4eef5a1b2.html

——— 'Eligibility Guidelines for Assessing the International Protection Needs of Iraqi Asylum-Seekers', 31 May 2012, HCR/EG/IRQ/12/03.

UNHCR Ex Com Conclusions UNHCR ExCom, Conclusion No. 65 (XLII): General, UN GAOR, 46th Sess., Suppl. 12A, UN Doc. A/46/12/Add.1 (1992), 6–8.

——— UNHCR ExCom, Conclusion No. 69 (XLVI): Cessation of Status, UN GAOR, 47th Sess., Suppl. 12A, UN Doc. A/47/12/Add.1 (1993), 10–11.

——— UNHCR ExCom, Conclusion No. 85 (XLIX): International Protection, UN GAOR, 53rd Sess., Suppl. 12A, UN Doc. A/53/12/Add.1 (1998), 6–10.

——— UNHCR ExCom, Conclusion No. 99 (LV): General, UN GAOR, 59th Sess., Suppl. 12A, UN Doc. A/59/12/Add.1 (2004), 6–10.

Other official documents

'Amended Proposal for a Council Directive on Minimum Standards on Procedures in Member States for Granting and Withdrawing Refugee Status' (2002/C 291 E/06), COM (2002) 326 Final, <www.europa.eu.int/scadplus/leg/en/lvb/133140.htm>

'Amended Proposal for a Directive of the European Parliament and of the Council on Common Procedures for Granting and Withdrawing International Protection Status (Recast) Amended Proposal for a Directive of the European Parliament and of the Council on Common Procedures for Granting and Withdrawing International Protection status (Recast)', COM/2011/0319 final – COD 2009/016.

'Commission Staff Working Document Accompanying the Proposal for a Directive of the European Parliament and of the Council on Minimum Standards for the Qualification and Status of Third Country Nationals or Stateless Persons as Beneficiaries of International Protection and the Content of the Protection Granted: *Impact Assessment*', COM(2009) 551, SEC(2009) 1374, Brussels, 21.10.2009, SEC(2009) 1373 Final.

'Communication from the Commission to the European Parliament, the Council, the European Economic and Social Committee and the Committee of the Regions – Delivering an Area of Freedom, Security and Justice for Europe's Citizens: Action Plan Implementing the Stockholm Programme', COM/2010/0171 Final.

Council Directive 2001/55/EC of 20 July 2001 on Minimum Standards for Giving Temporary Protection in the Event of a Mass Influx of Displaced Persons and on Measures Promoting a Balance of Efforts between Member States in Receiving Such Persons and Bearing the Consequences Thereof (2001) OJ L212/12.

Council Directive 2005/85/EC of 1 December 2005 on Minimum Standards on Procedures in Member States for Granting and Withdrawing Refugee Status, [2005] OJ L 326/13.

Council Directive 2008/115/EC of the European Parliament and of the Council of 16 December 2008 on Common Standards and Procedures in Member States for Returning Illegally Staying Third-Country Nationals, [2008] OJ L 348/98.

Council Directive on Minimum Standards for the Qualification and Status of Third Country Nationals or Stateless Persons as Refugees or as Persons Who Otherwise Need International Protection and the Content of the Protection Granted, 2004/83/E, [2004] OJ L304/12.

Council Regulation (EC) No 343/2003 of 18 February 2003 Establishing the Criteria and Mechanisms for Determining the Member State Responsible for Examining an Asylum Application Lodged in One of the Member States by a Third-Country National, [2003] OJ L 50/1.

Directive 2011/51/EU of the European Parliament and of the Council of 11 May 2011 Amending Council Directive 2003/109/EC to Extend Its Scope to Beneficiaries of International Protection, [2011] OJ L 132/1.

Directive 2011/95/EU of The European Parliament and of the Council of 13 December 2011 on Standards for the Qualification of Third-Country Nationals or Stateless Persons as Beneficiaries of International Protection, for a Uniform Status for Refugees or for Persons Eligible for Subsidiary Protection, and for the Content of the Protection Granted (Recast), [2011] OJ L 337/9.

European Commission, 'Report from the Commission to the European Parliament and the Council on the Application of Directive 2004/83/EC', COM(2010) 314 Final, 16 June 2010.

European Parliament, 'Report on the Proposal for a Council Directive on Minimum Standards for the Qualification and Status of Third Country Nationals and Stateless Persons as Refugees or as Persons Who Otherwise Need International Protection', 8 October 2002, A5–0333/2002.

Lambert, J. 'Working Document on Directive of the European Parliament and of the Council on Minimum Standards for the Qualification and Status of Third Country Nationals or Stateless Persons (Recast)', DT/830750EN.doc, 15 September 2010.

'Proposal for a Council Directive on Minimum Standards for the Qualification and Status of Third Country Nationals and Stateless Persons as Refugees or as Persons Who Otherwise Need International Protection', Brussels, 12.9.2001, COM(2001) 510 Final 2001/0207 (CNS), in [2002] OJ C 51 E/330, 26 February 2002.

'Proposal for a Regulation of the European Parliament and of the Council on Standards for the Qualification of Third-Country Nationals or Stateless Persons as Beneficiaries of International Protection, for a Uniform Status for Refugees or for Persons Eligible for Subsidiary Protection and for the Content of the Protection Granted and Amending Council Directive 2003/109/EC of 25 November 2003 Concerning the Status of Third-Country Nationals Who Are Long-Term Residents', 13.7.2016, COM/2016/0466 final – 2016/0223 (COD).

Regulation (EU) No 439/2010 of the European Parliament and of the Council of 19 May 2010 Establishing a European Asylum Support Office, [2010] OJ L 132.

UK Home Office, Immigration & Nationality Directorate, *Asylum Policy Instruction (API) on Refugee Leave*, 2 March 2017 <www.gov.uk/government/publications/asylum-under-immigration-rule-334-process>

UK House of Lords Select Committee on the European Union, Summary of Conclusions, *Defining Refugee Status and Those in Need of International Protection*, HL Paper 156, Session 2001–02, 28th Report.

Other

Department of Immigration and Multicultural Affairs, Australia, Refugee and Humanitarian Division, 'The Cessation Clauses (Article 1C): An Australian Perspective', A Paper prepared as a Contribution to the UNHCR's Expert Roundtable Series, Department of Immigration and Ethnic Affairs, Canberra, October 2001.

European Council on Refugees and Exiles (ECRE) 'Position on Exclusion from Refugee Status PP1/03/2004/Ext/CA March 2004', Reproduced in (2004) 16(2) *International Journal of Refugee Law* 257.

——— 'Guidelines for the Treatment of Afghan Asylum Seekers and Refugees in Europe', May 2004, Doc. No: PP3/05/2004/Ext/AP.

——— 'Information Note on the Council Directive 2004/83/EC of 29 April 2004 on Minimum Standards for the Qualification of Third Country Nationals and Others in Need of International Protection', IN/10/2004/ext/CN, 1 October 2004.

(The) Expert Panel on Asylum Seekers (Australia) *The Report of the Expert Panel on Asylum Seekers*, 13 August 2012, <http://expertpanelonasylumseekers.dpmc.gov.au/report>

Human Rights Watch, *Commentary on Australia's Temporary Protection Visas for Refugees* (Human Rights Watch, New York, 2003).

Index